T0373387

Moral Progress in Dark Times

Moral Progress in Dark Times

Universal Values for the Twenty-First Century

Markus Gabriel

Translated by Wieland Hoban

polity

Originally published in German as *Moralischer Fortschritt in dunklen Zeiten. Universale Werte für das 21. Jahrhundert* © by Ullstein Buchverlage GmbH, Berlin. Published in 2020 by Ullstein Verlag

This English edition © Polity Press, 2022

The translation of this work was supported by a grant from the Goethe-Institut.

Polity Press
65 Bridge Street
Cambridge CB2 1UR, UK

Polity Press
111 River Street
Hoboken, NJ 07030, USA

All rights reserved. Except for the quotation of short passages for the purpose of criticism and review, no part of this publication may be reproduced, stored in a retrieval system or transmitted, in any form or by any means, electronic, mechanical, photocopying, recording or otherwise, without the prior permission of the publisher.

ISBN-13: 978-1-5095-4948-1 (hardback)

A catalogue record for this book is available from the British Library.

Library of Congress Control Number: 2022934661

Typeset in 11.5 on 14 Adobe Garamond
by Fakenham Prepress Solutions, Fakenham, Norfolk NR21 8NL
Printed and bound in Great Britain TJ Books Ltd, Padstow, Cornwall

The publisher has used its best endeavours to ensure that the URLs for external websites referred to in this book are correct and active at the time of going to press. However, the publisher has no responsibility for the websites and can make no guarantee that a site will remain live or that the content is or will remain appropriate.

Every effort has been made to trace all copyright holders, but if any have been overlooked the publisher will be pleased to include any necessary credits in any subsequent reprint or edition.

For further information on Polity, visit our website:
politybooks.com

The evil in the world comes almost always from ignorance, and goodwill can cause as much damage as ill-will if it is not enlightened. People are more often good than bad, though in fact that is not the question.

Albert Camus, *The Plague*

Contents

Preface to the English Edition

I started thinking about the contours of this book in 2015 during a research stay at New York University. At that time, I began to wonder how the idea that ethics, and thus moral judgement, has some form of unconditional and universal scope that could be reconciled with the fact that many of our large-scale, socially orchestrated moral achievements are historically contingent. Let us call these achievements 'moral progress'. If, as I believe, there is objective moral value in reality which we are capable of grasping, how do we account for the equally important observation that such large-scale social formations as whole societies can miss them in systematic ways, with resulting harm to the victims of morally pernicious, evil practices?

My answer to this question of the relationship between the universality of moral judgement and the historical and social embeddedness of moral progress consists in realizing that moral facts concerning what we ought to do or ought not to do are never entirely hidden. Their truth can be repressed, distorted, twisted and violated in manifold ways, but this will never make it the case that the perpetrator who transgresses ethical norms of goodness can eventually win and gets it right by changing the moral code. Values are too objective (though they relate to human mindedness and are thus not fully mind-independent) for them to change at the will of any kind of group, let alone a single dictator.

In light of this conviction, I began to be worried about the historical trajectory of our era of nested crises (from populism, fake news, and the rise of authoritarian systems wreaking havoc in brutal wars, such as in Syria and now in Ukraine, to the environmental crisis, which always looms large in the background to any of our current global problems). In 2019 I returned for the fall semester to NYU as the Eberhard Berent Goethe Chair, where I wrote the first draft of the book you are about to read in its English translation. I remember talking to my German publisher about possible book titles and how they could not immediately see back then in what sense we live in 'dark times', times that require a serious return to the perennial ideas of moral realism, universalism and humanism – ideas that, despite a common narrative, are not in any interesting sense specifically 'European', let alone 'Eurocentric', as they originated in many different cultural settings long before such a thing as 'Europe' came into existence.

When I was about to finish the manuscript, the still ongoing coronavirus pandemic hit humanity and undermined several assumptions about our globally connected life form, our economic system, the role of nation states, etc. At the beginning, there was reason for hope. For it immediately became obvious that we needed moral notions (such as solidarity with the vulnerable) in order to bear through what had obviously become dark times. By the time I was adding thoughts on the pandemic to the almost finished manuscript, it had become clear to everyone that we are indeed living in dark times.

Unfortunately, moral progress is never isolated from the threat of powerful forms of regress. In various interviews and publications right at the beginning of the pandemic, I therefore warned explicitly against closing borders and rewinding human connectivity, regardless of the evident epidemiological truth that we needed some form of distancing (very inappropriately called 'social distancing') of human bodies in order to protect us from the virological threat. For this reason, I argue in the book that we actually need a 'metaphysical pandemic', meaning a gathering of humanity under the banner of different layers of universalism. These include the biological universalism of our animal species, which has been under attack by a virus which hits us regardless of our more local identities and forms of cultural belonging.

Instead of a 'metaphysical pandemic' as a response to the viral crisis, we have witnessed a series of backlashes accompanying various forms of moral progress over the past few years. On the one hand, we saw a heightened sensibility for modes of evil discrimination, which led to moral progress in the wake of #MeToo, #BlackLivesMatter, and so on (just think of the George Floyd case, which triggered further awareness of the urgency of moral progress during the pandemic). On the other hand, governments shut down borders, discriminated against many African countries (remember the recent reaction to the detection of the Omicron variant in South Africa), cut down civil liberties and hoarded vaccines for wealthy nations, who then even rejected this rich scientific resource on account of various forms of anti-scientific delusions, conspiracy theories, and so forth. In a word, very recent history is a turbulent struggle for moral progress, the detailed history of which has still to be written.

Today, I find myself writing this preface while Russia is raging an unjust, evil war of aggression against Ukraine. We all (including very many Russians, to the extent to which they still have access to the facts concerning attacks against civilians) feel the horror of historical evil in our bones, although we ought to have been feeling it for much longer: horrific crimes against humanity never ceased to take place, in this century or the last. Syria, like many other unjust wars (such as the invasion of Iraq in the fake news and bullshit era of George W. Bush), should have been our warning that the 'end of history' does not mean that from now on everything will be fine, in the sense that moral progress will eventually become automatic and no longer require our efforts and even our sacrifice for the higher ideals of human goodness.

By now, it should have become clear that we live in dark times. But I hasten to add that I have not become a pessimist. The project of a *new enlightenment* which I propose in this book is still entirely valid, as it is a normative recommendation, a call to action grounded in the idea that there are moral facts, that moral progress is possible, and that we can do better than we have been doing for the best part of modernity.

Here, I want to seize the opportunity to correct a widespread misconception of Francis Fukuyama's diagnosis of an 'end of history'.[1] It is not the case that he predicted that eternal peace would automatically be realized in the aftermath of 1989. Rather, he made a normative case according to which liberal democracy corresponds to the project of providing an institutional framework for enhancing the likelihood of moral progress.

During a fellowship at the Stanford Humanities Center in March 2022, I had the opportunity to talk to him about this. He had just completed *Liberalism and its Discontents*,[2] a book that clarifies the way in which he articulates a normative vision of intangible goods, of moral universalism, and of an informed optimism that allows us to read even the current critical situation of humanity as a potential contribution to history in Hegel's sense – i.e., to the 'progress of the consciousness of freedom'.[3] Hegel precisely does not argue that history takes care of itself. On the contrary, history for Hegel is a normative concept – i.e., a concept that permits us to see human action and institution formation in light of our human capacity to improve our condition.

The overall critical situation of humanity in the twenty-first century need not unfold as catastrophe. There is room for moral progress even in dark times. This claim is not naïve optimism but one of many modes of perceiving history through a normative lens, in this case the lens of our capacity for good and evil. Those who become pessimists about the human condition in the face of the various orders of evil with which we are confronted also apply a normative framework for making human action intelligible in terms of value judgements.[4] When thinking about human action, we simply cannot sidestep thick value judgement – i.e., judgement related to moral facts – whether we like it or not. Therefore, I am convinced that moral realism and a renewed philosophy of history can be combined without falling into the traps of the earlier dialectic of enlightenment. Thanks to the various interventions and ramifications of critical theory, it is now clear that history is not a single trajectory but a meshwork of social complexities. Yet this should not, of course, mislead us into thinking that history is an obsolete concept. Such is not the claim of an end of history. That I open the following book with the theme of a resurrection of history under novel conditions is not, therefore, in tension with Fukuyama's fundamental idea that history and thinking in terms of ends are compatible. In order to renew serious philosophical and ethical interest in history in the face of evolving catastrophes, we need a thorough commitment to the possibility of ethical insight and moral progress, a commitment strong enough to help us overcome the incoherent, erroneous and politically dangerous idea that morality is at best the expression of one's belonging to some kind of social group or other.

Stanford, March 2022

Introduction

There is great agitation. The values of freedom, equality and solidarity, which have been taken for granted in recent decades, at least since the fall of the Berlin Wall in 1989, seem to have become uncontrollably shaky along with their market-based realization. This process, which can be viewed as a *resurrection of history*, is accompanied by a confusion of moral fundamentals.[1] We seem to be in a deep crisis of values that has infected our democracy.

Before our eyes, countries such as the USA, Poland, Hungary and Turkey are moving further and further away from recognizing the democratic law-based state as a morally underpinned system of values. Orbán is allying himself with regressive autocratic rulers and the Polish government is attacking the separation of powers and weakening the independence of the courts. In Germany, far-right terrorism is on the rise; German society, somewhat like that of the USA, seems to be splitting up into progressive liberal forces and groupings that are sometimes openly racist, sometimes 'only' xenophobic and fond of German nationalism.

This crisis of values has been intensified by the coronavirus crisis, which infects not only our bodies but also our society. Admittedly, it initially had positive effects. From March 2020 onwards one could sense a new solidarity, triggered by an unprecedented moral decision in politics: in order to save lives, keep the health system running and break the pandemic's infection chains, the neoliberal principle that the logic of the market is the foremost rule of society would be suspended. While the far more disastrous climate crisis has so far failed to make us accept far-reaching economic losses for the sake of doing what is morally right, the novel coronavirus abruptly threw a spanner in the works of global production chains.

It is already clear for economic reasons, then, that we cannot go on as before when the crisis is over. But for that we need a new model of society, one with more stable foundations than the project of a purely economic globalization; for this project collapsed like a house of cards in the face of the coronavirus and, if one takes the financial crisis of 2008 and the foreseeable consequences of the 2020 coronavirus crisis together, it may even have incurred more costs than it has generated profits since 1990 compared to a more sustainable economic model.[2] Here it is a matter of not only the gigantic sums that the German state had to provide to save banks and other businesses, but also the collateral damage of an uncontrolled market logic, which significantly includes the negative effects of social media on the value concepts of liberal democracy. Digitalization, especially the rapid expansion of the internet and the smartphone's infiltration of our everyday lives, has set off a race for data, eavesdropping operations, targeted manipulations via tech monopolies and cyberattacks by Russia, North Korea and China with the aim of destabilizing liberal ideas.

Alongside the risks, every crisis also offers the chance to improve social conditions. The coronavirus crisis holds a mirror up to us: it shows us who we are, how we do business, how we think and feel, and thus opens up potential spaces for positive human change. Ideally this change is based on moral understanding; we can only improve social conditions if we pay more attention than before to what we should and should not do for moral reasons.

Identifying ethically untenable ways of thinking and formulating suggestions for overcoming them is one of the tasks of philosophy. But philosophy cannot carry this out alone; it must rely on cooperation with the natural, technological, life and social sciences, as well as the humanities. This is not simply an academic matter but a matter of who we are as humans and who we want to be in future. In order to work on this form of self-knowledge and the formulation of a sustainable 'vision of good', as the American philosopher Brian Leiter has called it, it is indispensable to build up a far-reaching cooperation between science, politics, business and civil society that is characterized by mutual trust.

This presupposes that we give up the deep-seated idea that a society is fundamentally controlled by competition and distribution battles that can only be kept in check through state regulation and supervision. Rather, the aim of an enlightened society is *autonomy* – the self-regulation of its members through moral understanding. Given the conditions of the modern division of labour, we need an equally global 'spirit of trust' – that is, more of what we commonly refer to as 'solidarity'.[3]

In the spring of 2020, an accumulation of crises (the crisis of liberal democracy, flaws in the health system, the global competition between systems or an increasingly out-of-control digitalization) revealed some of the systemic weaknesses of a world order based almost exclusively on the principles of economic globalization. In times of crisis, however, it becomes apparent that solidarity and cooperation do not work if the markets are the sole authority, since they rely on competition, greed for profit and increasingly also nationalism. This is demonstrated as much by Chinese state capitalism as by Donald Trump's 'America First' policies, and unfortunately this also applies to the intra-European competition for medical supplies that began immediately after the declaration of the pandemic and the catastrophic scenes in northern Italy.

In the last decade, at any rate, in the course of the increasing spread of social media (especially via the smartphone), it has become clear once more that history does not automatically lead to moral and legal progress. The more we can inform ourselves about world events every minute, the more clearly this seems to lead in the direction of unknown, alarming conditions: from the end of democracy, new pandemics and an unstoppable climate crisis to an artificial intelligence that threatens our jobs and perhaps even – as in *Terminator* – humanity as a whole with (self-inflicted) annihilation. In the light of these gigantic packing problems, the urgent question for all sectors of society is: *what on earth are we supposed to do?*

Yet before we decide whether this impression is accurate or not, we should first of all clarify our concepts. For how are we to speak of a matter if we have not clarified what we mean by it?

In the following, I will refer to something that we as humans should and should not do as a *moral fact*. Moral facts assert general demands that concern all people and define categories by which we can assess our behaviour. They show us what we owe ourselves as humans, what we owe other living creatures, and what we owe the environment shared by all life forms (to use a famous formulation by the American moral philosopher Thomas M. Scanlon).[4] Moral facts divide our deliberate, rationally controllable actions into good and evil ones; between these lies the domain of moral neutrality – that is, the domain of what is allowed.

These three areas – good, neutral and evil – are the ethical *values* whose validity is universal, meaning that it extends across different cultures and times. Values are not only positive; they also dictate both what we should and what we should not do. In addition, moral reflection naturally leaves space for actions that are neither good nor evil. Many of our daily activities are not subject to any moral evaluation, and one of the important tasks of philosophical ethics is to show the difference between morally charged and neutral actions. Only thus can we recognize where there is leeway for freedom that is not clearly morally regulated.

Not everything that we do falls into the categories of good and evil. Many everyday actions are morally neutral; in earlier times, humanity had to learn this with reference to human sexuality, for example. Much of what was once considered immoral (such as homosexual sex) has long since been recognized as morally neutral – which leads to moral progress.

Moral facts are articulated as exhortations, recommendations and prohibition. These can be distinguished from *non-moral facts*, which are explored and, in successful cases, discovered by the natural and technological sciences as well as the humanities and social sciences. Non-moral facts do not make any direct demands of us. We know, for example, that alcohol consumption is harmful to our organism, but this does not provide an answer to the question of whether we should drink alcohol or how much. We also know that the discoveries of modern physics and their technological realization can annihilate humanity or serve its continued existence. Yet it does not follow from the structure of the physically explorable universe that humans should exist or how we should treat them.

How we should treat people suffering from a neurodegenerative disease (such as Alzheimer's), for example, depends on the course of the illness and its effects on the personality of the sufferers and their loved ones. But examining the disease is certainly not sufficient on its own to determine an ethically responsible way of dealing with those affected. Moral progress is possible only if we acknowledge that what we owe ourselves, other people, other living beings and the environment is connected to non-moral facts, but it cannot be deduced purely from them.

We have long known in ethics that moral questions are not all limited to our spatial and temporal vicinity. In modernity, what we should and should not do directly or indirectly concerns all people of the present and the future – that is, also future generations that do not yet exist. Furthermore, our duties go beyond the human domain and affect other living beings and the environment (in the sense of non-animal nature).[5] Ethics deals with universal values and goes beyond the horizon of the small communities in which we move every day as members.

When people lament ever more loudly that the foundations of Enlightenment values and liberal democracy have been shaken and history is being turned back, they usually forget to say what *values* actually are and what exactly one means when one claims they are in *crisis*. Such fundamental conceptual clarifications have been carried out by philosophy for millennia and have repeatedly triggered advances in enlightenment.

The present book deals with *moral* values, which differ especially from *economic* values (see below, pp. 26ff.). Contrary to what one often reads, moral values are not subjective in the sense that their existence is an expression of value judgements that humans (whether individuals or groups) have made. Rather, values are the measure by which we assess *value concepts*. Value concepts can define individuals or groups and their way of life and group membership. Value concepts can then be classified as valid or invalid when they are measured against the moral facts.

Good and evil constitute the extremes of our moral reflections and are especially familiar to us in the form of fairly obvious examples. For millennia, saints, founders of religions and heroes who advanced humanity have thus stood for the principle that there is a moral compass. Conversely, since the atrocities of totalitarian dictatorships in the twentieth century at the latest, we have known examples of radical evil as manifested in the use of weapons of mass destruction, total war and extermination camps. Remembrance culture in Germany, which shows us the Holocaust as an incomparable extreme of evil that leaves us speechless time and again, performs the important function of reminding us that evil really exists. Evil did not disappear with the end of the Second World War but appears today in the guise of such figures as Assad and many other war criminals and mass murderers.

Good and evil are universal values: good is a universal moral imperative – regardless of group membership, historical juncture, culture, taste, gender, class or race – whereas evil is a universal moral taboo. Good and evil exist in each and every one of us and show themselves in our daily thoughts and deeds. These universal values and their application to concrete, unclear action situations in which we find ourselves daily are the subject of this book.

There would be no democracy, no democratic law-based state, no separation of powers and no ethics if humanity had not kept asking itself how we can jointly contribute – every person at every moment of their life – to improving ourselves morally as individuals and legally as political communities. Given the current heightened state of crisis, is it not high time for a *new enlightenment*? My aim in the following is no less than that.

I will argue that there are guiding moral principles for human behaviour. These guiding principles extend across cultures; they are universally valid and form the source of universal values in the twenty-first century. Their validity does not depend on being recognized by the majority of people; in this sense they are objective. Truth and facts exist in ethics just as in other areas of human reflection and research, and, in ethics too, facts are more important than this or that opinion. It is a matter of searching together for the moral facts that we have not yet registered. For every period presents new ethical challenges, and the complex crisis of the still young twenty-first century can be mastered ethically only with innovative tools of thought.

This book is a committed attempt to bring order to the actually existing, genuinely dangerous chaos of our time. I would therefore like to *develop a philosophical toolbox for solving moral problems*. It is my aim to breathe new life into the idea that humanity's task on our planet is to enable moral progress through *cooperation*. If we do not succeed in achieving moral progress in a way that incorporates universal values for the twentieth century – and thus all people – we will find ourselves in an abyss of unimaginable dimensions. The socioeconomic inequality on our planet, which will increase through the coronavirus crisis because many millions of people might slide into poverty, is not sustainable in the long term. Hence we cannot use the borders of nation states, for example, to keep away people who experience unimaginable suffering because of the consequences of our own actions. Such a strategy of defensive fortification is both morally reprehensible and doomed to failure in economic and political terms. Whether we like it or not, all humans are in the same boat – i.e. the same planet, which is surrounded by a thin, fragile atmosphere that we destroy through unsustainable production chains and irresponsible actions. The coronavirus pandemic is a wake-up call; it almost seems as if our planet had activated its immune system to curb the high velocity of our self-annihilation and protect itself from further abuse, at least temporarily.

Regrettably, it is absolutely true that we have fallen into a very deep crisis of values at least since the 2008 financial crisis. In the course of a palpable regression of liberal democracy, the last years have seen a rapid spread in models of authoritarian governance represented by Donald Trump, Xi Jinping, Jair Messias (*sic!*) Bolsonaro, Recep Tayyip Erdoğan, Viktor Mihály Orbán, Jarosław Aleksander Kaczyński and many other heads of state. On top of this we have Brexit, new forms of right-wing extremism in Germany (which have developed on the right wing of the AfD) and a general distrust in some parts of society towards scientific expertise in the face of partly anthropogenic climate change. Furthermore, advances in the fields of artificial intelligence, machine learning and robotics seem to present a genuine threat to employment, with the result that some people, such as the legendary entrepreneur and billionaire Elon Musk or the recently deceased physicist Stephen Hawking, even surmise that we humans will, in the near future, be surpassed, subjugated or wiped out by a coming superintelligence that will take control of evolution and the Earth in this manner.[6]

But climate change, which was made possible by scientific and technological progress, is not the only so-called *existential risk* – that is, a threat to the existence of our species through self-annihilation. In addition, the two world wars led to rapid armament in the realm of information technology, the coding and decoding of messages, which has resulted in a computerization of our lifeworld since the Second World War. The latest phase of computerization, so-called *digitalization*, is one in which smartphones, social media, search engines and control systems for our means of mobility (cars, aeroplanes, railways, etc.) influence our movements and our way of thinking.

This is a process that genuinely threatens our existence, for this entire architecture of control employs procedures from *artificial intelligence*. They are capable of infiltrating our thought processes in order to outdo us there, like today's chess or Go programs, which even the best human players have not had any chance of defeating for a long time. A few years ago, the company DeepMind succeeded in developing an AI system called Alpha Go that beats the best players of the ancient Chinese board game Go, even though it is yet more complex than chess.

Anyone who is active in today's social networks is kept in front of the screen by newsfeeds, text messages, images and videos selected by artificial intelligence. This means that we are playing a kind of social chess, as it were, against a superior opponent that will consume more and more of our time and attention. We are bombarded so relentlessly with serious information and fake news that we may one day have lost the ability to think for ourselves.

The rearguard action of liberal democracy and the analogue human, which is still resisting control by the software and corporate interests behind and inside artificial intelligence, threatens that ideal of modernity which relies on scientific-technological progress only succeeding when moral progress keeps in step with it. Otherwise, the infrastructure for a benevolent regulation of our behaviour (which includes the modern welfare state) turns into a dystopian horror scenario like those conceived in classics such as Aldous Huxley's *Brave New World* and George Orwell's *1984*, or – closer to our own time – in science fiction series such as *Black Mirror*, *Electric Dreams* and *Years and Years*.

What characterizes the *dark times* in which everything suggests we are living, and which will be at issue in the following, is that the light of moral insight is sometimes systematically concealed, for example by the dissemination of fake news, political manipulation, propaganda, ideologies and other worldviews.

Enlightenment helps to combat dark times; it rests on the light of reason, and thus moral understanding. An important foundation of enlightenment is the idea that, in reality, we usually know what moral demands a situation makes of us. Extreme cases such as ethical dilemmas are rare. An ethical *dilemma* consists in several possible courses of action being open to us yet leading to a situation in which we cannot fulfil what is morally necessary. If we do something good in a dilemma, we are automatically refraining from some other good, which means we are doing something morally wrong.

When such cases arise, we need clear moral understanding from other situations in order not to lose our moral orientation when faced with the great challenges of our life. If we then cannot gain access to our own moral understanding, things look dark for us.

It is the poorest of the world who feel most acutely what dark times we live in, for they often lack the bare necessities. While we have virologists who are employed to stem the spread of the novel coronavirus together with politicians and health experts, the poorest – who not only live far away but are also herded together in our refugee camps – are fully at the mercy of the coronavirus and many other diseases. We, the well-off, bear some of the responsibility for this, but we block it out in our daily lives because our transactions and consumer habits disguise the fact that we are all in the same boat, on the same planet.

The darkening of the moral horizon is not restricted to the global historical and economic developments of recent decades to which people in poor countries have fallen victim, for it has long since established itself among us, among people who grew up with the canon of values under-pinning the democratic law-based state, which would never have existed without the great wave of enlightenment in the eighteenth century. The coronavirus pandemic brought to light underlying weaknesses in our health systems, as well as revealing moral shortcomings in our way of thinking about one another. Nationalist politicians such as Orbán, Xi Jinping, Putin and Trump seized the opportunity and used the pandemic as a pretext to achieve political outcomes that would previously have been inconceivable (these include closing the USA's borders to European travellers, to which the EU responded with closures of its own). Without exception, the political state of emergency based on the *virological imperative* that we must interrupt infection chains and get statistical curves under control is, in one way or another, used by politicians in all countries to score points, but also by entire nation states. Germany, for example, displays the superior equipment and organization of its own health systems to the world – part of a symbolic arms race primarily with China, which is posing as the perfect crisis manager in order to spread its model of a capitalist dictatorship adorned with communist slogans.

It is worrying that, in Germany too, China's measures are admired and people are exploring digital 'surveillance capitalism', in the sense that, in the spatial isolation of a 'social distancing', we are all producing data like never before and thus giving up our privacy step by step.[7] For now we almost all of us sit in front of our screens all day; workplace and private retreat are merged into the new construct called 'home office',[8] and it is to be expected that many businesses will seize the opportunity to save costs for premises and continue to infiltrate private households after the coronavirus crisis. These are questionable processes that expedite a new 'structural transformation of the public sphere' (Habermas) by connecting the last place of privacy – the residence, the private home – entirely to the public network of data and commodity production.[9]

Such extreme measures exacerbate the crisis of values in liberal democracy, which was not so much overcome as deferred through the feeling of solidarity in the spring of 2020. The regressive forces of right-wing populism are already waiting for us at the other end of the coronavirus tunnel, and what is crucial is to vaccinate ourselves *now* against this danger by developing suitable intellectual formats that offer us better insight into what we should and should not do for moral reasons.

Modernity, initiated with a bang by the French Revolution, rests on the utopia of enlightenment, which essentially consists in the idea that our institutions – which means primarily the state – become instruments of moral progress. This is only possible if science, business, politics and every single citizen contribute through their daily behaviour to creating a situation in which we attempt in all conscience to do the right thing, both individually and collectively. The French Revolution made the utopia of enlightenment seem within reach, but it slipped away through a fierce backlash from mostly nationalist interests – starting from the waves of terror carried out by the different revolutionary factions in France and the subsequent Napoleonic tyranny.

However, we have progressed further than the late eighteenth and nineteenth century in many ways, both positively and negatively. We have seen the disastrous consequences of advancing scientific and technological progress without keeping step in moral terms. This has led to the development of weapons of mass destruction, for example, which were already unleashed on humanity at certain points in the twentieth century. And without the unfettered economic progress that goes hand in hand with modern technology, we would be not facing a climate crisis.

We can confront the twin dangers of new wars through the resurgence of nation-alism and the ecological crisis threatening hundreds of millions of people only through moral progress. What is required now is for humans to be mindful of their moral abilities, to begin to acknowledge that only a global cooperation beyond the egotisms of nation states can halt our ever accelerating movement towards a world-historical abyss.

Moral progress means becoming better at recognizing what we should and should not do. It presupposes insight and generally involves uncovering moral facts that were partially concealed. What we should or should not do is connected to the nature of reality – that is, the facts. What measures are suitable for reducing environmentally harmful emissions, how one diagnoses and heals diseases, how one distributes resources fairly, what forms of verbal expression must be classified as psychological violence, how one overcomes sexual harassment and other forms of gender discrimination based on power and violence, how we can regulate assisted dying – these are all moral and legal questions that can only be answered if one faces reality.

The character of non-moral facts can ideally be ascertained through cooperative research in the natural sciences, the humanities, the social sciences and technology, by giving universities and other research institutions the assignment of examining reality with reference to the urgent moral questions of our time. Philosophy also depends on natural science and technology; it must not ignore what we know about humans, other animals and the environment, of course, but it must integrate this knowledge into a philosophically informed image of humanity. Conversely, it is equally important for natural and technological scientists, but also economists who increasingly speak about philosophical issues, to acknowledge the state of philosophical research. Without such interdisciplinary cooperation, where all partners in the conversation take the others' insights seriously and translate them into their own language, the ideal of enlightenment is doomed to fail.

If we want to find out what we should undertake or avoid in the face of a morally striking, dangerous situation that may concern all of us, we must take on board every form of expertise that can help us to assess the non-moral facts as precisely as possible. For example, it is more urgently necessary than ever to acknowledge the massive environmental risks of our consumer behaviour and our global production chains so that we can take the corresponding moral, political and socioeconomic steps.

Whether we need more or less wind power to reach our climate goals as soon as possible is central to the question of how many wind turbines we should put up, and where. At the same time, we must take into account other non-moral parameters that also affect the environment (for example: How many storms arise, and where? How much woodland can we clear for wind turbines without attacking the green lung of a region?), so that we can ensure the best possible future both for our living children and yet unborn generations through productive cooperation between science, business, politics and civil society.

This aim has been undermined through an infiltration by postmodern arbitrariness, which still expects us to believe that there is ultimately no objective truth, no such thing as facts that can be brought to light using suitable research methods – only politically coloured opinions. Many even believe that science can never be liberated from ultimately senseless, politically motivated spin, such that it has meanwhile become a widespread belief, especially at leading universities in the USA and Great Britain, that universities are a place to wage identity-political conflicts.

It is in this spirit that the postmodern sociologist of knowledge Bruno Latour has claimed for decades that there are no 'matters of fact', only different 'matters of concern' that are examined or produced in laboratories. For example, he asserts that Ramses II cannot have died of tuberculosis, as examinations of the mummy have shown, as the tuberculosis pathogen has only been known since the nineteenth century.[10] Latour thinks that we should protect the environment not because we would otherwise be putting ourselves and other life forms in massive danger (as we have recognized through natural science) but, rather, because there is an ecological 'parliament of things' in which rainforests, insects and the ozone layer all have a vote.[11] Like many others among the first postmodern theorists, Latour has been insisting since the 1980s that we should forget about facts and instead take a stand in society for the oppressed, a group that, in his eyes, now includes the environment.

But this form of identity politics is verifiably nonsense, as it rests on a denial of facts. If Latour's theory of science were correct, we could simply do away with the coronavirus by ceasing to examine it in laboratories, as it would only be in effect – indeed, it would only exist – if it were discovered (or more likely invented). This is postmodern claptrap.

We cannot give meaningful answers to urgent moral questions without acknowledging reality. We all know this from experience: someone who denies facts for too long and evades reality will sink deeper and deeper into a life crisis. At some point one must face facts and ask *who one is and who one wants to be.* The postmodern denial of reality, facts, knowledge and truth is no help in this, as one can see in almost every speech by the current [2020] American president, who is no doubt in perfect agreement with the postmodern opinion that there is no such thing as truth or reality, only expressions of group membership.

On closer inspection, postmodern identity politics is no less destructive than a digitalization gone wild that toys with the notion both of replacing the welfare state, indeed democracy itself, with Chinese models of governance, and of expediting economic revival through computerization and automatization of industrial processes.

Modernity, as the Enlightenment ideal that led to the democratic law-based state, is under fire from all sides, and all of us are deeply unsettled by this shock in different ways. In this book, I combat the creeping erosion of the pillars of the democratic law-based state – which is closely connected to postmodern arbitrariness – by developing the outline of a *new enlightenment* that I will call *New Moral Realism.*[12]

As stated above, we are currently witnessing a darkening of the historical horizon. Globally interconnected humanity is currently working towards its own annihilation, assisted by the globalized production chains of sometimes pointless consumer goods that are produced at the expense of human beings purely out of greed for profit. No one needs a new car as often as the people who can actually afford one every few years, and who want one because they admire the latest interior options and technology. The same applies to smartphones, tablets, items of clothing and the many luxury items that we buy for ourselves and our children without noticing how it harms their future. We complain about plastic and know that it is destroying the oceans in which we want to swim and fish, yet simultaneously we buy plastic toys that replicate maritime scenes.

Our consumer behaviour is thoroughly contradictory. One relies on digitalization to reduce the amount of travel in the business world, for example, but easily overlooks the fact that digitalization also contributes to the ecological crisis. I was once invited to a conference that was held by a ministry in one of Germany's federal states to investigate the dangers of social media for the democratic law-based state, and the organizers were proud that it was being streamed live on YouTube. Treating social media as the problem while employing them as an act of resistance is a fairly obvious contradiction.

The many such contradictions that we encounter on a daily basis are far from harmless. The question of whether we achieve the necessary moral progress to guide a potentially dangerous scientific-technological progress in the right direction starts in everyday life. Physics and chemistry have given us modern infrastructure and the preparation of drinking water, but also the nuclear bomb and chemical weapons. Scientific-technological progress alone does not guarantee any more than economic prosperity that people will do what is morally right and implement it institutionally. At every moment of our life, each one of us is called upon to do good and thus reduce the magnitude of evil and devastation. Responsible action does not only take part somewhere 'out there' or 'up there' among influential people in politics, the media or business; it plays a role in the behaviour of each one of us.

As an example, we can present a fictional person I will call Antje Kleinhaus (in the hope no one really goes by that name). Antje lives in Berlin's Prenzlauer Berg district, sponsors an African child, donates to charity and generally feels empathy towards the migrant children who, as she sees on TV in the evenings, are harassed by some members of the public as well as the European border guards. Every day, she is appalled anew by the current dark times and tries to dissuade her acquaintances from voting AfD,[13] as she is in favour of tolerance and open-mindedness. One fine day her young daughter Luna wants to invite her new kindergarten friend Ayşe into the Kleinhaus household for her birthday party. Antje, however, feels that Ayşe does not quite fit in, and that she has a totally different culture, as both her parents came to Germany from Turkey and Ayşe speaks broken German. On top of that, they will be eating pizza with salami, and Antje is reluctant to confront Ayşe with pork. To honour Ayşe's culture, she is ultimately not invited, because Antje thinks it better for Ayşe to grow up happy in her own milieu – just as the donations for her sponsored African child serve to ensure that it can grow up in its homeland, in Africa, and will not have to brave the difficult journey to Germany.

This kind of mendacity shows that all of us, even the seemingly quite innocent and somewhat progressive Antje Kleinhaus, harbour potentially dangerous prejudices in some part of ourselves. If someone in the subway gives a start when a person who somehow looks 'like an Islamic terrorist' enters their train, this expresses a potentially racist, or at least xenophobic, prejudice. Please ask yourself: What does a typical German look like? If you think you have an answer, you have just become acquainted with a racist prejudice of your own – as there is no such thing as a typical German, let alone a typical German appearance.

We all pollute the environment, especially the Germans, whose history includes the invention of the automobile with a combustion engine by Gottlieb Daimler and Carl Friedrich Benz. The beautiful state of Baden-Württemberg has seen not only the founding of the Green Party but also the invention of the vehicle whose existence is a major reason why we need ecological policies in the first place.

To resolve all these contradictions, what we need is not only large-scale global and political solutions; we must also start with ourselves, with our own prejudices and our own actions. Moral progress is only possible if we acknowledge that evil is not only 'out there' – among the Americans, the billionaires, the Saudis, the Chinese, the Russian hackers or whatever actors one would like to blame for the dark times.

Next to the climate crisis, one important current danger in Germany comes from political extremism and the accompanying terrorism, which have led in recent years to political murders (of Walter Lübcke)[14] and terrorist attacks such as the recent one in Hanau.[15] This is, among other things, the result of a fundamental problem that will be one of the subjects of this book: *post-truth emotionalism*. This means that the creation of group memberships and majorities through sometimes targeted narratives of identity formation is more significant, both for minor and major decisions, than the attempt to work together on choosing a path of action that is recognizably correct by adducing rationally communicable reasons and establishing facts. Simplistically put, what matters today, often more than the relevant, verifiable facts that are at issue, are short, emotional messages in the Twitter format, pictures series on Instagram, or catchwords in a political confrontation blown up by the media.

That is why, as stated above, it is time to bring the central idea of the Enlightenment into play again: that, by means of reason, we can work *together* on finding out what we should and should not do. We need an updated form of enlightenment, however, one that is immune to edifices of ideas that attempt to convince us that there are, in moral matters, no universally acceptable solutions that are just for all people but only ever a defence of the law of the strongest. In the following, such edifices of ideas are accordingly subjected to clearly comprehensible criticism and rejected. This book, then, is an opening move of a new enlightenment whose necessity has already been pointed out by others.[16]

The new enlightenment aims for a *co-immunism*, to use a well-chosen formulation by Peter Sloterdijk (albeit with an entirely different meaning): the concern is to adapt the content of the canon of values comprising freedom, equality, solidarity, etc., to each period and to assess the respective dangers that are mobilized to bring about the fall of reason. Reason, after all, must always wrestle with unreason on account of numerous factors. The American philosopher Stanley Cavell was probably quite right when he suggested in his central book, *The Claim of Reason*, that 'Nothing is more human than the wish to deny one's humanity.'[17]

My book is aimed at the largest possible group of people who are both disturbed by the current palpable and observable coarsening of the sociopolitical discourse and open to an attempt to employ their reason for the purpose of moral judgements. One cannot speak to everyone to convince them that communicable reasons, grounds that can be shared with other people, form the moral foundation of successful coexistence. The power of arguments cannot, for example, help us combat violent far-right extremists and the intellectual agitators who encourage them any more than notorious climate change deniers or anti-vaxxers. In a society whose institutions fundamentally strive to ascertain the truth, to acknowledge facts, and to adhere to the principle that every person should treat all others as equal in moral questions, it is harder for the intellectual evil of these agitators to bear fruit than in a discourse where reasons are replaced by catchphrases and imperfect argumentation is overpowered by the evocation of emotional states. The post-truth age, which is deliberately reinforced via social media, is the soil in which radicalizations flourish, be they religious, political or otherwise. There is no point debating with an Islamic State hate preacher or a radical Stalinist to establish who is right through an exchange of reasons, since the basic rules of such an exchange are not accepted by the ideology of the interlocutor.

Radical intolerance whose aim is to undermine the foundations of the democratic law-based state by any means available (including violence against innocents) is nothing that one should tolerate. Therefore, this book is directed at those who wish to deal *rationally* – that is, not in a manner driven purely by their personal opinions – with the questions of whether there are such things as moral facts and moral progress in dark times and of how we can develop a system of values for the twenty-first century on the basis of universal values. The fact that increasing numbers of people are not interested in this is part of the problem, and I wish to contribute to the solution with these reflections from a philosophical perspective.

ONE

What Values Are, and Why They Are Universal

This chapter deals with the ethical fundamentals of the new enlightenment, which arise from a few core theses. The **core theses of the New Moral Realism**[1] are as follows:

Core thesis 1: There are moral facts that are independent of our private and group opinions. They exist objectively.

Core thesis 2: The objectively existing moral facts are essentially knowable to us; they are spirit-dependent. They concern humans and constitute a moral compass for what we should do, are allowed to do or must prevent. The central moral facts are obvious, and in dark times they are concealed by ideology, propaganda, manipulation and psychological mechanisms.

Core thesis 3: The objectively existing moral facts apply at all times in which humans have existed, do exist and will exist. They are independent of culture, political opinion, religion, gender, place of origin, appearance and age, and therefore universal. The moral facts do not discriminate.

I will address core thesis 1 as **moral realism**. Thesis number 2 concerns us humans as the free spiritual beings that are subject to moral demands. I therefore call it **humanism**. Finally, number 3 is usually referred to as **universalism**.[2]

We could coin a memorable slogan for this chapter by contrasting two fictional conceptions of the state. I will call the first PRN: P for pluralism, R for relativism and N for nihilism. I consider the constellation of value pluralism, value relativism and value nihilism harmful, because it amounts to the idea that moral codices – that is, value systems – arise and are maintained only because a more or less random group of people subscribes to them. According to this model, values are dogmas that keep a group together, which means that their validity is limited to only one group.

An example of this would be the value concepts of an evangelical Christian fundamentalist group that rejects all forms of abortion, any consumption of alcohol, same-sex intercourse and, in many cases, even tea and coffee as morally deviant, being deplorable in the eyes of God. Many Christian fundamentalist groups, such as the Jehovah's Witnesses, also believe that there are only a few chosen people whom God addresses with his moral commandments. In their eyes, most people are damned from the start and will either burn in hell or simply be exterminated.

A less radical (but equally mistaken) idea is that there are 'German' values such as punctuality and precision that do not apply in Italy, for example, where people do not follow the minute-to-minute rhythm of chronometric time and place no great value on carrying out work processes with German accuracy. This notion had fatal consequences: while Italy was in dire need of logistical and financial assistance from other European countries in the coronavirus crisis to prevent the overload of its health system through severe cases of COVID-19, its European partners initially refused to provide any. In Germany one increasingly heard it said that the problem in northern Italy was simply a result of cultural deficits – just 'Italian chaos'. A morally reprehensible, verifiably false stereotype. It is untrue that the northern Italian health system was pushed to the limit in the coronavirus pandemic by any *cultural* factors. The terrible tragedy in northern Italy and elsewhere is no expression of local cultural problems but could equally be explained by the logic of the virus's spread, which is still not fully understood because we lack the necessary data and studies. That Germany has more intensive-care beds per capita than Italy is due not to any 'German values' but, rather, to the organization of our health systems and our more generous state finances. Nationalist nonsense can be avoided if we remain morally clear-sighted; without this, there can be no ethics and no rational investigation of moral facts.

In opposition to PRN, the new enlightenment defends the ideal of a 'Republic of Humanistic Universalists' (RHU), whose basic moral-philosophical constitution, as we will see, fortunately corresponds largely to the German constitution [*Grundgesetz*]. Here R stands for realism, H for humanism and U for universalism.

In the last seventy years, one reason why the constitution has had a progressive effect is that it was a result of that dark time. Even the Nazi dictatorship was unable to extinguish the light of reason completely. This is not an argument in favour of either German nationalist hubris or a harmless constitutional patriotism but, rather, a reminder of a constellation that came about as a reaction to the darkest abyss of German history.

The constitution of the Federal Republic of Germany formulates a catalogue of values with a claim to universal validity that concerns not only German citizens (the obvious addressees of this text) but all people. It is far from a value-free foundation and could potentially lead to a party-political battle that might even result in an abolition of democracy. That is why today's crisis of values is at once a crisis of democracy: whoever damages universalism turns against the idea that our community is based on the fact that we are all human beings and already have certain rights and duties for that very reason. These include the right to develop our personalities freely, the right to life and physical integrity, gender equality, and the right not to be disadvantaged in court owing to gender, language, place of origin, income, etc.

People often overlook the fact that our basic rights also mean duties: if someone has the right not to be disadvantaged through racist stereotypes or homophobia, this also means that they have the duty not to disadvantage anyone else in the same way. Basic rights are meant to help us attain our human rights. Human rights include many things we have not legally codified: the right to living space, the right to environmental safeguards (allowing us to breathe air that is sufficiently clean and conducive to our well-being as humans), the right to leisure, the right to retirement, and generally anything to ensure that we can live in a community of solidarity whose goal is to encourage moral progress and cooperation.

In the present chapter I will argue that moral facts are justified not by God, by universal human reason or by evolution but, rather, by themselves. Like many other facts, they require no justification but, rather, a recognition that allows their contours to be grasped. There are self-evident moral truths, for example: you shall not cause pain to newborn children. No one, whether Chinese, German, Russian, African or American, whether a Muslim, a Hindu or an atheist, would seriously doubt this. There are a great many such self-evident moral truths that are immediately accepted by all people – yet we lose sight of this, because in moral matters we usually occupy ourselves with the difficult, complex moral problems which different communities seem to approach in divergent ways.

There is no moral algorithm, no rule and no system of rules that deals with all problems once and for all.

We can illustrate this with an example. Until recently, many people thought (and many still do) that it was entirely permissible, even necessary and desirable, to use corporal punishment on children. Perhaps some children in the past even thought it was good for them, since this is what they were told day in, day out, on the basis of supposed facts. Corporal punishment, one might have thought, is unpleasant but sensible, somewhat like a flu vaccination. But the disciplines of scientific psychology, sociology, theology and neurobiology, which came into being gradually only in modern times, have meanwhile shown us that corporal punishment has a traumatic effect, and that violence and cruelty in the family are even an important foundation for totalitarian regimes, which build on domestic violence.

It is conceivable in principle, of course, albeit highly unlikely, that there might be findings in fifty years showing that corporal punishment actually contributes decisively to maturation, and that children brought up gently in keeping with today's standards tend towards brutal, environmentally destructive capitalist consumerism, meaning that we must get out the rod again. But even if this were the case, the future reasons that would convince us as a justification for corporal punishment would be entirely different from those of the past, since people then were unaware of the facts that had yet to be discovered.

The fact that we can be mistaken about moral questions does not mean that there is no such thing as moral progress.

This first chapter is concerned with developing the three core theses of realism, humanism and universalism and defending them especially against value pluralism, value relativism and value nihilism – PRN. To give you an overview of the train of thought and avoid some possible misunderstandings from the outset, I would first like to explain in brief what exactly PRN is.

Value pluralism asserts the following about morality: when in Rome, do as Romans do. Every country is shaped by a culture with its own moral code, and some countries form groups that can communicate with one another. In this way, one thinks of the West in contrast to the East or Europe in contrast to Africa as orders of values. However one divides up the territories to which one thus assigns different value systems, the error lies in the assumption that there are separate value systems. This assumption quickly leads to the (false) assumption of **incommensurability** – that is, the notion that there are radically different moral systems that cannot be measured by the same standards.

Value pluralism is not automatically tied to the idea of incommensurability. It is first of all a form of ethnological assertion: on the basis of an examination of value concepts found in different places, it assumes that there is a plurality of value concepts. This does not necessarily mean that one of these systems of value concepts is not better or more right than the others; one could be a value pluralist while also claiming that one's own value system is superior to all others, perhaps even the only correct one. A value pluralist could say that most value concepts are simply wrong. The existence of different systems of opinions does not in itself preclude one of them being considered correct.

Value relativism goes a step further and assumes that what is morally recommended and morally reprehensible only ever applies in each respective value system, which is incompatible with the others. There is no overarching order that determines which system is morally superior to another. The choice of system, if made at all, is not made according to moral criteria. For the value relativist, then, there is no good or evil as such, only good and evil relative to one of the many value systems. This means that, strictly speaking, the exponents of these systems cannot assess one another by means of an independent standard.

If, for example, a Putin follower in St Petersburg is inciting against liberal democracy and sees it as Western decadence, while a value-relativist Dutchman considers liberal democracy a good thing precisely because many value systems can coexist in democracy, then, according to the relativist, no one is objectively right. To him, they both simply express what applies in their respective systems, and thus each is completely right. For the relativist, the confrontation between value systems leads no longer to a morally assessable ethical encounter but to a competition between systems and to concrete struggles for supremacy in determining the geopolitical narrative.

Finally, **value nihilism** takes all this to its logical conclusion and assumes that there are no values which determine our actions. It views all values as no more than empty words, at best simply excuses that are used so that particular groups can assert their preferences against competitors.

In this chapter I would like to convince you that all three assumptions are wrong while, at the same time, developing an alternative view in opposition to the postmodern, post-truth zeitgeist for which PRN is so useful.

There are moral facts that dictate what we should and should not do. Generally speaking, a **fact** is something that is true. Examples of facts are that Hamburg is located in northern Germany; that $2 + 2 = 4$; that you are currently reading this sentence, and so forth. **Moral facts**, unlike these descriptions of reality, usually contain demands dictating that one should or should not do something. Examples of moral facts are that one should not be cruel to children; that one should treat all people equally (regardless of appearance, place of origin or religion); that one should not push one's way to the front; or that one should help people whose lives can only be saved by oneself, as long as one does not endanger oneself by doing so. A moral fact is an objectively existing moral situation that determines which concrete actions are necessary, allowed or impermissible. Moral facts and values can exist without being correctly recognized, let alone followed. People often push their way aggressively to the front in everyday life, after all, whether on the motorway or at the supermarket, and unfortunately many children, in Germany too, are subjected to abuse and cruelty. If there are such moral facts, they do not come into existence only when we pay attention to them, let alone because we somehow invent or agree on them.

Moral facts are neither social compromises nor cultural constructs, because they exist *sui generis* and must be held to universal value standards that can be employed for an overarching evaluation of compromises and cultural constructs. Moral facts apply across cultural boundaries and have always done so – which does not mean that there are no difficult or new moral questions, as we will see. The task in our moral reflection on what we should and should not do, and on what is optional (that is, what we can equally do or not do without harming the moral order), consists in finding out together what the relevant moral facts are. Moral reflection, then, means *convincing* ourselves and others of the right way to act, not *persuading* others to follow our own prejudice- and interest-based perception of the social situation.

The good, the bad and the neutral: basic moral rules

Before we can address concrete moral questions of our time on the basis of examples, we must first clarify a few basic concepts; for, if our concepts are unclear and hazy, we can easily make logical mistakes. This prevents us from formulating well-founded and, in the best case, true and coherent opinions. This is especially grave in the realm of practical philosophy, which is concerned with our actions, because it has consequences for our lifeworld. If we have only hazy notions of happiness, duties and rights, we will all too easily make mistakes because we fail to understand the fundamental definitions of these concepts. One of the main tasks of philosophy is therefore the clarification of concepts, which has been closely connected to the modern ideal of enlightenment at least since Kant.

Ethics is the philosophical subdiscipline that, since the term was coined by Plato and Aristotle, has been occupied systematically with the question of what constitutes a good, well-lived life. The traditional name for a good, well-lived life or a correspondingly successful phase in one's life is ***eudaimonia***, which one would translate today in a simplified form as **happiness**. The first systematic, rational ethics that claimed scientific status, that of Aristotle, is therefore primarily a contribution to happiness research. The term 'ethics' comes from the Greek word ēthos, whose range of meanings encompasses 'whereabouts', 'residence', 'custom', 'habit', 'character' and 'mentality'. The examination of ēthos has therefore always dealt with the formation of human character, in order to answer the question of how we can attain happiness and sustain it despite the adversities and hardships of life and survival.

This must be distinguished from **morality** as a response to the question of how humans should act, both in general and in particular situations. Of course there are norms and sanctions in other areas of the coordination of human actions, especially in the form of legal systems. The universal values of general ethics are a form of norms; there are also other norms, however, that are tied to ethical ones but apply largely to realms of non-morally regulated, neutral actions. They include traffic regulations, as well as aesthetic norms that concern the assessment of a given art genre (such as opera). Our preferred choice of art genre is not a morally charged problem. It is neither good nor evil to prefer *House of Cards* to Beethoven's *Fidelio* (though it does show poor taste ...).

The theory of norms encompasses more than philosophical ethics. Legal norms, for example, are not automatically moral in their meaning. In the case of a state that is illegitimate in moral terms, it is morally reprehensible to follow its legal norms. Yet there are legal norms, both in democratic law-based states and in morally questionable ones, that are morally neutral: someone who walks across a red light is not in any sense making a *moral* mistake – unlike a driver speeding through empty city streets at night, who could overlook someone and run them over.

Morality and law are thus connected, but far from identical. The validity of legal norms, their power over actors, still applies even when the prevailing legislation and the underlying laws are recognizably immoral. Stalinist show trials were *legally valid*, even if we consider them *morally illegitimate*. That is the fundamental **difference between legality and legitimacy**.

Morality articulates rules that concretely determine which actions are forbidden, necessary or permissible. In this way one can abstractly mark two extremes, two poles, and a moral centre. Whatever is clearly morally forbidden is **evil**. One should refrain from evil actions under any circumstances. Whatever is clearly morally necessary is **good**. The centre of this moral spectrum is the permissible. As the permissible is neither good nor evil but simply permissible, I call it **neutral** (from the Latin *ne-uter*, meaning 'indifferent' or 'neither'). The neutral lies not beyond good and evil but, rather, on this side, as it were, by being neither the one nor the other. Good, as the extreme on the moral scale – that is, something that is clearly necessary – is not permissible in this sense, since something can only be permitted if one can either do it or refrain it. But one must never refrain from doing good. It is morally necessary – something to which there is no real alternative. It is in the nature of good that every alternative to it is worse.

Of course, we do not consider all human actions recognizably and unambiguously good, neutral or evil, as these are only three central reference points on the moral spectrum. For the most part, to grasp the moral space more generally, I will therefore speak in the following of what is morally necessary, permissible or reprehensible.

The **morally necessary** is what one *should* do in a given situation (but not automatically in every situation).[3] The **morally permissible** is everything that one *can* reasonably do in a given situation, without any obligation to do so. In each situation, there are many permissible options without moral significance. The **morally reprehensible** is what one should not do in a given situation (but not automatically in every situation).[4]

One of the central concepts in this book is that of values. Generally speaking, **values** are standards of assessment. In the special case of universal courses for action that concern us as humans, there are *moral* values: to the extent that we *morally* assess actions that have actually been carried out, or actions that are possible in the light of the facts, by applying recognizable standards, we rely on moral facts. The evaluation of actions in terms of whether they fall into the category of good, neutral or evil refers to moral and non-moral facts, assigning them to one of these value categories with a fallible knowledge claim.

A knowledge claim is **fallible** if one uses it to assert something that could certainly be false and there is no compelling reason to accept it. Most knowledge claims are fallible, since we are never sufficiently aware of all circumstances for us to be absolutely secure in our judgement. For example, I think Angela Merkel is currently in Berlin. But I could be wrong.

The more complex the reality about which one is trying to gain information, the more likely it is that even the most secure of our knowledge claims are ultimately false. This is no different for moral matters, for here, too, the nature of reality is at issue. We want to find out what we should do in a difficult situation, which is different from creating courses of action by arbitrarily positing them.

Moral values are universal. They apply to everyone, everywhere and at all times, even if not everyone is necessarily fully aware of this. That is why we can be wrong about values. The fact that they are universal does not mean that everyone recognizes them all the time.

There is a particular difference between *moral* and *economic* values. **Economic values** are measured on the stock market, in currencies and by banks. They express the results of negotiation processes tied to the production and exchange of commodities. Economic values do not apply universally or across different times. In addition, some of the rules of play in the economic realm are highly immoral, since it is customary to make profits by deliberately inflicting losses on other people, or at least withholding profitable information from them.

In a good society, political measures expressed in legal rules serve to establish the right hierarchy between moral and economic values; for example, the law-based state ideally ensures that the production and exchange of commodities does not violate minimum moral standards. Then ethics takes precedence over economic accretion, and immoral economic growth is considered worse than a recession. Human trafficking is prohibited in Germany and many other states, for example, and we also have a minimum wage, universal healthcare and further welfare structures ensuring that not everything and everyone is subject to the rules of the market. If economic values alone rule, however, and are more important than moral values, we find ourselves in an immoral, reprehensible form of society – one can observe this to an extent in the USA, but in some details also in Germany and, if one looks closely, ultimately everywhere. Especially in the USA, the dollar counts for more than the health of human beings who quite simply cannot afford patient care.

Naturally, economic values are indispensable for the implementation of moral values, something that has been pointed out especially by the American philosopher Martha Nussbaum.[5] Morality and economy need not, and indeed should not, be mutually exclusive. However, this presupposes that the economic aims of an enlightened society are subordinated to its moral principles. A morally reprehensible economy must be rejected at all costs – a fact that ideally informs economic theorizing and its political implementation in the market economy.

In this sense, the famous line from Bertolt Brecht's *Threepenny Opera*, 'Food is the first thing; morals follow on',[6] is only half true: moral standards can only be met if we create the economic conditions for it, for we cannot generally expect humans to behave like moral heroes under all circumstances. Conversely, it is the duty of the economy to create the conditions in which moral actions are possible without heroism, being quite ordinary and possible for all people.

However, it follows from this that the economy should follow moral aims, not vice versa. Morality is not subject to any market logic, but market logic should be guided by the overarching goals of an enlightened society geared towards moral understanding and moral progress. If it is not, then the market's logic is unfettered, and this leads to moral injustices that grow in an uncontrolled fashion – which includes the rightly criticized spread of plutocracy, the rule of money, which is especially drastic and rampant in the USA and Russia.

Moral facts

A *fact* is an objectively existing truth. It is true, for example, that the trains of the Deutsche Bahn are often delayed. It is also true that the Earth has only one moon, that it orbits the sun, that, at the time of writing, Angela Merkel is federal chancellor, that over a million Indian citizens own sneakers and that I am just finishing this sentence.

But there are facts in the realm of values too: moral facts. Many people today believe, implicitly or explicitly, that there are no moral facts, that it is not objectively clear what we should or should not do in a given situation for moral reasons. Instead, people then say something like (to quote Jean-Paul Sartre): 'Indeed, everything is permissible if God does not exist.'[7]

This raises a fundamental question that appears in a number of variations: do objective values actually exist? This question is closely connected to what we should do. If pure reality did not issue any demands, if demands only ever came from the voices of authorities (teachers, parents, churches, governments we have internalized, etc.), then ethics would really be pedagogy, psychology or sociology. We could replace ethics with spiritual guidance or behavioural economy, which is used to control us as irrational herds.

In addition to virological suggestions, we therefore see behavioural-economic models being employed in the time of the coronavirus crisis: in many countries – especially those where curfews have been imposed – people are being viewed as herd animals that are not really capable of moral decisions. Morality is left out of this perspective, as the authorities implicitly or explicitly doubt that people are capable of genuine moral understanding.[8]

This is a more or less mild form of value nihilism known in philosophy as anti-realism. To understand this misconception better we must undertake a brief excursion into political theory.

The philosophical discipline that examines the question of whether there are (more or less) objectively existing moral facts that we can recognize, or perhaps not recognize, is **metaethics**. It considers the important question of what form of existence moral values exhibit, or whether and under what conditions the moral statements with which we express the forbidden, the permissible and the reprehensible are true or false. The most prominent schools of thought in current metaethics can be divided into *moral realism* and *moral anti-realism*.

Moral realism assumes that the principles such as 'You shall not kill' or 'You shall reduce your CO_2 emissions so that the generations after you can have good lives too' are true, since there are moral facts represented by these postulates.

Moral anti-realism, on the other hand, asserts (as formulated in the title of a famous book by the Australian philosopher John Leslie Mackie) that ethics is a matter of *Inventing Right and Wrong*.[9] Anti-realists, also known as subjectivists, believe that there are in fact no moral values, no prescribed or reprehensible actions. From this point of view, moral principles in everyday thinking seek to pretend by grammatical means that moral standards exist. Thinkers from the Sophists of antiquity via Nietzsche and the National Socialist constitutional scholar Carl Schmitt to the present day have tried repeatedly to expose this (supposed) illusion.[10]

Anti-realism is a dangerous step towards value nihilism, which leaves behind all moral obligations. Though it does not have to be interpreted nihilistically, it can scarcely explain why we as humans have the impression of being called upon by a higher morality, why we experience a phenomenon that we all know as the voice of our conscience. To the anti-realists, this voice is a form of grammatical deception.

The limits of free speech: how tolerant is democracy?

The idea of a parliamentary democracy is geared towards reaching, through debate, a consensus that did not previously exist. As in a compromise, this consensus should incorporate different perspectives in order to represent as many sections of the electorate as possible. In the space of free expression, then, one opinion is initially as good as another. Whether it is actually true seems to be unimportant, which is why, in ethically urgent and difficult matters, this notion leads to a replacement of the value of truth with strategies for reaching compromises.

This can have fatal consequences, for, in politics too, complex moral issues are debated and moral judgements reached. And that is a good thing, since our elected representatives are also human beings and also bear great moral responsibility.

In politics, as in public debates, it is a matter not only of forming opinions but also of finding out which opinions are good – that is, true and morally defensible. It soon becomes clear that something is rotten about a conception of absolutely free expression in which every expressed opinion is truly considered as good as any other.

Let us assume, for example, that paedo-criminals decided to found a party in order to procure votes for the so far oppressed, even legally persecuted paedo-criminal minority and thus allow them to voice their opinions within the framework of parliamentary democracy. If you think this is a good idea, you will rightly face a number of accusations. You are certainly allowed to express such opinions (and will by no means be punished or otherwise pursued by the state), but you will not get far with any attempt to give paedo-criminals a voice and find open spaces for them. If, for example, one suggested opening up a few kindergartens to visits by paedo-criminals so that they could live out their sexual diversity, one would soon find not only that this opinion lacks anything convincing but also that many people who wanted to be tolerant and acknowledge all opinions will suddenly pass harsh moral judgements and mount the barricades.

This extreme example illustrates the fact that the idea of democracy cannot consist in giving every minority that is restricted by institutions in carrying out its free will (which, in addition to paedo-criminals, would also include burglars, murderers and enemies of the constitution) the moral and legally enshrined right to found a party in order to shift the political guidelines of society.

There is a value framework of democracy *legitimacy* that differs from merely factual *legality*, which is why the legislature has to revise a few laws in each new legislative period whenever it becomes apparent over the years or decades that they contradict the value framework of democracy by no longer keeping up with the moral progress of society.

A recent example for this is the removal of paragraph 103 from the penal code, which demanded a different punishment for insulting the sovereign than for insulting other persons. When Erdoğan invoked this paragraph and instructed his German lawyers to bring the full weight of the law to bear on the comedian Jan Böhmermann and put him behind bars for writing a mocking poem about him,[11] even Angela Merkel decided he had crossed a line (despite feeling that Böhmermann's genuinely morally questionable work of art had gone too far). This led to a rapid parliamentary consensus, and the paragraph has meanwhile been removed. The Böhmermann case had shown that it was no longer in keeping with our times to require an especially grave punishment for *lèse majesté*. Thus an instance of moral progress actually came about thanks to Böhmermann and his highly questionable intervention.

Unfortunately we have not yet learned to prosecute other forms of defamation appropriately, as demonstrated by another German case: the legal dispute over the clearly morally unacceptable verbal abuse of the Green Party politician Renate Künast. Meanwhile she has had partial success, in that 'only' sixteen of twenty-two comments directed personally at her are classified as legal. According to a report in the *Berliner Morgenpost*, however, these include the remark 'Pfui du altes grünes Drecksschwein' [Yuck, you dirty old Green pig]. According to the *Morgenpost*, the chamber argued that not every animal comparison constituted defamation.[12] This would be almost cynical, since 'dirty pig' is not an animal comparison but an insult used to cause a personal emotional pain (pigs are in fact very clean animals, so saying 'dirty pig' as an insult is also insulting to the pig).

What is true is that not every utterance directed at a person in public life that looks like defamation really is defamation and that we should not prosecute every defamatory utterance for reasons concerning the democratic law-based state (which is complex legal territory). One characteristic of the democratic law-based state is that leniency in the use of sharp penal instruments is as significant as the attempt to strike a balance between warring legal parties. Ideally, the democratic law-based state strives for social peace and does not, fortunately, constantly attempt to lure people mercilessly into the complex traps of jurisprudence.

That is why the law-based state is not a rigid corset of iron paragraphs but, rather, the expression of a negotiation process that takes into account our moral reflections. Jurisprudence develops in dialogue with the public and works with moral deliberations. Then judges pass verdicts that are legal rather than moral, but, in ethically relevant cases, moral arguments can nonetheless have a bearing on the opinion of the court.

It is clearly morally reprehensible, however, and thus belongs to the realm of the morally forbidden, to call Renate Künast a 'dirty pig', even if this expresses the opinion that, like other members of her party, she had not distanced herself unambiguously from paedophilia in the past (the context was a series of events in the 1980s), which is a different discussion. But the fight against a moral evil (in this case, sexual abuse of defenceless children) does not automatically justify resorting to other moral evils (such as insults).

If one abandons the idea that the democratic law-based state should be involved in encouraging moral progress and reflecting it in the revision of paragraphs or via new legal systems (to regulate digitalization, for instance), then one can abandon the rest of modernity, and hence, along with it, the democratic law-based state, since this cannot be reduced to merely defining particular selection processes and procedures.

Time and again, it is viewed negatively when jurists reach verdicts that are not purely morally and not purely legally grounded. Yet such criticism is predicated on a fallacy; for it is possible to rely mostly on legal argumentations only *because* these have already been morally grounded in a democratic law-based state. The rules of juridically defined justice must not come into conflict with moral justice, otherwise we would be morally compelled to change them.

The National Socialists and the Soviet and Chinese communists also had, or still have, processes and legal frameworks, but we reject them because, among other things, they were or still are immoral. If *legality*, namely juridical judgement, is not ultimately grounded in *legitimacy*, it is morally hollow.

In a democracy there are limits of tolerance, and hence of freedom of expression, that are tied to the level of moral understanding reached by society. We do not, for example, seriously discuss whether we should allow cannibalism. Many courses of action are located far beyond the reach of what the modern democratic law-based state would even consider. Social, socioeconomic, moral and political mechanisms of selection narrow the space for what public opinion defines as being worth discussing. An interim goal of the new enlightenment must be to make explicit the value system that we have institutionalized in the form of a democratic law-based state. Every citizen should be in a position to present arguments as to why it is better to live in a democratic law-based state than in the *ancien régime* of the eighteenth century, for instance, which was overcome through the French Revolution, to say nothing of the Third Reich or the GDR. If citizens do not accept this view and see no reasons for it, then democracy is irredeemably damaged, as it rests on historical experiences based on moral progress – which would clearly not have been lasting in such a case.

A meaningful debate in society about tolerance and freedom of expression must start there in order for the truth and the facts, not least in the moral domain, to be heard. If our current constitution as a community were no more than a posited principle, a resolution that could not be justified independently of arbitrary juridical rules, we would no longer have any intellectual foundation to defend the idea of a social market economy and the democratic law-based state in the competition of systems against unfettered neoliberal global capitalism, on the one hand, and Chinese surveillance communism, on the other.

Morality trumps majority

Certainly, one cannot always grant minorities the demand to be heard and have a seat at the table for decision-making processes. Because of their moral deficits (whatever explanations there might be in individual cases), paedo-criminals, anti-democrats, clear enemies of the constitution, murderers, etc., quite simply do not have the right as minorities to be protected from institutional severity.

If we are rightly concerned with protecting minorities, then, this by no means implies that every subgroup of people who share a particular characteristic, or a form of behaviour that is less common in the rest of society, should automatically constitute a protected minority. Rather, minorities worthy of protection are usually those who have suffered or are suffering demonstrable injustice, meaning that one has to give them special support in order to afford them the full moral and legal rights of which they have been or are being deprived. One of the commendable aspects of democracy is that it lets unjustly oppressed minorities be heard after suffering exclusion because the shaping of public opinion has not taken them into account. This is morally necessary under certain conditions, and thus a genuine democratic value that one would wish to protect and advance by state means through the value of free expression.

But who deserves to be heard? Who can rightly claim to be oppressed? As it is not generally a positive moral value, not morally necessary, to provide every minority with a platform for free expression so that its thoughts and feelings can flow into institutional processes of democratic decision-making, we must ask especially urgently today where the limits of free expression and the restructuring of social conditions are located.

One factor in this is the opinion in some quarters that we should actively undermine the basic liberal democratic order on which Germany is based, or not even recognize it in the first place. Far-right terrorists, *Reichsbürger*[13] and advocates of a communist dictatorship on the model of North Korea (to name only a few obvious examples) are not among the minorities whose opinions should be allowed to contribute to the democratic decision-making process.

Democracy is entitled and even morally obliged to ensure its own survival, because it rests on the universally valid canon of enlightenment values. Its goal is to provide acceptable and ideally favourable institutional conditions for the free development of all human personalities that are conceivable within the framework of moral legitimacy. The minimum foundation for this is the basic principle for a law-based state formulated by Kant, namely that my freedom ends where the freedom of others begins, meaning that infringements on the free spaces of others that prevent their development must be sanctioned.[14]

This simple argument can be used to undermine the **paradox of democracy**, which states that a democracy can vote for its own abolition if a qualified majority decides it. Many people believe that democracy means the majority decision; this is short-sighted, however. If, for example, a party convinced the majority of Germans that we should expel Muslims or treat them with even greater cruelty, or if we were to establish a new National Socialist dictatorship through a majority decision, these decisions would not be justifiable within the framework of our democracy and would accordingly be contested by the state. *Morality trumps majority*: this is a central rule of the game in modern democracy and distinguishes it not least from the classical democracy of the Athenians, who had not yet recognized this moral fact and made rather cruel judgements as a result.

The mere fact that a majority decides on something does not automatically make it morally legitimate.

In the canon of values, moral legitimacy comes before political legality, which in no way means that it is easy in every case to ascertain which option for action is morally legitimate. This justifies the idea of a parliamentary democracy that makes the distribution of financial resources dependent on public opinion as well as the state of the debate in the Bundestag. The aim of political debates should always be to establish the moral and non-moral facts through dissent – that is, by comparing different opinions and consulting experts. Only when a majority of equally justified courses of action has emerged as morally legitimate and politically legal can the decision be brought about by forming a majority.

It is far from true, then, that democracy means 'anything goes'. The notion of postmodern arbitrariness in the decision-making processes of the individual groups that constitute the people, in the sense of democratically legitimized citizens, is deeply misguided and contradicts the concept of democracy defined by the constitution.

Cultural relativism: the law of the strongest

It seems that there are more and less clearly delimited cultures. Furthermore, drawing boundaries between cultures often seems tied to the borders of nation states. For example, it is common to speak of German, Chinese, American or Russian culture. Some even believe that there has been a world-historical battle of cultures or civilizations raging for millennia, and that it is unfolding in the twenty-first century as a conflict between civilizations whose rivalry has been intensified by globalization. This idea was promoted in the late twentieth century especially by Samuel P. Huntington, a political scientist who teaches at Harvard University and, in a book on American identity published in

2004, applied the idea of culture wars to the USA; like Donald Trump in more recent times, he argues that the USA should have an Anglo-American Protestant identity and therefore considers Latin American immigration a problem. This intellectual construct was refuted in detail by, among others, the Nobel laureate Amartya Sen, who likewise teaches at Harvard.[15]

One especially obvious lacuna in the argumentation of Huntington and other culture-war theorists is that they do not clarify what defines a culture, resulting in an inflationary use of the word 'culture' that, on closer inspection, does not stand for any clear concept but, rather, hides a dangerous confusion. Huntington claims that there are major civilizations, such as Islamic, Western or Latin American ones. According to him, these civilizations are in a state of conflict that leads to wars. He does not, however, provide any theological or culture-philosophical criteria for the way he defines civilizations and delimits them from one another. Ultimately, this only results in **stereotypes** – false ways of thinking that divide human beings into groups (such as Hindus and Muslims, Europeans and Chinese, North Americans and Latin Americans).

These groupings are not supported by the facts.[16] It is by no means the case that all Europeans think and act in the same way, for instance; they are fairly diverse. This is apparent at a very regional level: for people from northern Germany, Bavaria sometimes seems more culturally alien than regions of other countries. And even this is a stereotype, since there are also groups of people in Hamburg who set themselves apart from other groups of Hamburgers. The idea that people belong to groups such as Hindus or Christians is an abstraction that can become misleading, even dangerous, if we believe that it enables us to understand a person or to predict that we can assign them to such an abstract group. This is how stereotypes come about.

Value pluralism based on a nebulous concept of culture is a widespread opponent of universalism. It essentially claims that all values, including moral ones, are ultimately an expression of group membership. This means that there are German values (stereotypes include diligence, honesty and a tendency towards tinkering) in contrast to American, Chinese, Russian or whatever other values. The last decade has seen frequent references to Judeo-Christian values or Western values, which supposedly differ especially from Muslim values. This makes the situation even more complicated, for the task of precisely defining religious value systems is at least as difficult as the delimitation of cultures.

Before we can set about the task of rebutting the nebulous cultural relativism that underlies value pluralism and value relativism, we must first let it speak in order to establish what it might actually mean.

So let us assume the following: **cultural relativism** is the thesis that all values – hence also moral ones – are nothing but an expression of a group membership. The relevant groups chosen by cultural relativism as a point of departure are cultures. It thus argues that values are relative to cultures that divide people into groups. Generally speaking, **relativism** is a theory that applies to a particular area of speech and asserts, firstly, that statements in this area are true with reference to a system of assumptions, secondly, that there are several such systems, and, thirdly, that it is essentially impossible to adopt an independent position towards the question of which system is better.

One can approve of relativism regarding various matters. Someone who is a relativist about human references to beauty believes that beauty lies purely in the eye of the beholder; something that I find beautiful might seem ugly to you, and vice versa. A beauty relativist also believes that there is no independent party that could mediate between us and establish who is right. Perhaps my assumptions about beauty could be explained neurobiologically and psychoanalytically by my sexual preferences, sociologically or in some other way related to the story of my life. Or perhaps I only consider the things beautiful that people who mean something to me recommend. According to the relativist, the same applies to you. The relativist reduces statements about beauty to idiosyncratic, individualized judgements of taste.

In the case of moral values, which are the central concern of this book, the cultural relativist holds the following opinions:

Cultural relativism 1: Moral values are relative to a culture. There are no absolute moral values.

Cultural relativism 2: There is a multitude of cultures that can never be brought under an all-encompassing, universal cultural roof.

Cultural relativism 3: There is no culturally independent, unbiased (transcultural) position in the matter of which culture to follow.

Relativists usually believe that cultures are in a state of war that cannot be settled on the basis of moral values, since these values, just like the cultures, are irreconcilably antagonistic. In this culture war, there is no overarching moral order in force; relativists consider this notion an illusion because, to them, morality is at most something that one of the many cultures imposes on itself. A moral recognition of the enemy in the culture war would lead, if anything, to weakness in the competition of systems and is therefore rejected by cultural relativists (be they on the political left or the right).

In the Netflix series *House of Cards*, the atmosphere of this worldview is expressed in a slogan uttered by the fictional US president Frank Underwood: 'There is no justice, only conquest.' This idea is admittedly far older than Netflix and is advocated not only by fictional presidents. Unfortunately, it prevails at the time of writing in the genuine, by no means fictional White House, which is supported by a Republican Party that sees itself in an implacable culture war with an equally implacable Democratic Party.

The first clear presentation and defence of the idea of the law of the strongest, which is regularly evoked by Donald Trump in particular, is attributed to Thrasymachus, a speaker in Plato's central political work, the *Republic*. According to Thrasymachus, what is just (justice, *dikaiosynē*, is the classical name for the highest moral value) is defined by the one who is victorious in battle. In Book 1 of the *Republic*, Socrates speaks first of all to a certain Polemarchus about political ideas before Thrasymachus, a famous Sophist, interrupts them. Plato portrays the Sophists as demagogues – almost as the inventors of fake news, one might say – whose oratorical skills consist merely in using clever rhetoric to weave a stronger argument out of a weaker one, enabling them to overwhelm their opponents with sheer chatter.[17]

In Plato's *Republic*, Socrates is just developing a universal view of justice when Thrasymachus butts in: 'Why are you deferentially bowing and scraping to each other like simpletons?'[18] Thrasymachus thus accuses Socrates of being a do-gooder (as some people put it today with this terrible term) and wants to make short work of the subject of justice. This leads him directly to the following definition of justice: 'All right, then, listen to this,' he said. 'My claim is that morality is nothing other than the advantage of the stronger party ...'[19] For this purpose, he uses an argument that is far from unknown today and which is rearing its head once more on the world stage: he assumes that state power is nothing other than the self-assertion of a government determined by a form of governance. Thrasymachus distinguishes between dictatorship (*tyrannis*), aristocracy and democracy.

> Now, each government passes laws with a view to its own advantage: a democracy makes democratic laws, a dictatorship makes dictatorial laws, and so on and so forth. In so doing, each government makes it clear that what is right and moral for its subjects is what is to its own advantage; and each government punishes anyone who deviates from what is advantageous to itself as if he were a criminal and a wrongdoer. So, Socrates, this is what I claim morality is: it is the same in every country, and it is what is to the advantage of the current government. Now, of course, it's the current government which has power, and the consequence of this, as anyone who thinks about the matter correctly can work out, is that morality is everywhere the same – the advantage of the stronger party.[20]

One finds the idea of a law of the strongest in numerous variations over millennia. It not only serves the political right as a justification of the use of force but is equally prominent on the left. Karl Marx ties moral ideas to classes, which he famously sees entangled in a struggle.[21]

Like the Sophists of antiquity, today's left- and right-wing activists are not usually concerned with the truth of their opinions so much as with the aim of keeping the upper hand in their struggle, at least rhetorically, and then gaining power by taking office before ideally annihilating their political opponent entirely by means of purges; this is the nature of political extremism, whatever its persuasion.

Anyone who considers the law of the strongest the basis for expressing moral value judgements has left morality far behind. If moral values were nothing but an expression of affiliation according to class, gender, generation, political party or culture, there would actually be no such thing as moral values. Then it would simply be a matter of winning the political struggle while giving morally eloquent speeches so as to place oneself on the bright side of history, while hiding the violence by which one has risen to power and attempts to stay there.

Boghossian and the Taliban

The fact that cultural relativism has feet of clay is evident from a number of arguments developed over the last few decades by Paul Boghossian, a philosopher who teaches at New York University.[22] One of his examples is a moral conflict between himself and a member of the Taliban.[23] Boghossian believes the following characterization to be accurate:

> Boghossian: School education for women and girls is morally necessary.
> Taliban member: School education for women and girls is morally impermissible.

The cultural relativist would assert that, in reality, Boghossian and the Taliban are involved purely in a conflict of interests. Boghossian, they might suppose, is representing American interests and values, which includes compulsory schooling that makes no difference between different genders, since everyone should profit from education in order to have equal opportunities later in life. The relativist could analyse Boghossian's opinions further by placing the system of American assumptions and the accompanying culture in the larger context of Western values. The Taliban, on the other hand, would simply be seen as having a different culture in which female persons are assigned completely different tasks in society, based on the Taliban's interpretation of the Qur'an as well as other local customs.

The relativist probably thinks they are helping all parties with this argumentation and somehow declaring everyone in the right. In their eyes, after all, everyone is right: both Boghossian and the Taliban consider certain moral statements to be true, albeit based not on genuinely moral grounds but, rather, on their respective group membership.

But this argumentation is less robust than it seems. Boghossian points out that the relativist ultimately has to reinterpret the statements of the conflict parties. To the relativist, then, Boghossian does not actually believe his own statement 'School education for women and girls is morally necessary.' For the relativist, unlike Boghossian, believes that nothing is absolutely morally necessary. Because of this, the relativist hears a different statement in Boghossian's words, as it were, namely this one: 'School education for women and girls is morally necessary according to American value concepts.' The same applies to the other moral opinions under consideration. So what the Taliban member really means is this: 'School education for women and girls is morally impermissible according to the Taliban's interpretation of the Qur'an.' The fatal problem of this manoeuvre becomes clearer if we take another step back. One would normally assume that there is an obvious moral conflict between A and B if A believes that φ is morally necessary, while B believes that φ is morally forbidden.

In this case, φ stands for a morally charged act. It would be an entirely different matter if moral conflicts actually consisted in A asserting that φ is morally necessary in Germany (for example), while B claims that φ is morally forbidden in Saudi Arabia (for example). In this case, a German cultural relativist in Saudi Arabia could do something they would never do in Germany – take part in a stoning, for example – without committing a moral error. But even a hard-line Western cultural relativist would never do this; for the cultural relativist accepts that they themselves have their own moral stance, which is that torture is wrong under any circumstances.

Otherwise, the conflict the cultural relativist wishes to describe would not exist. If the cultural relativist thought that one should not stone people except in Saudi Arabia, and the Saudi Arabian thought that one should stone people only in Saudi Arabia, not in Germany, they would be in agreement and there would be no different systems of opinion, but simply locally valid rules of conduct. If, on the other hand, the cultural relativist in Germany thought that one should not stone people, this would naturally also apply to Saudi Arabia.

And why should one's morals change when one goes to a different place where the majority opinion on what is morally necessary or forbidden is different? Another decisive factor is that those who are stoned in Saudi Arabia are most probably not of the opinion that stoning is morally acceptable in Saudi Arabia, which points to a fundamental problem in cultural relativism: cultures are not usually homogeneous but can develop certain majority opinions. There are no self-enclosed cultural areas in which unambiguous, universally accepted value concepts prevail. Cultures are always diverse, even if they define only small groups. Everyone knows this from family celebrations.

Moral facts about what we should and should not do are not territorially restricted; they apply everywhere and to everyone. That is why, for example, the so-called Ghetto Law introduced in Denmark is morally reprehensible. In 2018, Denmark classified twenty-eight urban neighbourhoods as ghettos and applied specific laws to these areas. In so-called ghettos, according to the *Tagesschau* report from 28 December 2018, kindergarten is mandatory and there are harsher punishments for 'offences such as theft and vandalism'. In addition, there are mandatory pre-school language tests and a greater police presence. In this way, groups of people are systematically disadvantaged because they are measured against a notion of Danish normality that is used to justify a harsher assessment of their behaviour. This egregiously goes against the idea of a blind justice that judges without distinction of person.

The proposal by the right-wing nationalist Danish People's Party was implemented by a centre-right government and is an example of a morally reprehensible interpretation of legislative texts. In this case, the Danish state behaves rather like a moderate form of aristocracy in which some people are considered better than others, meaning that one section of the people, not the people as such (all Danes), sets itself up as the sovereign. This is no longer a democracy, at least not in that area.

Once again, this shows how inadequately the vague word 'culture' is to refer to nations. The Scandinavians, supposedly such political role models (another misleading stereotype), show their teeth by turning against people they have declared different, shamelessly disadvantaging them and demoting them to second-class citizens. So one does not necessarily have to cite North Korea or Saudi Arabia as examples of harsh, unjust measures; moral injustice begins at home, in this case within the EU. It is not only a foreign phenomenon to which one can feel morally superior in the West.

There are no Judeo-Christian values – and why Islam is clearly part of Germany

Cultural relativism is an instrument in the toolbox of populism (regarding this contentious term, see below, pp. 169ff.). It is often used by governments or opposition parties with a strong populist bent in order to justify and implement concrete plans of action. One example consists of the widespread references in the previous decade to 'Judeo-Christian values', the 'Jewish–Christian tradition' or indeed the 'Judeo-Christian West'.

The starting point for the most recent bluster about the Judeo-Christian West was the speech given by the federal president at the time, Christian Wulff, on the twentieth anniversary of German reunification in 2010, a speech with surely unintended consequences. It contains the following notorious passage:

> But first and foremost, we must adopt an unequivocal stance. We need to view German identity as something that is not defined merely by people's passports, family background or faith, but is something broader. Christianity is without a doubt part of German identity. Judaism is without a doubt part of German identity. Such is our Judaeo-Christian heritage. But Islam has now also become part of German identity. As Johann Wolfgang von Goethe put it nearly two centuries ago in his *Poems of the East and West*: 'He who knows himself and others, here will also see, that the East and West, like brothers, parted ne'er shall be.'[24]

The speech ends with the words 'God save Germany', which would probably not have been entirely to the taste of polytheists and atheists, who also belong to Germany. At any rate, the speech invoked a supposedly 'Christian–Jewish' history without specifying when it began and exactly which periods of overall German history it encompasses. (And what about the pre-Christian history of the Germanic tribes? Or the terrible waves of anti-Semitism in German history, which are a central part of actual Christian–Jewish history?) It is well known that German history as a whole is anything but pleasing, and, in actuality, the dogmatically fixed articles of faith in Judaism and Christianity are partially irreconcilable, which also applies to the value systems explicitly described in the holy texts of these two world religions. It is certainly not the case that Christianity and Judaism have always coexisted peacefully; the history of Christianity is full of anti-Semitism, which has applied in the past to all Christian confessions. There is quite simply no clearly 'Christian–Jewish history'.

Wulff's speech caused immense confusion, especially because he did not give the slightest explanation of the decisive attribute of 'belonging'. As a result, we have been forced to endure a nonsense debate that has gone on for years, and which is unfortunately still active, about the question of whether Islam does actually belong to Germany (as asserted by Wulff and later Chancellor Merkel) or not (as their noisy opponents complained, especially the agitator Thilo Sarrazin).

It is quite obvious, however, that Islam does not in any relevant sense belong to Germany any less than the other monotheistic religions. Of course, the speech and the chatter that followed it failed to take into account the atheists, agnostics and polytheists, whose right to exist is unambiguously guaranteed by the basic human right to freedom of religion. Articles 4.1 and 4.2 of the German constitution state:

(1) Freedom of religion and conscience, as well as freedom of religious and ideological orientation, are inviolable.
(2) Undisturbed exercise of religion is ensured.

The concept of religion is not limited to monotheism, or indeed to Christianity and Judaism (which would be absurd). The question of where religions stand vis-à-vis democracy and how one justifies and defends freedom of religion as a value has not been conclusively resolved.[25] In the heat of the Islam debate, assertions were made time and again, sometimes using terribly unscientific arguments, that Islam as such is a danger to the basic liberal-democratic order und its values were irreconcilable with our (whose?) understanding of human rights, and so on. This was supported with interpretations of the Qur'an popularized by Sarrazin, without possessing any expertise in the field Islamic studies.

What do blanket references to 'Islam' and 'Christianity' actually mean? Certainly not simply the totality of what is in the Bible or the Qur'an. Do these words mean that one cultivates a tradition, gives alms, celebrates Christmas or Ramadan? A strict fundamentalist reading of the Bible, at any rate, is just as irreconcilable with the democratic law-based state as the fundamentalist reading of the Qur'an that many consider dangerous, while ignoring or downplaying Christian and Jewish fundamentalism.

Let us recall that the great monotheistic world religions of Judaism, Christianity and Islam all came into being long before the modern democracies that grew in the wake of the revolutions of the eighteenth and nineteenth century. None of the founders of world religions could be well-disposed to modern democracy, since such a form of governance was simply unknown in their time. Many recommendations and rules for behaviour found in the holy texts of all world religions (including Hinduism and Buddhism) explicitly call for the violation of human dignity and are therefore clearly irreconcilable with our insights into the structure of human rights. One off-putting example is a passage from the Book of Leviticus on the subject of male homosexuality: 'If a man lies with a man as one lies with a woman, both of them have done what is detestable. They must be put to death; their blood will be on their own heads' (Leviticus 20:13).

Under Mosaic conditions, a slightly less draconian punishment such as banishment is even easier to incur: 'If a man lies with a woman during her monthly period and has sexual relations with her, he has exposed the source of her flow, and she has also uncovered it. Both of them must be cut off from their people' (Leviticus 20:18).

Infidelity is not taken very lightly either, as we read in the same context: 'If a man commits adultery with another man's wife – with the wife of his neighbour – both the adulterer and the adulteress must be put to death' (Leviticus 20:10).

Things also look bad if one curses one's parents: 'If anyone curses his father or mother, he must be put to death. He has cursed his father or his mother, and his blood will be on his own head' (Leviticus 20:9).

The *Bhagavad Gita*, an important holy text in Hinduism, is set in a bloody context.[26] It is part of the *Mahābhārata*, a major verse epic that tells of the brutal war between two groups of cousins, the Kauravas and the Pandavas, who are fighting over dynastic succession and for territorial power. In a complicated situation it transpires that the god Krishna, an avatar (incarnation) of the god Vishnu, appears as the charioteer of Arjuna, a Pandava prince. Arjuna is hesitant to wage a brutal war against his own family, but the god Krishna reveals himself to him. The initiation into divine knowledge by no means leads to the end of the war and reconciliation between the families but, rather, emboldens Arjuna to go to war, for he believes that the presence of his divine charioteer shows that the war is just.

In this sacred Hindu text, the conversation between Arjuna and Krishna revolves around justifying a war between families, not some peace mission. Based on this source text, Hinduism is as bloodthirsty an affair as the Old and New Testament.

Things are not much friendlier in Christianity. Jesus, we read in the New Testament, 'did not come to bring peace, but a sword' (Matthew 10:34). 'Do you think I came to bring peace on earth? No, I tell you, but division' (Luke 12:51). In this context, speaking as an end-times prophet, Jesus is urging his listeners to abandon their own families and love him more than their father and mother, even more than their own children. The apocalyptic mood of the New Testament comes from the assumption that the world will soon end and this will be followed by the Day of Judgement, which means that continuing a conventional family life under these circumstances (which have not yet come to pass ...) would simply be futile.

Arjuna is not Gandhi, just as Matthew is not Pope Francis, which indicates the moral progress in the field of religion. Gandhi's interpretation of Hinduism and Francis's interpretation of Christianity have a pacifist and universalist orientation, and they strive from the outset to oppose the misguided ways of fundamentalism – though the situation is not quite so simple for a number of reasons, since both could be accused of a reactionary view of women.

The point of all these examples is that the texts of all world religions contain many passages with instructions and worldviews that are clearly incompatible with a democratically enshrined respect for human dignity. If one were to follow these incitements to violence, some of them explicitly formulated, which require trampling on human dignity (stoning homosexuals and adulterers, treating women and serfs as property, etc.), it would be a violation of the basic rules of the modern democratic law-based state, especially as found in Germany today. Anyone who thinks that Islam does not belong to Germany because of the brutal passages and calls to violence in the Qur'an should accordingly concede that Judaism, Christianity, Hinduism and Buddhism likewise do not belong to Germany. Then the CDU [Christian Democratic Union party] would be incompatible with the constitution and require examination by national intelligence – which is obviously nonsense. There is freedom of religion in this country, which is incompatible with fundamentalism but not religion as such. As there are an indefinite number of non-fundamentalist interpretations of Islam (as of the other religions), Islam naturally belongs to Germany every bit as much as a Buddhist meditation centre or churches. It would be a sign of great moral progress if this no longer needed to be emphasized.

Modern states define freedom of religion in general in such a way that exercise of religion is restricted for *all* religions. A person who wishes to adhere to the exact text of the Bible cannot exercise their religion freely in Germany any more than someone who follows the Qur'an to the letter, although things are admittedly far more complicated than they sound, since it is not entirely clear what actually constitutes the exact text of these writings. This already depends on an act of interpretation.

This is why the discipline of **hermeneutics** (from the Greek *hermeneia*, 'interpretation') emerged in the modern age. With the aid of this method, the holy scriptures were read in a way that could be reconciled with modern insights. Hermeneutics developed from the theology that is supported by taxpayers' money in countries such as Germany in the form of theology departments at public universities. The purpose of this support in the Enlightenment project was to keep this religious interpretation concentrated at state institutions (such as theology departments) in order to establish how far it was compatible with the universal values that characterize a modern law-based state and which are neither tied to nor based on any religion.

The same rules apply to Islam that apply to every other religion. There has also been closer theological examination of Islam since the Federal Ministry of Education and Research set up centres for Islamic theology at several German universities in response to the fact that there are at least 4 million Muslims living in Germany, many of whom are Germans in exactly the same sense as the author of these lines: German citizens.

Let us not forget to recall a further self-evident fact: the basic rights described in the constitution, which rest on the idea of human rights, are limited neither to Germany nor, within Germany, to Germans alone. The human dignity of French tourists, refugees and others who reside in Germany must be protected no less than that of the descendants of the Hohenzollern, a family that has demonstrably lived in the state territory of today's Germany, even though some of their ancestors carried out crimes against humanity in colonial times and in the First World War.

The universality of human rights is expressed in Article 1.2 of the constitution: 'The German people therefore commits to inviolable and inalienable human rights as the foundation for every human community, for peace and for justice in the world.' Incidentally, this reveals one of the criteria for belonging to the German people: embracing human rights as the foundation for every human community and so forth is part of the definition of the German people. Obviously this is not enough on its own for citizenship, which is regulated according to other criteria.

The law-based state defines the rules for freedom of speech, nationality and the basic rights that can be applied as the foundations for protecting the constitution. That is why Reichsbürger or religious fundamentalists who dispute human rights are neither automatically banished nor stripped of their citizenship, since this would be irreconcilable with human rights and would amount to the dictatorship of opinion or GDR 2.0 that is feared by many populists but does not exist at all.

Human rights include the possibility of spaces for freedom of speech, even to the point that one is allowed to express the opinion that there is a lack of human rights in this country, which is verifiably false and at odds with the constitution. Despite this freedom, it is still a mistaken opinion. And the debate about whether Islam belongs to Germany is nonsensical, as the answer is laughably simple: yes.

North Korea and the Nazi machine

Some will object that it is part of the democratic canon of values to tolerate an unlimited plurality of opinions. After all, one can express opinions that are at odds with the constitution. One must take into account that there is a multiplicity of value systems, and hence values. This seems like an ideal situation for value relativism, which formulates a principle of tolerance so broadminded that it is even tolerant towards intolerance. But the fact that one must tolerate the expression of false opinions does not mean that the value concepts underlying these opinions are tolerable and that there are hence relative values.

It is in the nature of opinions that they can be true or false. Whoever holds the opinion that Bill Gates wants to vaccinate humanity by force is wrong. It is equally wrong to believe that Angela Merkel wanted to set up a GDR 2.0. She quite simply did not.

We tolerate false opinions. This is generally a good thing, since no person has exclusively true opinions. On the contrary, we all have plenty of false opinions, since no one can know everything. This does not, however, mean that we should tolerate all opinions; for, on closer inspection, one sees that there cannot be any good reason to be tolerant towards intolerance. Part of intolerance, after all, is fighting tolerance. Why should tolerance accept being replaced by its antithesis? This would be akin to a pacifist automatically accepting a bellicist (warmonger) campaigning against pacifism. Rather, the pacifist is entitled to employ all available means (provided they are proportionate and morally permissible, which rules out violence) in order to limit and ideally prevent the bellicist's activities. The whole point of pacifism is that there should be no wars at all, which means that pacifists are not obliged to show any tolerance towards bellicists.

It is exactly the same with tolerance. The positive moral character of tolerance stems from the fact that one affords people whose way of living and thinking strikes one as outlandish, perhaps even repulsive, the right to live and think as they see fit within certain boundaries. The criterion for these boundaries is that such a different way of living and thinking does not infringe on the space for my own living and thinking. It is morally necessary to be tolerant towards models for life and decisions that are morally neutral. It is, however, morally reprehensible to be tolerant towards morally reprehensible models for life (such as sadism or right-wing terrorism).

It is in the nature of intolerance that it opposes tolerance and can attempt to destroy it. The tolerant do not have to stand for this. If those who live and think differently are verifiably living and thinking in a morally wrong way (consider the Holocaust-denying Bavarian Reichsbürger, followers of the Ku Klux Klan, paedo-criminals or the Cannibal of Rotenburg),[27] there is a moral right to restrict their actions if they infringe on the scope of action of those operating within the spectrum of legitimate diversity of opinion.

There are better and worse states, better and worse laws, better and worse forms of governance. The moral standard we apply when we compare the legal systems of North Korea and Germany, or of today's Germany and the German Empire (which was rooted mostly in what is currently German territory), often provides clear results. No one would willingly relocate from Germany to North Korea to be brought to trial. Unfortunately, there are people who believe that they would like to travel back in time to the German Empire or even the Nazi dictatorship.

One could counter this with an argument that is a variation on a famous reflection by the American political philosopher John Rawls. This argument shows that there is a moral compass which we activate if make morally meaningful decisions under clearly formulated conditions. We will call this argument the **Nazi machine**. Let us imagine that we give a convinced neo-Nazi, someone who wishes for a return to the conditions of the Nazi dictatorship, access to a time machine that allows him to travel back to the year 1941 and live in the Third Reich. Perhaps our neo-Nazi will welcome this and immediately want to board the machine. But there is a little catch to the time machine: our neo-Nazi will be sent back to the past not as himself but, rather, as someone who actually lived in Germany during that time. He does not know beforehand who he will be. So he could be Adolf Hitler, Ernst Röhm or Martin Heidegger, but he could also be Anne Frank, Hannah Arendt, Primo Levi or any of the millions of victims of the Nazi dictatorship – though he would not notice, since he would lose his own identity in becoming someone else. He could also be a poor 'Aryan' German sent to the front at some point as cannon fodder. So the likelihood of being on what he would view as the good side would fall rapidly, considering that the majority of Germans and those residing in Germany at the time did not exactly benefit from National Socialism. Despite its name, the National Socialist German Workers' Party (NSDAP) was anything but socialist, let alone a workers' party – at least not one that would make ordinary workers better off than in the Weimar Republic.

Given the choice to enter the Nazi machine on these terms, the neo-Nazi will probably think twice. It would be much better to have the chance to travel to a utopian land, a place one could participate in shaping beforehand. As one does not know in advance who one will actually be or in what situation one will find oneself, it is advisable to develop a social order that allows everyone to be in a good position.

Anyone in the position of designing such a society at the drawing-board should act rationally and neutrally. This is possible because we humans are capable to varying degrees of putting ourselves in other people's position. That is why using thought experiments and plans for ideal state scenarios to exercise one's imagination is part of ethical training.

The idea Rawls used here is known as the 'veil of ignorance'. It has a long history in moral philosophy, of course, but became especially well known as a result of Rawls's much debated political theory.[28] We can take the idea that he makes fruitful for political theory as a way of approaching the foundations of ethics. This provides evidence of the possibility to make moral judgements that exceed our culturally and socially conditioned perspective.

Rawls's thought experiment does not supply the desired result on its own, but it points in the right direction: in our consideration of the reasons for what we should and should not do, we are capable of abstracting from the fact that we sometimes have immoral interests which interfere with our behaviour under the normal conditions of practical life. We can put these interests aside for the sake of others because we can imagine being the other. This never succeeds completely, because we usually take ourselves up into the equation, so to speak, by imagining what it would be like for us to inhabit the other's body. But we can recognize this and use it as a corrective in our reflections on what we owe ourselves and others for moral reasons.

That is why art and the culture sector are indispensable for the development of our ethics. Moral education is impossible without fictions and their dissemination in society as a whole. It is no coincidence that totalitarian systems restrict artistic freedom; they want to limit the imagination of their subjects.

Value pluralism and value nihilism

Value relativism is thus incoherent, and consequently untenable. What we should or should not do for moral reasons cannot be simply an expression of group allegiance.

Because it makes less forceful claims, value pluralism is in a slightly better position. **Value pluralism** is first and foremost the initially harmless assumption that there are different value concepts which cannot be reduced to a common denominator, since they are fundamentally contradictory. Yet this assumption overlooks the fact that, in humanity as a whole, there is far more unity than it would appear if one thinks that there are fundamental discrepancies between the moral convictions of different subcultures and subgroups of people. This assumption is simply false. Social plurality and multiculturalism do not automatically lead to divergence between people of different cultural affiliations on relevant moral issues.

By now there are moral-psychological studies based on large cross-cultural data sets showing not only that there are abstract universal principles that can be found across different cultures but even that decision-making in real-life situations displays universal patterns.[29] This should not come as a surprise, since there are no fundamental biological differences between different human groups; rather, one should expect substantial similarities between our basic emotions, which are also ethically important.

Universalism is biologically rooted, though this does not apply to all its aspects, since the biological prehistory of higher morality took place in close quarters and small groups, meaning that today's ethical problems can no longer be meaningfully solved on this basis.

Yet even if value pluralism were correct, the existence of numerous incompatible value concepts would not disprove the existence of universal values. It is true that there are different, in part irreconcilable value concepts, though these do not define cultures; at most they spell out statistically determinable groups. However, the fact that different groups of people have different value concepts does not indicate that these are all right or justified. For some value concepts are deplorable, such as those presented by Hitler in *Mein Kampf*.

Next to the dangerous value relativism and the mostly harmless value pluralism, the third myth that obstructs the recognition of moral realism and will be examined here assumes that, in truth, there is no such thing as values or moral facts at all. This is value nihilism, which denies that there is any form of moral objectivity.

Value nihilism has adherents in all political camps: there are far-left and far-right nihilists as well as nihilists in the political milieu known today as the 'middle-class centre' [*bürgerliche Mitte*].

It is clear that there is a line of far-right nihilistic tradition in Germany that remained significant in the post-war era, for example in the thought of the philosopher Martin Heidegger and the influential constitutional scholar Carl Schmitt. Both had a personal biographical interest in white-washing their own entanglement in different phases of the establishment and maintenance of the National Socialist dictatorship. One factor in this interest was no doubt that, for both of them, it was a psychological and moral strain suddenly to find themselves clearly on the side of the criminals of world history; thus an ideology such as value nihilism was like a balm for the two thinkers' souls. If there were no moral facts existing outside of the power struggles and the whims of individuals who imposed their value concepts through acts of force such as the seizure of power, then there would seemingly be less guilt attached to the atrocities in which one was indirectly or even directly involved. Even before the National Socialist takeover, admittedly, Heidegger and Schmitt had demonstrated value nihilism with their views, which goes some way towards explaining their political positions (and takes us towards a broad field of research that has not yet been cleared).

Carl Schmitt himself penned a clearly formulated polemic against the idea of objectively existing universal values. It was written in 1959 and bears the almost cynical title *The Tyranny of Values*. This text draws on thinkers including Heidegger, whom Schmitt even knew from the legendary Committee for Legal Philosophy, which, since its founding in 1934, had met at the Weimar Nietzsche Archive under the direction of one of the highest Nazi jurists, Hans Frank. There is no need here to go into the historical details of this at times highly controversial constellation.[30] What is interesting and genuinely perverse is the argumentation of Schmitt, who – like Heidegger – maintains that the Holocaust was a result of neo-Kantianism, which was represented especially by Jewish, universalistically inclined and politically mostly left-wing philosophers. In this context, the **basic principle of the neo-Kantian philosophy of values** is that the natural sciences describe a value-neutral area of the universe, while philosophy, the humanities and the social sciences explore a domain of the validity of norms, including such foremost moral principles as the famous Categorical Imperative (see pp. 99ff.); though not causally observable, this domain exists objectively nonetheless. Schmitt refers to the philosophy of values in its entirety as 'an attempt to assert the human being as a free, responsible creature, indeed not in itself, but at least, in its valuation, what one called value. That attempt was put forth as a positivistic substitute for the metaphysical.'[31] Schmitt is cheating here, for a thing is metaphysical only if it cannot be examined using the best available means from the natural sciences – that is, if it eludes physical exploration in particular.[32]

Now, there are so many things that cannot be physically explored, such as numbers, justice, general elections or art history. The methods of physics can only be used to explore what can be experimentally ascertained; it cannot speak about anything it cannot measure. That is not a weakness, but actually the true strength of physics, which, through experimentation and formation of mathematical theories, gathers impressive insights into the universe and can make them technically applicable.

In this way, like Kant long before them (who was following the Scottish philosopher David Hume), the neo-Kantians reject the so-called naturalistic fallacy. The **naturalistic fallacy** attempts to derive rules for our behaviour from what we can already be observed as doing. It confuses forms of being that can be examined via natural and social sciences with what should be done, mistaking nature for norms.

So physics can at most describe what can be measured and is thus the case; it can accordingly predict the future trajectories of certain measurable processes. Yet value judgements do not relate to anything measurable, let alone predictable, as they are normative – they prescribe what *should* happen rather than predicting what *will* happen. This is the famous **is–ought problem**, which became a central concern for the neo-Kantians. They considered what ought to be a matter for metaphysics – that is, the form of reflection that deals with objects and facts beyond the domain of physics – an idea already found in Kant, who employed it for the grounding of his ethics, which he himself referred to as the 'metaphysics of morals'.[33]

The distinction between 'is' and 'ought' is meant to prevent the reduction of moral facts, which at times make demands of us for radical changes of behaviour (consider the demand to live more sustainably in order to slow climate change), to factual behaviour. The way in which humans behave in empirically verifiable terms never proves that they are doing what is morally right. The way we are is not automatically the way we ought to be.

If one reduces values to value concepts and moral obligation to measurable being, then, values lose their validity. People constantly violate moral norms; unfortunately, countless moral atrocities occur on our planet at every moment of the day, and inhabitants of rich industrial nations such as ours contribute to it with our consumer behaviour. One cannot conclude from this, however, that we are incapable of doing what is morally right. That would be sheer cynicism.

What this precisely does not mean is that whatever we factually do represents the norms. Rather, norms come into play when observed human behaviour does *not* correspond to them, which means that they are never adequately scientifically verifiable. Norms that were always followed could not become the object of sociological examination – a central idea in normativity theory that has been elaborated especially by the renowned Berlin legal scholar Christoph Möllers.[34]

That is why the great physicists in the first half of the twentieth century on both sides in both world wars could produce weapons of mass destruction and architectures of extermination in unprecedented forms without being bad physicists. It was precisely because they were excellent physicists that they succeeded in building weapons of mass destruction that were used for acts of mass murder, such as dropping nuclear bombs on Nagasaki and Hiroshima. Physicists certainly do not have insight into what is morally right by virtue of their profession. That is not an accusation, and it does not mean that physicists are morally better or worse than other people. It only shows that knowledge of how subsystems of the universe function physically does not in itself lead to the moral progress of humanity.

This is precisely one of the points of neo-Kantianism, which is why it does not, as Schmitt claims, replace the metaphysical but, rather, defends it by pointing out that the dimension of values has a different ontological status, a different level of being, from what we can perceive with our five senses and within scientific-technological experiments.

Schmitt's kindred spirit Heidegger, as we have known for some years, does not hold back with anti-Semitic constructions that even blame the Jews for their own extermination. In 1942, for example, in a comment on current events that is muddled but no less abhorrent for it, he notes:

When the essentially 'Jewish' in the metaphysical sense fights against the Jewish, the climax of self-annihilation in history is reached; assuming that the 'Jewish' has completely seized control everywhere, such that the fight against the 'Jewish', and this fight above all, comes under its dominion.[35]

'Dominion' here means submission; Heidegger means that anti-Semitism is a submission to the rules of the Jewish. It claims, in his typically convoluted way, that the Jews annihilated themselves by developing, through their logical-mathematical and economical-strategic abilities, the conditions for modern extermination systems that were then turned against them when the anti-Semites, driven by the Jews, entered modernity and carried out the Holocaust by the Jews' own means.

Like Schmitt, Heidegger transforms moral good into a form of terror. What we ought to do suddenly becomes tyranny, and the roles are reversed. For this terror and tyranny did not in fact come from the neo-Kantian philosophy of values, let alone the millions of Schmitt's and Heidegger's Jewish fellow citizens who were abominably humiliated, tortured and executed. It was rather the National Socialists who were responsible for the terror and tyranny. We must never forget what happened in the Third Reich, for it revealed to us that human beings are capable of systematically organized radical evil driven by scientific-technological progress.

Unfortunately, the mentality that considers values purely arbitrary and leads some to insult those who do good cynically as 'do-gooders' is still widespread, and it is no coincidence that Schmitt, Nietzsche and Heidegger are invoked today by someone such as Björn Höcke[36] to advance the inversion of the perpetrators and victims of the Nazi past (as in the slogan 'monument of shame').[37] In this manner, the political discourse propagated by parts of the AfD gradually contributes to a downplaying of the Holocaust and National Socialism by reversing the roles of victims and perpetrators.

Downplaying the atrocities of the Nazis is a morally reprehensible act too. This is one of the reasons why the remark made at the national convention of the AfD's youth organization by Alexander Gauland,[38] that 'Hitler and the Nazis are just a speck of bird shit in over a thousand years of successful German history', was morally unacceptable. Although Gauland underlined Germany's 'responsibility for those twelve years', he simultaneously urged his listeners to acknowledge the period of over a thousand years that he described as glorious. Many elements of the speech are muddled, absurd and false, including the fact that Germany (Gauland does not say exactly what that means) has not actually existed for a thousand years. Either there is something called 'German history' that has existed for over one thousand years, in which case one is referring to what happened on the territory of today's Federal Republic, or 'German history' refers to everything that has taken place since the founding of a German nation state, though this period is shorter than a thousand years.

Of course, there have been many favourable achievements on the territory of today's Federal Republic: the invention of printing, Beethoven's symphonies, modern physics, the discovery of infinity in mathematics, the philosophy of German Idealism, the emergence of a politically effective ecological movement, and many other things. But none of this is a reason to envision a thousand successful years in the past and minimize National Socialism by restricting it to twelve years and referring to it as mere bird shit (Gauland also overlooks the fact that the Nazi Party existed for more than twelve years). I am only mentioning Gauland's well-known confused claims to illustrate how someone can also be wrong by combining false claims about non-moral facts with errors of moral judgement.

Naturally, value nihilism is not found only among far-right thinkers such as Schmitt, Heidegger and, more recently, Höcke. It is widespread wherever people assume that values do not exist in reality but are invented by us. The cynical politics of the Trump administration likewise made use of it. Obvious lies, unpredictable decisions, shamelessly ignoring better arguments, and contempt for the idea of moral progress are the foundations of the postmodern media performance of Donald Trump, the figurehead of value nihilism. His goal was to preserve and increase the power of the USA in the international system of forces with the aim of strengthening his clientele and potentially wiping out his enemies, or at least limiting their room for manoeuvring so that they cannot obstruct the realization of his interests.

Nietzsche's ghastly confusion(s)

On the whole, **nihilism** is the view that nothing actually has objective value, not even life. Nihilism sees reality as a value-free place in which a struggle for survival rages between species and individuals. The central principle of nihilism is that value exists only if someone assigns a value to something that has no intrinsic value.

This idea was formulated especially emphatically by Friedrich Nietzsche, who used it for his large-scale project of dethroning the supposed Christian–Jewish system of values (which, as we have seen, does not actually exist!) he termed 'slave morality' in favour of a new 'master morality'.

Strictly speaking, Nietzsche offers only a single argument for his radical gesture and employs it in different variations in his moral critique. The one he uses is the following, which is ultimately a rhetorical trick: he presupposes that values exist only if there are value judgements, which he interprets as inventions of values. For example:

> Fortunately, I have since learnt to separate theology from morality and ceased looking for the origin of evil *behind* the world. Some schooling in history and philology, together with an innate sense of discrimination with respect to questions of psychology, quickly transformed my problem into another one: under what conditions did man invent the value-judgements good and evil? *And what value do they themselves possess?*[39]

But Nietzsche here assumes the very thing he should be proving, namely that moral values are *invented*, which means he is adducing the false proof known as *petitio principii*, or begging the question. If one person (A) wants to prove something to another person (B) of which B is not yet convinced, it is not enough simply to assert what B does not yet believe. A ***petitio principii*** is a circular argument that presupposes what should be proved. Nietzsche thus fails to provide any logically convincing reasoning, instead relying on his (certainly impressive and effective) skills of persuasion to slip the central thesis of his book *On the Genealogy of Morals* past the reader.

In so doing, he commits a further error known as ***equivocation***. This consists in using two linguistically related expressions with different meanings in a conclusion and pretending they mean the same thing. Here is an obvious, easily identifiable case of equivocation:

1 Angela Merkel is a clever fox.
2 Foxes are predators.
Conclusion: Angela Merkel is a predator.

The first proposition uses 'clever fox' as a metaphor. The second describes foxes as an animal species, however, which means that the conclusion does not follow from the two premises. The conclusion appears logical, but it is not.

Nietzsche's equivocation lies in the fact that he constantly mixes the moral and economic meanings of the word 'value', suggesting that every morally argument hides a power tactic. He also relies on the following simple fallacy:

1 People invent values.
2 Values have value.
Conclusion: people invent the value of values.

To support the first proposition, Nietzsche states that we invent value judgements – which is actually true in a certain sense. If I condemn a given action as evil, I am calling this judgement into existence; it did not exist until it was passed. In this sense it is an invention. It does not follow from this, however, that the being-evil of the action as such is an invention. So proposition 1 already contains a confusion. The fallacy becomes clear if one formulates the following similarly constructed 'conclusion':

1 People invent medications.
2 Medications have chemical properties.
Conclusion: humans invent the chemical properties of medications.

Nietzsche's second proposition above ('Values have value') confuses two different meanings of value. The first is moral, the second strategic or economic. People invent *economic* values (such as the prices of goods) because they depend on objectives and negotiation processes. We do not invent moral values, however, only value judgements that can be right or wrong. And what exactly is it supposed to mean that the moral value of good or the counter-value of evil has a value? Good is simply good and evil is evil; there is no second value here attached to the first. Neither is good automatically useful or evil automatically harmful, as Nietzsche claims. It is possible, after all, that evil people might not achieve their goal and, in the attempt to do so, might unintentionally create conditions for good. Perhaps the force invoked by Goethe actually exists: 'that power which would / do evil constantly, and constantly does good.'[40]

Not everyone who seeks to harm us succeeds. But this does not, as Nietzsche thinks, mean that moral values automatically have another value that is the real concern.

Nietzsche claims that moral values have an instrumental value, something that would need to be proved but which he tacitly presupposes. Admittedly this argument, which operates in the background (which builds on Schopenhauer), does have a semblance of plausibility. Consider a morally charged everyday situation such as the following: you walk through an underpass and see a homeless man sitting on a blanket. He holds out his hand to beg for money. Various thoughts go through our mind: 'One can't help everyone', or 'I don't have time right now', but maybe also 'The poor guy, I should help him!'. Unfortunately, there are also people who, faced with this scene, will think that the man is to blame for his own predicament and even argue that such people cost 'us' too much money anyway.

Let us now imagine that we give the homeless man a few pounds. In this case one can always ask oneself why one actually does that. Does one want to feel good and decent? Does one think that this is at least some small help? Is one trying to repress the knowledge that, aside from small donations, one does not usually help anyone in need?

In the act of decision-making, our true motives are often hidden from us. When we act in a morally charged everyday situation, we do not usually undertake any complicated psychological self-exploration in order to ensure that we are acting out of purely moral motives.

That is why Arthur Schopenhauer (following Kant) already supposed that most, if not all, human actions are driven by non-moral motives. The reason for such an act is more likely that one is trying to rid oneself of a guilty conscience, for example, or that one happens to find this particular homeless man likeable because he bears a resemblance to one's grandfather.

Nietzsche now argues that not only our actions but *all* moral value judgements perform an entirely different function from being an expression of moral thinking. Behind every moral value he suspects a strategy, an instrumental or tactical value.

Let us articulate this *new demand*: we stand in need of a *critique* of moral values, *the value of these values itself should first of all be called into question*.

This requires a knowledge of the conditions and circumstances of their growth, development, and displacement (morality as consequence, symptom, mask, Tartufferie, illness, misunderstanding: but also morality as cause, cure, stimulant, inhibition, poison); knowledge the like of which has never before existed nor even been desired. The *value* of 'values' was accepted as given, as fact, as beyond all question. Previously, no one had expressed even the remotest doubt or shown the slightest hesitation in assuming the 'good man' to be of greater worth than the 'evil man', of greater worth in the sense of his usefulness in promoting the progress of human *existence* (including the future of man). What? And if the opposite were the case? What? What if there existed a symptom of regression in the 'good man', likewise a danger, a temptation, a poison, a narcotic, by means of which the present were living *at the expense of the future?*[41]

Yet, once again, Nietzsche makes many minor and major logical errors that are all expressions of equivocation. He plainly confuses the economic and moral senses of value. *Economically*, a value is the result of a negotiation or of several complex measuring processes. The property value of real estate is a result of supply, demand, economic policy, buying power of a potential clientele, attractiveness of location, quality of soil, urban development plan and many other parameters. In itself, however, a property has no particular value that could be measured in any currency. The monetary value is determined by all these elements, which are in a state of constant change, and this in turn leads to property speculation and state control measures.

But a *moral* value is intrinsically non-negotiable. The fact that torturing infants (as well as torture in general, but the case of infants is even more obvious for most people) is evil is not a result of complex negotiations; it has always been the case. Whenever children were tortured, a great moral error was committed – whether the torturers realized it or not.

At this point one might ask who decides that one should not torture children, considering that they were tortured in the past (e.g., in witch trials) and are sadly also tortured in the present (e.g., in Syrian torture chambers). This question contains an error of reasoning: facts exist independently of stipulations. No one decides that the Earth has a moon or that our organisms consist of cells. The objectively existing scales of values cannot really be influenced by humans; we can only recognize them. They are not facts of nature, but this does not mean that we can change them by thinking differently. Majority opinions have no bearing on whether they are true or false, since even the greatest number of people can be mistaken. The truth or falsity of an opinion does not rest on the fact that many others share it; in the digital age of fake news and new, highly skilled forms of manipulation and propaganda, we must keep emphasizing this.[42]

The validity of moral demands does not stem from the fact that God, a group of people, evolution or human reason in general have determined them. Rather, the validity of moral demands comes from themselves. This is what it means to recognize that there are moral facts that cannot be reduced to anything else, be it majority opinions, divine commandments, adaptive evolutionary advantages, or competitive advantages of altruistic behaviour that are measurable in behavioural-economic terms.

That something is morally good or morally evil need not be apparent to all persons concerned. It is possible to do something evil without noticing, which is an important aspect of the climate crisis and the morally reprehensible excesses of global capitalism and its systems of exploitation. It is difficult, however, to imagine doing something radically evil without knowing it is evil. Anyone who tortures or executes a person knows that the associated actions are deplorable but takes them on board for the sake of a supposedly higher goal.

The problem is precisely that it is possible to do something radically evil while knowing that it is radically evil. It is unimaginable for most of us what moral-psychological state existed among the perpetrators in concentration camps, and I will not make any attempt here to put myself in their position. We can assume, however, that there were and still are genuine sadists, people who have become enforcers of radical evil in the full awareness of their responsibility.

As with nihilism, what causes value nihilism to fail is that it is simply at odds with reality. It is a fatal mistake to believe that only what can be scientifically measured exists or is real, and that the rest is a pure invention of the human spirit that has no genuine counterpart. The senselessness of this is already evident in the fact that the claim that there is such a thing as pure inventions of the human spirit is itself not based on scientific measurements and is thus, by its own standards, a pure invention of the human spirit that has no genuine counterpart.

TWO

Why There Are Moral Facts but Not Ethical Dilemmas

When we have to make difficult ethical decisions, the circumstances are usually unclear. This especially concerns people in morally demanding and responsible professions such as doctors, clinic directors and politicians. The coronavirus crisis has demonstrated this very starkly in some countries. If not everyone can be saved because the health system is not prepared for a pandemic, it must be decided who can live and who might have to die – decisions that will traumatize many people.

This emergency only reveals what is universally the case; for the resources of our planet are scarce and controlled by international politics and the global production chains of affluent societies. Markets based on competitiveness constantly determine life and death, just as the partly impermeable, but contingently placed borders of nation states strive to gain advantages over their neighbours. And all of us, through our consumer behaviour as well as our very ordinary attitudes towards other people, make morally charged decisions, though we have grown so accustomed to them that we no longer find them so serious.

It seems to be a facet of our complex global situation that we are constantly entangled in ethical dilemmas; at every turn, each of us is faced with urgent moral questions. How can we produce and consume fairly and sustainably? What products can we even buy nowadays without harming someone? How do we organize our mobility? Where do we drive or fly for our holidays?

Our everyday lives are fundamentally structured by the fact that we are embedded in the consumption and production chains of our own prosperity. The only reason we do not constantly experience this as an imposition and a burden is that it is tied to the promise of holidays, leisure, luxury, health and freedom. We receive (sometimes generous) compensation for working so that we can consume, not noticing that our consumer habits have already become work through the internet. Anyone who is active on social media produces data from which major software companies profit. Every click and every like eventually ends up as dollars in the accounts of people like Jeff Bezos and Mark Zuckerberg.

This economic order is not a natural given. It was created in the last two hundred years, in the modern age, through waves of industrialization and huge historical upheavals – most recently the digital revolution. The coronavirus crisis makes this order in its current state especially clear and shows all of us that we have grown uncritically accustomed to being data points in economic systems. The many global production systems in our everyday lives ensure that we are constantly making morally charged decisions. Before the coronavirus crisis our way of life was not *normal* but, for many people, actually *lethal*.

We are all familiar with the problem that the complexity of modern everyday life is so great that we can no longer understand how to make the right decisions at an individual level. Many people respond by giving in to cynicism and believing that a politics with high moral standards is impossible and we simply have to ensure our own prosperity at the expense of others. Whoever thinks in this way is justifying themselves in the face of moral contradictions that are difficult to tolerate when viewed clearly.

However, the impression of an irresolvable tangle of ethical difficulties is deceptive. In this chapter I will show that, on closer examination, there are no true ethical dilemmas, no irresolvable situations in which we inevitably become morally guilty because every option we choose has morally reprehensible consequences. If this were the case, we would no longer be able to reflect or act in a morally coherent fashion; there would be no *ethics*, but at most forms of *strategic calculation* that help us to give a modicum of stability to our society, even though they automatically cause suffering and moral harm.

No, we are not figures in a large-scale tragedy in which all of us, like Oedipus, become guilty against our own will and despite our best efforts; rather, we are in a complex situation that calls for systematic rethinking but does not make ethically sound decisions impossible. We are fallible in ethical matters, but humanity has also accumulated a substantial amount of moral knowledge over millennia because moral facts cannot be hidden from us entirely. Our daily routines are shaped by moral understandings: we stand more or less patiently in line, yield to people who need our help, smile at infants who look at us on the bus and greet our colleagues cordially (even those we like less).

That we have a moral order based on mutual respect becomes visible whenever it begins to crumble, as in the spring and summer of 2020 during the massive social unrest in the USA triggered by racist police brutality and other factors (such as the rapidly increasing unemployment resulting from the coronavirus crisis and a divisive president). The feeling of normality is, after all, closely tied to safety, peace and somewhat fairly distributed wealth – and all these factors are absent if the majority of humans reject moral understanding and the corresponding actions.

The moral progress of modernity that has so far been achieved, and at times even fought for, must become the foundation for a reformatting of the global order: the scientific-technological progress that drives our economy must be brought into alignment with our moral understanding, which has long been a step ahead of it. This is why many people despair in the face of the appalling injustices on our planet and think that we cannot escape tragedy. We must therefore demand an alignment of scientific-technological progress with our moral level: research must be geared towards the moral good of humanity.

If our everyday situations were morally irresolvable and ridden with dilemmas, it would be impossible to do the right thing intentionally. If we did actually do the right thing, if we did good, it would be pure coincidence in a complex situation. But this would mean that we were never capable of acting morally. Our actions would be at the mercy of chance, something one could at best describe with models from behavioural economics or evolutionary biology in order to produce statistics about how people behave and how they can be controlled.

Fortunately, however, this impression is false. In reality, we act and think more morally today than in the past; there is moral progress, though it is not automatic. Moral progress includes a recognition of animal rights, child protection, the possibility of same-sex marriage as well as the processes of gender equality, which are generally desired in society but far from complete.

But there is a greater cause for hope: *it is fundamentally impossible that we cannot do the right thing, otherwise it would not be the right thing.* A morally relevant demand, an ethical imperative that we cannot possibly fulfil because our situation is too complex, would be an absurdity.

What follows from this philosophical argument, which runs through the history of philosophy since Plato's and Aristotle's establishment of ethics as a rational philosophical discipline, is surprising to many:

We humans largely act as we please. In so doing, we keep recognizing new non-moral facts and produce morally charged facts, such as the digital products of today's lifeworld and artificial intelligence. This raises new ethical questions, which in turn introduces the possibility of moral progress. We are not radically evil in the sense that we only follow egotistical, even violent impulses by nature. Humans are neither good nor evil by nature but, rather, free. And, in moral matters, freedom means that we have the capacity to do the right thing or the wrong thing.

A society that is evil in the majority of its actions would destroy itself; this is one of the central insights in the moral philosophy of Immanuel Kant. Admittedly, it means that we must concede that humanity is currently still working diligently towards radically evil self-destruction by producing masses of plastic waste, emitting unimaginable amounts of CO_2, consuming cheap meat from factory farming and cutting down the rainforest. As long as we do not recognize that these activities are radically evil, the moral progress we urgently need – especially in the realm of environmentalism – will fail to materialize.

For if we systematically do what is morally wrong, this can only succeed because the moral demands that are evident to us in daily life are concealed. A society in which we predominantly did what is morally wrong would be just as unstable as a group of people who were mistaken about all non-moral factual matters. If we were always mistaken we could not even buy bread in a shop, since we would not recognize it if it were in front of us.

Universal values are an expression of the fact that we cannot always be mistaken, that we, as humans, have always been in touch with moral reality. Famous formulations such as the Golden Rule ('Do unto others as you would have them do unto you') or more advanced variations on this theme, such as Kant's Categorical Imperative and modern principles of equality among all people, demonstrate the human understanding of the basic structure of our actions and thoughts that the American philosopher Donald Davison has termed the 'principle of charity'.[1] It simply cannot be that the absolute majority of our opinions and actions is wrong, since we would then be incapable of existing or acting in a coordinated fashion. The acquisition of language and mutual understanding via language already rely on a minimum of moral insight, since one cannot constantly hit one's educators and thus prevent them from teaching one anything. The basic learning situation that begins after birth, when people wait for us who help us to survive, presupposes that we are doing what is morally right. Without successful moral action, there can be no society.

That is why even the worst moral monsters – figures from the novels of the Marquis de Sade, or world-historical actors of regrettably great importance such as Adolf Hitler, Mao Zedong or Kim Jong-un – sometimes act morally, even if it is only towards groups of people with whom they feel kinship or whom they need in order to maintain their tyranny.

The coronavirus crisis has revealed the dynamics of moral progress in dark times. We can already venture a prediction: the decisions made by many governments in that time have proved that it is possible to conduct politics with high moral standards – with almost no regard for the cost. The German government, like many others, proved willing to accept hitherto unimaginable economic losses for the sake of protecting our health. We, the citizens, accepted this because we could assume that the reasons motivating our politicians were not based purely on tactical calculation but, rather, stemmed from genuine moral concerns. This triggered a wave of solidarity, of social cohesion.

This offers world-historical proof that it is merely an excuse if we say that in complex democratic societies we are automatically forced to follow the imperatives of the markets, the lobbyists and the neoliberal economists. Politics is not automatically morally corrupt – after all, it is carried out by human beings, who are capable of moral understanding and responsibility.

Universalism is not Eurocentrism

The French Revolution was the bang that initiated modernity. One part of it was the moral verve with which different groups in society sought to do away with the notion that people could be divided into classes and assigned value depending on race, religious affiliation and gender. Modernity thus began with the attempt to overcome the value relativism of the *ancien régime* – the cynical absolute monarchs and the privileged classes shielded by them – and demand human rights that applied to all demographic groups, which were largely trampled on by the rulers of the time.

Yet it is precisely the genesis of modernity that is often used as an argument against moral universalism, for the wake of the French Revolution saw outbreaks of violence and state terror, totalitarian warfare in the Napoleonic campaigns and new systems of exploitation. Indeed, according to the postmodern and postcolonial critics of modernity, the whole of modernity was a process of European colonialism that used language evoking universal morals to wreak havoc in other parts of the world.

The idea of universal values is not a modern European invention, however, but was (a) already found in pre-modern periods and (b) also outside of Europe.[2] Besides that, it is also a fatal act of Eurocentric presumption to believe that the idea of universal human rights was a European invention. This assumption would undermine their universal validity from the outset and raise the question of why people outside the tip of the Eurasian plate we inhabit today would not have noticed that their moral standards apply to *all* people. It is downright absurd to believe that, without us Europeans, the Aboriginals, the Chinese, the Indians or the indigenous populations of the American continents would never have noticed that they were humans and differed from other life forms in, among other things, the fact that they make moral demands that concern all humans as such.

It is true, however, that, in all documented periods in which complexly organized major cultures encountered one another, some group of people had the idea of viewing another ('the Russians', 'the Yellow Terror') as less than fully human. If someone believes that Jews, dark-skinned persons, Sumerians or Aztecs are somehow less human than they are, they are overlooking the fact that all people have more or less the same DNA and, biologically speaking, cannot seriously be divided up into different races (see below, pp. 134ff.). One of the origins of racist thinking lies in these verifiably false assumptions about the biological nature of humans.

A false universalism, then, makes universal claims while overlooking that it seeks to universalize attributes that are found only in some people. Accordingly, it would be wrong to try converting all people to Christianity, since this is a universal aim, but also a wrong one that corresponds neither to moral nor to non-moral facts. To convert people, at times by force (as in the Crusades or colonialism), is clearly morally reprehensible. In the worst case, such behaviour would constitute the universalization of an error, since it would rest on the belief that only certain people are fully human.

That there is false universalism does not mean that universalism as such is false.

Before we examine and refute the widespread suspicion that universal moral standards and values are always a cover for particular group interests, we must first gain a better understanding of the idea of universalism.

Value universalism is the assumption that there are universal values – an idea that I take as meaning that human actions can be divided into three categories that merge into one another. As explained above, the three categories in the system of universal values are the following: good, neutral and evil. This division applies across all historical and cultural boundaries and can (in different linguistic articulations) be found wherever people engage in moral reflection.

Universalism is the opposite of relativism. It states that moral values apply independently of group membership, and thus to all people (and ultimately even beyond the human realm). So there is only one system of universal values: good, neutral and evil.

Universal values are the guiding principles for our moral judgements in complex situations where not all moral facts are immediately obvious. Let us consider a complex action situation such as a visit to the Munich Oktoberfest (before the coronavirus crisis) involving a variety of morally charged episodes. Let us imagine that we are in a tent, sitting at a table with a group of friends and some Japanese visitors. It is morally permissible in this situation to order beer, greet people cordially, wear appropriate shoes and so forth; no one at the table will find any of these actions morally reprehensible. It is morally permissible to make integrating gestures towards the Japanese visitors, such as helping them to order the right beer and not to be at a disadvantage when competing for the attention of the waiting staff. If one sees someone at the table drinking so much that they are at risk of alcohol poisoning, or someone from the group groping a waitress or one of the Japanese visitors, it is morally necessary to intervene.

The moral conditions of an Oktoberfest taking place in China or the USA are not significantly different. Regardless of who is sexually harassed by whom and at what celebration in the world, it is a morally impermissible action – whether the person who sexually harasses another is a man, a woman, a Bavarian transsexual, a Japanese minister, a village priest or Donald Trump. There are quite simply no places where truly, radically different moral convictions govern events, otherwise communication would be impossible.

In general, one can say that there is a crucial difference between *value concepts* and *values*. **Value concepts** are answers to the question of what one believes one should do both in general and in certain particular situations, and how this is connected to what is good, neutral or evil. Good, neutral and evil, on the other hand, are **values** that exist irrespective of what value concepts a given group of people or individual has. In order to establish in a given action situation what we should or should not do, it is not sufficient to refer only to universal values. For we must acknowledge the non-moral facts structuring a situation and find out, together with other people, how the situation's participants assess the state of things. How people judge a situation is one element of moral reflection.

Universal values do not relieve us of making concrete decisions. The moral compass shows us in which direction to go, but we must still take the individual steps as individuals that remain fallible. Otherwise we would not be free, since our actions would be predetermined by the moral forces of universal values, as it were.

The **central thesis of moral realism** in this context is that value concepts can be true or false. It is possible, of course, for different groups with irreconcilable value concepts all to be wrong. If National Socialists and Stalinists discuss what people to crush in torture camps, they will disagree because each would like to imprison the other group. In such a case, however, the value concepts of *both* parties are mistaken, as it is evil to put any person whatsoever in death or torture camps. The value concepts of National Socialists and Stalinists are based on historico-philosophical principles. Both believe that there is an automatic world-historical mechanism that can be uncovered through economic analysis (as traditional Marxists believe), or which consists in a race war and has, in accordance with destiny, sent a leader who will protect us from the enemy takeover of our nation's racial corpus (as the National Socialists believe). They derive concrete measures from these (verifiably false) assumptions in order to achieve their aims through morally reprehensible actions.

Universalism is not Eurocentrism or any other elevation of our own culture (whatever that means) over others. In all human cultures, there is a difference between what one absolutely should and what one absolutely should not do – though every culture develops a zone of tolerance in which something that is actually morally reprehensible and impermissible is tolerated for non-moral reasons.

That universalism is not Eurocentrism follows quite simply from the fact that it contains a universal precept: not to take whatever one considers one's own 'culture' as the basis for an imperialistic subjugation of foreign cultures. Imperialism, enslavement and colonialism belong in the spectrum of evil and are therefore universally morally forbidden – which does not mean that they do not exist (and that there were even complicated legal systems to regulate them).

It would be a fundamental mistake to object here that different cultures make different moral judgements. This is true: the vast majority of citizens in the German Empire around 1900 had no problems with colonialism, and may even have hoped for more colonies. But this does not legitimize colonialism, any more than the Earth becomes flat because the members of the Flat Earth Society, founded in 1956, believe it to be flat. Rather, we have undergone moral progress in comparison to the empire and the dictatorships on German soil.

That does not remotely mean that we live in morally perfect surroundings. There are manifold moral deficits in our own culture (whichever culture you, the reader, might consider yours) that we studiously overlook at times.

These include the continued existence of forms of slavery, even though slavery is officially illegal.[3] It is morally reprehensible to deny the existence of slavery and human trafficking in today's world order, because then one cannot help the enslaved and also ignores conditions bordering on slavery for too long; among these are the cramped conditions of abattoir workers and the sometimes irresponsible hygienic standards among seasonal harvest workers, who supplied Germans with asparagus and strawberries during the coronavirus lockdown while often having to work under unacceptable conditions, including exposure to the virus. Our everyday behaviour thus falls short of the highest standards of moral reflection, and in many situations we fail to see how wrong our behaviour actually is.

Moral progress does not have a finishing line. It is an eternal, never-ending process, not least because the non-moral facts are constantly changing. Because we are intellectual, historical creatures and nature is likewise in perpetual transformation, there is no ultimate moral result, only a never entirely fulfilled call to do what is right and refrain from what is wrong. Morality does not take us to an earthly paradise, and universal values do not automatically lead to a final state of reconciliation with nature and all humans.

Ageism towards children and other moral deficits in everyday life

There is a very human tendency to view one's own behaviour as morally right and that of others as questionable and to blame the 'powers that be' for our misery. This too became dramatically apparent in the coronavirus crisis: the state must do what we think is right, and some people are evidently surprised that Angela Merkel, Jens Spahn and Markus Söder are not superheroes but politicians who take responsibility within a democratic division of labour and follow a clear, albeit fallible line.

Moral deficits begin at home and reveal themselves under quite ordinary circumstances. They also take effect, and especially so, where one might think everything is in order.

Here is an example from my own life in which one can identify a considerable moral deficit: I recently wanted to go to a large swimming pool with my daughter on a Sunday. Our ritual includes having lunch together in our dressing gowns after a round of swimming. The pool in question offers everything necessary, even an indoor area with palm trees. Without my knowledge, however, a new rule had been introduced stipulating that children could no longer enter the large indoor pool on Sundays, only on Saturdays; this information is found only in the small print, as I was told upon arrival. As if that were not enough, the only way to access the cafeteria is via said indoor area, which means that children under the age of sixteen can eat at the pool on only Saturdays, since they are not admitted to the cafeteria on any other day.

Discussion was futile; we were told that my extremely hungry and downcast daughter would not be allowed into the indoor area, and would therefore not get any pizza. As it happened, my daughter and I had just had a conversation about racism, which she does not understand at all, as she can barely even discern differences of skin colour, and certainly does not see why such a difference should constitute a reason for people to treat one another 'unfairly' (as she calls the immoral). Then, after a five-minute discussion at the ticket counter, my daughter full-throatedly told the unfriendly yet principled cashier that she was a racist towards children! Told that these were simply the rules, my daughter said that in that case, the rules were racist.

Now, obviously this was not a case of *racism* but a clear, morally reprehensible case of *ageism towards children* – which is, unfortunately, very widespread in Germany. For, unlike other age groups, children are democratically represented only indirectly via the voting choices of their parents or through protest movements such as Fridays for Future. Children under the age of six do not have a say in any of that, of course, and their parents or adults by necessity make decisions for them.

Our children are excluded from many activities because adults think that, on Sundays, they are entitled to be free of children's noise and children's behaviour in the sauna or pool area (or in the first-class area of trains, in business class on flights or in hotels).

Of course, it is morally permissible to offer leisure facilities to certain groups and exclude others. Such measures can also express social and moral ills, however – such as discrimination towards children; the only reason it does not strike us as particularly bad in Germany is that it is so widespread. But we owe the upcoming generations an unambiguous moral progress, something that became especially clear in the discourse around Fridays for Future, in which children and young people have been showing considerably more progressive thinking than the vast majority of adults.

Racist discrimination at swimming pools is morally graver than ageism towards children because racism has already led to systematic mass murder, and still does, such that we have finally reached a more or less shared understanding of the moral fact that racism in all its forms is morally reprehensible. If it had not led to slavery and mass murder, 'only' to everyday exclusion and disadvantages for certain people (which is still the case in Germany), it would not be recognized by the majority as something unambiguously evil. Racism and slavery are historically intertwined; this too, over the centuries of modernity, has gradually made the terrible effects of racist discrimination clear to almost everyone.

Pointing this out is not, incidentally, similar to saying that there is a problem with old white men. Old white men are human beings just like young black girls, radical feminists or middle-aged transsexual Bavarians. The fact that, both in the past and the present, the statistical probability that certain professions or positions are occupied by white men over the age of fifty is, because of its background history, the result of morally reprehensible decisions. But it would be equally morally reprehensible if one consequently disadvantaged white men of a certain age out of revenge or simply to correct the relevant statistics – which no one is demanding. Disadvantage through discrimination is the overarching problem that must be solved, not the fact that it is often carried out by old white men. It is no better for young dark-skinned women to exclude white men from jobs with high responsibility and good pay than for old white men to do this to young dark-skinned girls. It is simply the case, because of many past and present circumstances, that the latter is vastly more common.

Nor should this lead to the mistaken assumption that young dark-skinned girls are morally better than old white men. The state, society and thus every individual must work against discriminatory thinking. We need rules not for successful discrimination, but for fighting it. Where state-prescribed quotas are introduced, the concern is not to take revenge on groups of people whose earlier representatives excluded other groups but, rather, to balance out a demonstrably untenable, unjust distribution of resources. It would be morally reprehensible to discriminate against old white men, for example by denying them access to resources (certain jobs, intensive-care beds, ventilators, etc.) purely because they are old white men and old white men have had unfair advantages in the past. If a majority that comes about through contingency rather than innate necessity in certain social or economic branches (as in the American film industry) abuses its power for the moral humiliation of other people, this is the real problem, not the fact that this majority consists primarily of old white men. If the majority abusing its power consisted of young dark-skinned women, the moral situation would not be one iota better.

Moral progress is achieved if we acknowledge that morally reprehensible patterns of behaviour are reprehensible independently of the age or appearance of the persons responsible, otherwise we merely set up systems of revenge, which would only lead to a backlash among old and young white men, for example, who felt wronged. One does not balance out historical injustices by doing what is reprehensible to those whom one justifiably accuses of moral ills.

This is not meant to suggest that quotas in general are wrong. They serve to introduce balance at a certain point into systems that have led to an unacceptably unequal distribution of resources in the past. This does not, however, mean that every person can or should carry out every human activity with the same justification.

The reason why the government participation of women is a case of genuine moral progress (like some other recent breakthroughs in real-world gender equality) is that women make up around 50 per cent of voters but have hitherto been underrepresented in the German government. There is no reason to believe, as the antiquated assumption has it, that women govern differently because they are more gentle, empathetic and circumspect. Women are as fallible as men or non-binary persons. All humans sometimes act in a morally good way and sometimes do not. The notion that one group of people should automatically consist only of saints or sages is a distortion of moral and non-moral facts.

Moral tension

Every human action situation that is directly or indirectly shared with others has moral aspects. When one crosses the street, one usually avoids barging into the oncoming pedestrians. When standing in line, one does not simply kick the person in front in the heels. Even in a situation where something evil happens, those involved know the moral rules and choose to break them. A torturer in a secret Syrian prison knows exactly what he is doing to his victims and deliberately attacks their human dignity, inflicting not only unspeakable bodily pain but also mental torment and unbearable fear on their victims in order to break their will as fully as possible. The torturer is fully aware of what is good, but actively turns against it. Torture would not work otherwise, as it would simply be sadism.[4]

We change between social systems several times daily. In the morning, for example, one might speak to one's partner or housemate. Then one takes the subway, attends meetings, meets someone for lunch, and so on. Because we are social creatures, other people are almost always involved in what we do. The retreat into solitude usually serves only as a temporary breather from society and is itself socially organized and morally charged. Consider all the complex expectations one has of a holiday (also known as 'relaxation stress') in which one can withdraw and leave one's cares behind, free of all social strain. Someone will always bother other people by talking in the sauna, banging the door or putting the towels away. This disturbs one's expectation of a perfect holiday. And even a completely solitary visit to the sauna at a less busy time holds potential for disturbances, since there is still someone operating the sauna, supervising the electronics of the lighting systems, and so forth. Nor does it help to withdraw to a Buddhist monastery to live in silence, for the silence there is ritualized and determined by social rules. One can only partially relieve oneself of society and its demands, which always include moral ones.

As soon as a majority of people belong to the same social system (which is already the case if one is sitting in the same subway carriage), they begin to observe one another and form an image of the overall situation in order to predict the behaviour of the others; then they base their own behaviour on these predictions. As human animals, we detect danger and pay attention to whether anything about other people's behaviour points to a threat. At the same time, we are equally attentive to any prospects of friendly encounters, or at least to maintaining a neutral atmosphere.

One can flirt in the subway, though this is practically always inappropriate, as it is part of subway etiquette almost everywhere to pretend the others are not there, only to observe them secretly and cautiously. Anyone who tries to make explicit social contact in the subway will come across as intrusive.

Such descriptions apply across cultures. Wherever one sits in the subway, whether in Stuttgart, Mumbai or London, the people there will coordinate their actions – which is why taking the subway does not usually result in civil war-like situations. Humans are peaceful under the vast majority of circumstances but usually also exude an implicit threat of possible violence; this is why everyone steers clear of everyone else and ensures through politeness that no one will notice that they could just as easily pounce on one another.

Human socialization proceeds via glances, gestures and bodily contact (or its avoidance), but naturally also through language. As soon as some kind of social system exists, those participating in it can feel how it is morally charged. One *senses* normativity, the balance of expectations that allows us to recognize that we should do some things and refrain from others. There is no moral understanding without empathy with others and an awareness of the expectations that define a common, shared situation.

Generally speaking, **normativity** is no more than this: sensing (and thus realizing) that one should do some things and refrain from others. A **norm** is a specific regulation that divides behavioural patterns into categories of what one should and should not do.

Not all norms are moral, and not all norms exist objectively. One can violate the norms of German spelling without committing a moral error. Someone who makes an illegitimate move in chess is breaking the rules, but this is far from a moral error. Some norms, such as table manners, are simply contingent rules. There are social norms that have no moral meaning whatsoever and are laid down by people to pass the time. These include such things as trivial party games and small talk – both are subject to rules, but violations are not subject to strong sanctions. So norms are not discovered as a totality but can be imposed on a whim, which makes them a potential object of sociological research.

However, every situation of human action involving other people contains moral elements for which we have a complex assortment of sensors, some of which have come about through millions of years of evolutionarily transmitted environmental adaptation. For several hundreds of thousands of years, humans have been living in groups in which they act out different social situations. All human groups structure their daily lives and assign different roles in the community to different members. This leads to the creation of normativity.[5]

As soon as normativity exists, moral options become visible. If a person living in some small group in the Amazon region five thousand years ago took on the task of supervising the assignment of roles in their group, this always raised the question for the whole group of whether the division of tasks was fair and one should really follow the chieftain's instructions. Moral questions arose that were in part responded to silently or through rituals, in some cases with explicit instructions in the form of stories and other traditions.

There is no such thing as a completely amoral society or a society so different in its morality that *every* action carried out in it as a stranger could be a dangerous misstep. Wherever people encounter people, they can empathize with them to a certain extent. There is a bond of humanity that can be empirically observed. Ethics investigates the universal structures of social cohesion and then seeks to develop ideas for improving our moral circumstances. How we can achieve moral progress only emerges in the context of genuine decision-making situations. Here we are fallible, otherwise we would be morally perfect (which is far from the case).

The moral charge of our action situations is the palpable presence of universal values. With our thinking organ we perceive that reality places moral demands on us that are not always easy to grasp, as our action situations are interwoven with many systems of which no one can fully keep track.

Susceptibility to error, a fictional messiah and the nonsense of postmodern arbitrariness

We are susceptible to error in moral matters. If, in dark times, we keep an eye out for moral progress, whether to react to a merely perceived crisis of values or a truly verifiable one, we must live with the fact that the concrete value judgements we consider right might turn out to be wrong in the near future, or perhaps only fifty years later. If moral realism is correct and there are moral facts that we can and should acknowledge, it follows that we have to deal with uncertainty: we can posit truth claims in moral contexts, but these can also come to nothing. A truth claim fails if one is mistaken – that is, if one believes something false to be true (or vice versa). No one and nothing can guarantee that we will not be mistaken even in very important, morally relevant questions.

These include the genuinely difficult question of whether we have an immortal soul that is tested in this life to ascertain its morality – an assumption that is certainly not off the table. It would be a mistake to think that research in the field of natural science had proved that there is no immortal soul, for such research can neither prove nor disprove the claim, as shown by Kant in the *Critique of Pure Reason* as well as his beautiful text *Dreams of a Spirit Seer*.

If one opposes cultural relativism, one is sometimes accused of being intolerant of other people's opinions, since one could be mistaken. What I and many others consider morally right might in future turn out to be wrong, even evil. After all, many people in the past have similarly acted in all conscience yet made grave moral missteps.

So why should we trust our moral judgements at all? Should our tolerance towards those who live and think differently extend so far that we might, for example, consider the Chinese variety of communist dictatorship morally superior to the liberal understanding of the democratic law-based state?

It is indeed a consequence of moral realism that one can be wrong in moral matters. As a rule, one can follow the universal philosophical principle that, wherever one can be right, one can also be wrong.[6]

There is a simple reason for this: among other things, 'true' and 'false' are norms for evaluating our thinking behaviour. To make an assertion is a form of behaviour; one does something when one makes an assertion. When someone makes an assertion, they automatically commit to the fact that what they are asserting is true; the assertion is then measured against this.

An assertion can be an **error** if it is wrong. Not all errors are equally bad. A medical error can have fatal consequences; if, on the other hand, I am mistaken and think that my key is in my right jacket pocket rather than the left, this is of little significance.

An error is different from a lie. A **lie** is usually an assertion that is made in a way that is visible (or audible, readable, etc.) to another person and is considered false by the person making it, though they present it as true by asserting it. Whoever lies is deliberately saying something false. To be mistaken is not to lie, since one fails to see the truth if one is mistaken. For example, I do not know at this moment where Anne Will is.[7] If, however, I mistakenly believe for some dubious reason that she is in Munich, call a friend on the telephone and adamantly claim that she is in Munich, then I am not lying, since I do not know that she is not in Munich.

When one asserts something, one is making a truth claim; after all, what one says is supposed to be true. A *claim* to truth is not a *guarantee* of truth, of course, but a normative status. This means that a truth claim can be judged by whether it succeeds or fails. Someone who makes a truth claim can subsequently be measured against the facts: if what they say is true, they were right and thus spoke the truth; if not, they were mistaken. This expresses the oldest known definition of truth, which is found in Aristotle:

> Well, falsity is the assertion that that which is is not or that that which is not is and truth is the assertion that that which is is and that that which is not is not. Thus anyone who asserts anything to be or not to be is either telling the truth or telling a falsehood.[8]

We humans are susceptible to error in our truth claims, something referred to in philosophy as **fallibility**.[9] One reason for our fallibility is that we always reach judgements under time pressure and are never in a position to take into account all the factors that actually exist if we are to reach an interesting, informative judgement. It is not interesting for me to state that I am stating something, since it is largely uninformative. It is equally uninformative for me to state that Berlin is the city called Berlin.

One can divide assertions into those that contain no information whatsoever and those that contain a great deal of information. This division depends partly on our interests; human claims to truth and knowledge are rarely made in a vacuum of pure thought but take place in reality, which we attempt to grasp and also communicate with our assertions. Truth claims, then, are not free of all interests.

Yet this does not mean, as the relativists among you might counter, that there is no such thing as objective truth. It is correct that there is no absolutely neutral perspective, no 'view from nowhere', as the American philosopher Thomas Nagel calls it.[10] If it is true that it is raining in Berlin, this information has different practical significance depending on who expresses it to whom or on who observes it at what point. If I travel to Berlin as a tourist and learn that it is currently raining, I will pack an umbrella and might be saddened. If I am on summer holidays in Greece, however, I might be relieved or even pleased; I might feel sympathy with my fellow citizens in Berlin or be happy for the Brandenburg farmers. And if I engage in urban gardening in Berlin or make a living with farming myself, this information is actually important for me and will guide my actions. Yet none of this changes the fact that it is raining in Berlin if it is true that it is raining in Berlin. In the vast majority of cases, the truth is not a matter of interests but, rather, objective in the sense that something is the case, and thus true, independently of our interests.

Anyone who can be mistaken can also be right. This can be quickly shown using a slick argument made by René Descartes: if we were exclusively mistaken, if we were never right, then we would also be mistaken about the fact that we were always mistaken. This would mean that we could not even ask whether we were always wrong, since we would then not be mistaken about asking whether we are always mistaken. To put it even more concisely: whoever asks themselves if they are mistaken is not mistaken about the fact that they are asking themselves whether they are mistaken.

So ask yourself with the look of a straining thinker whether you are always mistaken. If you tried to follow my request, you were not mistaken: you genuinely asked yourself a question. This is the trick behind the most famous proposition in modern philosophy: *cogito, ergo sum* (I think, therefore I am).[11]

Let us return to the subject of values. In our everyday lives, values act as guiding principles for our moral assessments. The values we consider our own say something about who were are and who we want to be. However, we can be mistaken about two things: firstly, what values actually exist and, secondly, how we genuinely remain faithful to our values in a given situation.

To illustrate this, let us consider a morally weighty decision about the right treatment for a severely ill relative. One learns that a close relative is suffering from a complex, probably terminal form of cancer. At the same time, there is constantly renewed hope, because new therapies keep becoming available, though they are not yet clearly supported by studies or cases of successful treatment. In addition, there are still the options of enlisting a faith healer or using an alternative medical method to get the problem under control.

In such extreme situations of human life, we find out who we really are. We learn something about how deeply we are actually connected to this relative and what our values and belief systems really are. For we have to make difficult judgements with far-reaching consequences under time pressure: do we want to make a terminally ill relative go through the hardship of chemotherapy, even if there is little hope of success? How do we advise people in such difficult situations without taking away their hope, yet avoid letting them live under illusions? What someone means to us and who we really are in relation to this person are things that we learn at the latest through the shared painful experience of this person's passing. In the extreme situations of life, which in all societies include birth and death in particular, we learn first-hand what ethics is about, because our judgements about ourselves, about others and about what we should do have the greatest possible weight.

This becomes especially clear in the age of the coronavirus crisis, for now our socially shared and politically implemented moral judgements count. If it comes down to choosing which human lives should be saved in the light of scarce medical resources, a doctor in the intensive-care unit is confronted with the question of whom to help first if she does not have enough ventilators: the young mother of three or the Nobel laureate who might be on the verge of a further ground-breaking discovery? This is in fact an intolerable situation, since every possible decision is ultimately morally reprehensible.

This is not actually a moral dilemma, however, because it is impossible in this scenario to do the right thing. A genuine dilemma would involve a situation in which one can do the right thing only by simultaneously doing the wrong thing in another respect, which is not the case here. If one can only do the wrong thing, if one has to choose between several evils, then this is not a moral dilemma but a genuine tragedy.

If someone who is capable of saving people's lives and is even employed to do so must choose which of the persons arriving they should save first, this decision cannot be fully covered by moral reasons, because here the value of one life is inevitably compared to that of another.

Yet the accompanying moral blame cannot be placed on the doctor, since she is not responsible for the scarcity of resources. Therefore, appropriate committees issue guidelines designed to help the doctor, whose goal will always be to save all human lives, to make decisions based on a bureaucratically legitimized document. This relieves her psychologically of the immense responsibility, meaning that we can expect her to perform actions that must be carried out as quickly as possible but which ultimately cannot be morally justified.

In the light of all this, it is morally necessary for the state administration of our health system to recognize since the coronavirus – at the latest – that we cannot subject our hospitals to the logic of the market, since this is currently resulting in a large, as yet unknown number of people dying because health systems are not equipped to survive a viral pandemic.

In the coronavirus crisis, ethically complex decisions have been made in order to redistribute resources. These decisions were made with the primary goal of containing the viral pandemic and preventing an overload of the health system. Among other factors, this is morally right because it helps the doctor to avoid the situation of triage: she will not be confronted with weighing up human lives against one another. At the same time, this redistribution of resources puts politicians in a difficult ethical situation in a different area, for they have to take on board the fact that the special measures, some of them drastic (such as curfews or school closures), will cause people to suffer.

The ethical decisions of the executive could scarcely be different in the light of the virological prognoses, which is why the government's actions were largely welcomed in this country because of their factual transparency. But they are justified only to the extent that they are supported by genuine moral considerations. This cannot succeed merely by pointing to the *virological imperative*, which demands the protection of as many lives as possible from the coronavirus. For, in the past, the political system has generally failed to respond adequately to much greater crises – first and foremost the climate crisis – and instead, for example in the context of the unacceptably slow shift towards electric mobility, has placed the value of the German automobile industry above the people's quality of life. This is changing in the course of the coronavirus crisis, which had made it clear that there can be no return to the previous 'normality', which we have long known is not sustainable.

Alongside the virological imperative, then, there are also other scientifically and medically grounded moral imperatives, such as the urgent demand to develop new forms of sustainable, humane mobility that do not lead us to pollute the air that we need to breathe. There is a fundamental human right to breathe.

Unlike the non-man-made coronavirus, most of the environmental pollution that causes immense damage to people's health is purely our own doing. The responsibility is spread among numerous actors, and each of us plays a small part in the fact that people must suffer and even die at certain nodes of our global production chains.

It is unacceptable to push aside this fact with the cynical remark that those people do not belong to our immediate social environment and do not concern us. This form of argumentation only shows a morally reprehensible way of thinking that cannot be glossed over convincingly with any excuse.

Extreme situations of life and death do not exclusively concern doctors, who work in particularly morally demanding professions and therefore deserve particular appreciation, because not only their medical but also their moral knowledge plays an important part in moral progress. The moral hardships of everyday life are illustrated by a fictional, yet nonetheless instructive example from the Netflix series *Messiah*. In this series, a man appears (first in Syria) whom many take for the messiah. He seemingly even performs miracles (by driving Islamic State out of Damascus by means of a sandstorm, reviving a child wounded by gunfire or walking on water in front of cameras in Washington). The series is especially good at raising repeated doubts (especially among the viewers) about whether the protagonist truly embodies the (re)appearance of the messiah or is simply a deranged, dangerous charlatan, perhaps even a terrorist.

One plot thread shows a mother bringing her cancer-stricken child to the presumed messiah to be healed. For this, she breaks off chemotherapy and risks the life of her child because she cannot bear the woes of the chemotherapy and hopes for a miracle cure through divine intervention. She does not inform her husband before leaving with the child to find the messiah, for she knows that her husband does not support her decision and would probably ensure that the child remain in medical treatment. After the two return, the husband decides to file for divorce and sole custody of the child.

In this situation, complex value judgements and truth claims clash. The mother wants her daughter to be healed at any cost and is emotionally unable to subject her child to the suffering of chemotherapy. Instead, she puts her trust in the religious belief that the protagonist is truly the messiah and that he is also willing to heal her daughter. The father does not believe this, preferring to rely on the prospects of chemotherapy. These starkly conflicting value judgements are connected to truth claims and belief systems that extend so far that the marriage cannot be continued and the law-based state is called upon to pass legal judgement. One point of the thought experiment in the series is to show us what is at stake in the moral life of humanity and how the seriousness of life would become visible if someone appeared and, as the messiah, propagated in a credible and media-friendly way that the meaning of life is to be tested by God.

In ethical discussions, we must not forget that billions of people genuinely believe that ethics and morals are closely connected to the presence of the divine, or even the personal god of the Abrahamic religions (Judaism, Christianity and Islam). As we know, when it comes to gods, the divine or God (in the eminent singular), things can get serious. When we reflect on fundamental moral questions, we must not forget that we by no means live in a secular age in which religions are merely a sideshow. Rather, taken as a whole, there are still more people with religious worldviews than atheistic ones. An ethics that did not speak to our religious fellow humans – whatever their faith – would be a case of false universalism.[12]

Religions are firmly rooted in the human process of finding self-images, something that must be taken into account in ethics without being dependent on religious authorities; whatever is objectively right does not become more right because religious authorities also believe it. Yet we must not underestimate how substantially religious thought has contributed to moral progress, indeed moral revolutions, through such disparate elements as the Buddhist ethics of compassion, which includes other animals, or the Christian notion of a human kindness that knows no bounds.

The indisputable seriousness of the extreme situations of human life is a further, and indeed sufficient, reason to reject the abstruse logic of postmodern arbitrariness, which presupposes a fluid value pluralism in which one can ultimately choose for no particular reason which value system to follow. Those who subscribe to this misconception believe in particular that we can choose between value systems. Yet our freedom does not by any means consist in trying out different value systems before we decide on one. The principle of postmodern arbitrariness – which involuntarily expresses a value system itself – comes from a complete overestimation of the scope of value pluralism. When it comes down to it, human value judgements are not as different as one might think. This is precisely what the fictional story of the series *Messiah* demonstrates: both the mother of the child brought to the messiah and the father, who relies on a medical cure, want to save their child.

It is impossible to avoid far-reaching prejudices. Anyone who thinks one could choose between value systems has, in the process, already chosen a value system: value pluralism. Therefore, there is no value-neutral position from which to assess values. Even value nihilists have value concepts, because they consider it a value to cling to the truth of their opinion that there are in fact no values (which is naturally a contradictory position). A mistake regarding the ontology of values (their mode of being and scope) is already a mistake within the objectively existing system of values, the moral order.

Understanding that there are universally shared human value judgements – which naturally also connect us to the Chinese, who are governed not democratically but by a dictatorship – does not necessarily require invoking God. Considering the relatively minor significance of monotheism in the whole of Asia, this would fail in any case. Alongside other factors, monotheism is also an unsuitable basis for a universal ethics because universal values do not require divine support.

Rather, it is sufficient to understand that we humans are living creatures that are capable of morality – a principle that can be supported just as easily in China and Japan without recourse to the Bible as it can here. Our moral judgements are closely tied to our way of life – that is, the fact that we are animals of a particular kind, namely humans. When we make decisions under time pressure (which happens constantly), biologically measurable parameters prearrange our courses of action. This is evident in the fact that we feel horror even when we see *fictional* terrible suffering, for example in *Messiah*. Even though we know that what we see in the series is not happening 'for real', only 'on television', we go through an emotional rollercoaster because most of us have an innate capacity for empathy developed over several hundred thousand years. Our moral judgements and values are closely connected to the fact that our organism inherited forms and processes that came about through the evolution of species on our planet. One of the reasons why humans are evolutionarily successful and strategically superior to other animals through their intelligence is that they have moral feelings (and thus the foundations for a conscience). This is certainly not the limit of our moral power of judgement, but it favours it, because its origin is intertwined with the social nature of humans.

The vast majority of humans (whatever their origin) are startled by scenes of extreme physical violence. Similarly, everyone is pleased by universally recognizable accommodating gestures, such as compassion, hospitality or helpfulness. If there were no shared moral foundation for the perception of human action situations, people who had never met before could not remotely communicate or understand one another. We continue to develop our morally charged feelings (such as shame, outrage, anger or pride), so it does not follow from the evolutionary history of our moral judgements that we can explain our contemporary moral system – the moral facts we acknowledge – only in purely evolutionary terms. This important idea was summed up in particular by the famous Australian ethicist Peter Singer:

> From these intuitive responses, shared with other social mammals, morality has developed under the influence of our acquisition of language. it has taken distinct forms in different human cultures, but there is still a surprisingly large common ground .... Understanding the origins of morality, therefore, frees us from two putative masters, God and nature. We have inherited a set of moral intuitions from our ancestors. Now we need to work out which of them should be changed.[13]

What is overlooked by proponents of postmodern arbitrariness is how serious a matter life is: in every action situation a living creature experiences, everything is at stake. We could die at any moment, we could contract a lethal disease any time. We have no certainty that our life will proceed happily and healthily, for we are always playthings of forces, powers and processes that none of us commands. As living creatures, we are at the mercy of reality.

Non-human nature knows no mercy – with the notable exception that other, non-human animals also know systematic moral behaviour and judgements. Even in the animal kingdom there are traces of morality, which should not be surprising, for nature is gradually constituted; it does not make leaps, as Leibniz succinctly put it: *natura non facit saltus*.[14] That is to say that new, primarily biological forms that develop in nature do not come into existence overnight but emerge in small steps, and usually in a sequence of imperceptible changes that take up a great deal of time.

It is therefore a well-supported, albeit not fully confirmed hypothesis that the behavioural spectrum of other living creatures is likewise guided by the fact that they experience their surroundings as morally charged. Humans also have a complex language of emotions because we describe and assess our behaviour with language and have preserved these assessments for millennia in cultural artefacts comprising images, writings, stories and more recently videos, as well as social media. This is tied to our ability to abstract, and thus to develop systems of universal norms that we can encode symbolically through language, but also by other means, for example in works of art.

Human morality stands 'above' that of other animals in so far as our historically developed patterns of behaviour display a level of complexity that leads to the constant revision of previous moral judgements, and thus the possibility of moral progress (but also regression). Humans develop radically new patterns of behaviour that they must later bring back into the space of previously rehearsed practices of moral assessment. In the Stone Age there were no urban neurotics, hipsters, right-wing extremists, hotel managers or parliamentary secretaries of state, and we cannot predict what possible courses of action humanity will develop in the future.

Moral feelings

Not all truths are objective in the sense of existing completely independently of human interests. In moral matters, after all, the concern is first and foremost with ourselves and, indirectly, with other life forms, the environment, and so on. One can easily see that the *objective* and the *subjective* are not mutually exclusive from the fact that our subjective feelings, emotions and evaluations can be examined from the objective perspectives of other people. The fact that something is subjective does not mean that it cannot be objectively understood; we cannot, however, explain our subjectivity from the objective perspective in exactly the same manner as natural science. This is something constantly attempted by Sheldon Cooper in the popular series *The Big Bang Theory*, but his failure shows primarily that what counts is knowledge of human nature, empathy and life experience, which can never be replaced by a purely scientific or psychological perspective. For one cannot become and remain a natural scientist or psychologist if one does not expand one's knowledge of human nature, empathy and life experience. Such disciplines as psychology and sociology can only exist on the basis of these forms of knowledge, which are not conferred by scientific studies.

The fact that something is subjective does not mean that it is not true or actual. Subjectivity is as much a part of reality as objectivity.

Let us define this idea a little more precisely in order to come closer to understanding the nature of universal values. Some truths concern circumstances that have almost nothing to do with the human spirit (our consciousness, thoughts and feelings). The mass of physical elementary particles, the Big Bang, the basic forces of nature and much more most likely do not depend on our existence. Thoughts relating to such truths can be classified as maximally objective. **Maximum objectivity** thus refers to facts and processes that are entirely independent of humans, especially in non-human nature.

Other truths, on the other hand, are completely subjective. So, at the opposite end of the spectrum, there is **maximum subjectivity**, which consists in phenomena such as feeling a sharp pain in a fleeting moment, or seeing a coloured surface in a dream, without ever remembering it.

Some consciousness theorists believe that our mental life has a base layer consisting of the sensations we experience directly and only in the moment. This base layer is known as **the phenomenal consciousness**.

The American philosopher Sharon Hewitt Rawlette has written a wonderful book whose title expresses its central thesis: *The Feeling of Value: Moral Realism Grounded in Phenomenal Consciousness.*[15] Her basic idea is plausible and easy to understand: when we make moral statements and assert that something is morally necessary or forbidden, we always take into account how we ourselves and other people (including other living creatures) feel as a result of an action. Feelings are indispensable for ethics; they play a decisive part in the moral assessment of courses of action.

One can see this from the fact that there is a crucial difference between kicking a Japanese robot dog and a Maltese puppy. If one kicks a robot dog, one will not hurt it, while giving the poor puppy a firm kick would torture it, which is morally forbidden. It is therefore morally permissible to kick a robot dog but morally reprehensible to mistreat a Maltese puppy. Perhaps one would hurt the feelings of the robot dog's owner, which does have moral significance, but never those of the robot dog itself, since it has none. In contrast to the robot dog, we owe the puppy direct moral respect because it is a sentient creature.

In the past, ethics of compassion were developed on a similar basis (especially by Schopenhauer) that viewed our compassion with others as the foundation of morality. Yet this falls short, as Rawlette shows, for it is not only a matter of developing sympathy with other creatures. Ethics takes place not only in negative zones of life but also under conditions of joy, love and enjoyment. Ethics is not *ascetic*; its function is not merely self-discipline for the purpose of reducing violence, as the bleakly pessimistic Schopenhauer believed, but is rather, taken as a whole, *hedonistic*: it is geared towards feeling happiness. There is an ethics of joy as well as one of suffering, an ethics of love and one of anger. Doing good to oneself or others is a matter not only of reducing suffering on our planet but also of multiplying joy. If one smiles at people whose gaze one meets as one walks through the city centre, one increases one's own wellbeing and that of others. One is then doing something good even though it may not be necessary. There is no absolute rule dictating that one must smile at other passers-by. Nonetheless, one improves the overall happiness of society if one makes a point of granting joy to oneself and others.

A positive attitude towards other people, defined in this minimal fashion, is necessary. For one factor in the darkness of our time is that the urgent moral problems all appear hopelessly irresolvable – even though they are not, fortunately. The climate crisis, which puts an excessive strain on advanced life on our planet, the systemic competition between the liberal democratic law-based state and authoritarian, even dictatorial regimes, as well as unfettered global capitalism, cannot be dealt with overnight. In particular, we feel overwhelmed by these problems on a daily basis because we simply do not know where to begin. If one stops buying plastic bags and volunteers to look after refugee children, but flies to the Caribbean in the summer and wears designer clothes manufactured under dubious conditions, the overall moral balance of our actions tends towards the negative. As an individual, one can no longer see all the things one would have to do in order to have credit in one's moral 'karma account': we generally know what we should do but are structurally overtaxed when it comes to putting our goodwill into practice.

To overcome this dilemma, Rawlette takes the approach of locating ethics closer to ourselves, in the emotional foundations of our everyday conduct. In doing so, she is able to draw on the classical tradition of ethics that revolved around the concept of happiness, *eudaimonia*. We should try to base our actions as a whole on how we and others feel towards ourselves. Proceeding from this, Rawlette advocates a form of **hedonism** (from the Greek *hēdonē*, 'pleasure' or 'joy') – that is, the idea that ethics is about the feelings of pleasure and displeasure. If Rawlette were right, moral statements would deal with actions that are to be assessed primarily in terms of the resulting pleasure. The object of ethics would then be maximally subjective facts. Unfortunately, this does not quite work; not every source of joy is morally commendable, and not every feeling of unhappiness merits moral respect. It is more fun to speed along the motorway in a Porsche than a Prius, and a Wiener schnitzel is delicious but requires the killing of a calf. If a brutal dictator enjoys efficiently torturing his subjects, this also inflicts moral harm on humanity. And many of the feelings we experience as positive – feelings of home and belonging, for example – are ultimately always in part an expression of reprehensible systems of discrimination that we fail to notice only because we have grown used to them.

Even compassion is not a morally commendable feeling in all cases. It is not necessary, at any rate, to feel compassion when war criminals are punished harshly and suffer because they know they have committed morally monstrous acts. Like other feelings, suffering and joy should only be assessed in moral terms if we also consider a context that does not consist only of maximally subjective states. Ethics does not directly concern the sensibilities of particular groups at particular times, then, but always also the context that explains these sensibilities and legitimizes or delegitimizes them.

Not every feeling merits moral respect. Some feelings can legitimately be hurt; indeed, it is even morally necessary to take on board the fact that some feelings, for example those of terrorists such as the hookah lounge murderer of Hanau,[16] will be hurt if their atrocities can – in successful cases – be prevented by capturing them in time. After the reactions of many AfD politicians to the Hanau attack, the party was accused of trying to gain votes with rhetoric and propaganda based on morally legitimizing feelings that guide the behavioural patterns of far-right terrorism.

There is a politics of affect that is ethically evaluable; we all accept this on a daily basis by teaching ourselves and others to control our own impulses. Philosophy is a universal voice; as a rational, systematic and scientific discipline, it has attempted for centuries under changing historical circumstances to find out what principles are valid from a non-partisan perspective. Moral reflection strives for universality, and hence non-partisan neutrality. No single party is always right, least of all in moral questions. Philosophy, on the other hand, is as partisan as mathematics – that is, not at all. If the result of a philosophical consideration comes about only because the person in question has a particular party membership card or votes for certain parties in regional and national governments, it is thus falsified.

That is why we need more, not less philosophy today in the realm of public opinion, which is currently highly politicized, reinforcing the impression of a division of society into groups with different values and thus encouraging value relativism. A number of politicians can profit from this in the short term, in keeping with the old Roman motto 'divide and rule', since it enables them to divide society and thus gain votes. Fortunately, however, this old tactic cannot succeed in the long term with an enlightened public; this is part of the crisis among the mainstream parties, which, in a time when their actions and decisions are digitally visible, should strive to follow the truth and reality that unite us. As Goethe already put it in 1804: 'Divide and command, a wise maxim; / Unite and guide, a better.'[17]

Ethics is concerned with the question of who we are and who we want to be. Our self-portraits as humans are thus under scrutiny; yet the universal values that emerge from this do not guarantee by themselves that we will apply them adequately. It is therefore indispensable to bear in mind as many non-moral facts as possible in order to identify the moral facts in complex action situations.

Because this is about ourselves, subjectivity must be taken into account. That is why ethics cannot be turned into an objective calculation that could be represented by an insentient machine in the form of an algorithm. Rather, it is crucial that we can empathize with other living creatures, whether they belong to our species or not. Ethics creates a relationship between subjectivity and objectivity that can shift according to situation. It confronts us with a task that can never be completed once and for all.

Doctors, patients, Indian police officers

Ethics would not exist if we did not have feelings. We do not have any *direct* moral obligations towards the moon, amoebas, robot dogs or gravity, as they have no feelings. Nor am I committing a moral error if I scratch my desk or destroy some inanimate object out of frustration, unless this inanimate object happens to be a Dürer painting or someone's favourite teddy bear. Direct moral obligations exist only towards sentient beings; hence ethics and morality are closely intertwined with phenomenal consciousness, as we can learn from Rawlette. We have indirect obligations towards the atmosphere and the world's oceans, since their condition affects living beings (including us).

The example of a far-right or Islamist assassin, however, showed that not every emotional state deserves moral respect. Anyone who feels racially motivated disgust towards a group of people thus has morally reprehensible feelings that they should overcome through cognitive work on themselves.

A decisive factor in the present context is that there is a middle position located between maximum objectivity and maximum subjectivity. This position is the New Moral Realism.

> The **New Moral Realism** proceeds from the assumption that moral statements deal with actually existing circumstances involving feeling and thinking living beings. These actually existing circumstances are never maximally objective or maximally subjective but are located somewhere between these extremes. Their location depends on the concrete circumstances of our action situations.

This somewhat abstract suggestion can be illustrated using an everyday situation: a visit to the doctor because of a painful affliction in an intimate area of one's body (I will not go into further detail). The doctor has moral obligations towards their patient, as they advise us in matters of life and survival that obviously belong to the most urgent moral issues, since the clearest moral commandment of all is 'Thou shalt not kill'. Doctors must not kill us but, rather, do everything in their power to preserve our lives and bring about our recovery as best they can. The doctor is, however, entitled to cause us pain. They can do this in order to find out what illness we have – for example, so that we can describe the specific pain they deliberately inflict ('How does it feel if I touch you here with this instrument?', etc.). We will undress before them and show parts of our bodies that we do not usually display, perhaps not even to our intimate partners. In the concrete action situation inside the consulting room, the doctor and the patient will establish what touches and questions are acceptable, desirable and even indispensable for the common goal of diagnosis and recovery.

This overall situation in which we engage in moral considerations consists, on the one hand, of maximally objective facts that the medical practitioner knows as a result of their science-based training; some parts of our body and the processes taking place in them are unaffected by our mental disposition towards them. Not everything that happens in our bodies is psychosomatic; some things are simply somatic (such as the growth of fingernails or the biochemical composition of some skin cell). On the other hand, every visit to the doctor, especially in intimate contexts, involves maximally subjective facts: sensibilities, feelings such as worries and hopes, feelings of cold, pain, shame, and so on. Doctor and patient must work out together what courses of action are in the morally acceptable realm.

Here one can observe moral progress in the sense that, today, we are all sensitized to the fact that our mental states also play an important part in doctor–patient relations. In addition, scientific-technological progress has taught us more (though certainly not everything) about which processes are maximally objective and which are maximally subjective. Going to see a gynaecologist or urologist in the Wilhelmine Empire was no doubt considerably more stressful than is usually the case in Germany today.

Here we should note that there are no profound cultural differences that would suddenly confront us with Chinese values if we went to the doctor in China, for example, and automatically give us reason to expect a violation of our supposedly Western human rights. As I write these lines, Chinese doctors and authorities (in so far as the communist dictatorship allows) are cooperating with authorities worldwide to contain the spread of the coronavirus. A Chinese doctor does not view fundamental questions of medical ethics much differently from their Bavarian colleagues, and, if they do, we can reproach them rather than downplaying it as a matter of cultural differences.

Of course there is such a thing as cultural differences in action situations. Religious ideas about gender roles, reproduction and life itself, political circumstances and much more play a major part in explaining action situations. This can be elucidated with an example from my own personal experience. While travelling in India, I realized in Goa that the same taxi route from the hotel to the beach, under the same traffic conditions, always had a different, seemingly random price. To the German customer, such a situation immediately arouses the suspicion that different standards are being applied.

Instead of relying on prejudices towards Indian taxi drivers, I wanted to find out what was going on. So I asked several taxi drivers why the price varied. One particularly amusing answer on a Saturday was that the prices were slightly higher on Saturdays because one has to pay a sum to the policeman who patrols a particular corner on Saturdays. I cautiously pointed out that this sounded like corruption, but this was dismissed by the taxi driver with the remark that it was simply a rule that one had to pay this sum to exactly this policeman, and only on Saturdays. After making further cautious enquiries of Indian friends, I discovered that what I had perceived as the corruption of a police officer was in this case an act of grateful support towards a policeman who was always especially helpful to the community. I did not check if this was legal in Goa, but the overall moral context did not entirely confirm my strong suspicion of corruption. There are simply socioeconomic conditions under which something that would be legally classified as corruption is morally necessary.

We have well-grounded opinions, adapted to our society, about the fact that even such forms of well-meaning financial support for police officers should be considered corruption and lead in small steps to an undermining of the democratic law-based state as the institutionally effective founding values of our society. Here the first rule should be: when in Rome, do as the Romans do – though this by no means implies that neither of the two options is better. One would have to take the overall moral context into account.

Other customs do not imply fundamentally different values but involve different non-moral facts that we must take into account; in other places, different social and socioeconomic conditions apply.

In India, a police officer's salary can be so low that they have to rely on non-state support from other group members, whereas, in Germany, the dominant idea is that the state should take on as many of the organizational tasks in public life as possible, preventing any form of corruption through the appropriate remuneration of the respective officials. In addition, there is a completely different gift culture in India (as also in China or Japan) that involves bringing presents for guests in many situations that we would consider inappropriate, seeing them as attempts to influence persons who are obliged to neutrality, even if they do not have this significance in their context.

In Germany we rely on the state as a vehicle of moral progress – an idea that came about in the context of the German nation state's emergence and is rooted not least in the thought of Kant and Hegel. Precisely because the history of the German nation state involved unimaginable harm, it is crucial for us to remember the foundational gesture of the Enlightenment and effectively implement its moral impulse on an institutional level.

It is part of the trajectory of the German Enlightenment that we assign tasks of moral education to the state, which is why we also make moral demands of the state. Things are quite different in the USA, for example, where private schools and universities usually fulfil this task considerably better than state institutions, which are fundamentally distrusted because the state has a different function in the USA compared to Germany. By contrast, the idea of the state that forms part of the German constitution comes from the Enlightenment and is based on the principle that there are tax-financed institutions that are judged by moral standards; they do not simply serve the purpose of protecting borders and roads in order to give free rein to the logic of the market.

Because there is a fundamentally unbridgeable gap between universal values and their conditions of application in complex action fields and individual situations, the **principle of leniency** applies:

Before we condemn others whose moral assessment of a situation is different from ours, we must examine the reasons they give for reaching their divergent judgement. This also applies to us: we change our own opinions because we are fallible. Therefore, everyone has the right to be corrected before being condemned unnecessarily harshly for moral missteps, and possibly even punished by legal means.

However, this circumspect moral tolerance towards other value concepts and their institutional manifestations ends if we establish that police officers in an authoritarian regime are arresting clearly innocent people, and even making additional money doing so. No one, whether Indian or German, will consider this morally legitimate on closer inspection; self-evident moral truths remain valid. The principle of leniency is not carte blanche for value relativism. To be clear: no cultural difference between groups of people can ever be cited to justify the Nazi concentration camps or the atrocities of other totalitarian regimes. The Nazi murderers did not belong to any other culture than the people they persecuted.

Remembering, historically researching and documenting dictatorships (including the SED[18] dictatorship in the GDR) is a crucial part of our moral progress. Germany was the scene of one of the worst episodes of moral education in human history. The extreme cruelty that ensued is a deterrent example of what can happen when one devotes oneself to the revaluation of all values. We are therefore especially vigilant when basic values are violated, as the termination of the Nazis' reign of terror was a form of moral progress for which many people even gave their lives to create a better world order.

The same applies to religiously motivated human sacrifice, circumcision of women and girls, slavery and forced prostitution, as well as less ghastly but unacceptable forms of gender inequality, which in Germany include the proven pay gap between men and women or the way successful and powerful women are still spoken about in the media and direct communications (as in the cases of Angela Merkel or Renate Künast).[19] Complete equality would exist only if no one noticed the gender of the person fulfilling a professional function any more (except in professions where gender attributes play a central part). There is much to be resolved before we come closer to this goal, as it is not fully clear which professions are tied to which gender attributes. In many ways, we have only just begun to explore the issue of gender.

The rejection of a widespread value pluralism is not a denigration of foreign cultures but, rather, the recognition of universally shared humanity. Cultures are not clearly demarcated from one another; they are not even defined by political boundaries. It is simply not true that there is a single German culture or dominant culture [Leitkultur] that unites all those who belong to or believe in it. We are a multicultural society and have always been. It is impossible, after all, to coordinate the attitudes, wishes, ideas, talents and actions of over 80 million people in such a way as to produce a monoculture. Even a totalitarian dictatorship like that of the Nazis was internally multifaceted and divided. It is certainly not as if people had agreed at some point in an imagined past on what exactly everyone should do. The Nazis also persecuted and killed one another – a feature of totalitarian systems, where no one, not even the dictator, is safe from persecution.

This does not mean that the project of multiculturalism has failed, for it cannot fail. A monoculture cannot remotely be brought about under the conditions of a modern mass democracy. At the same time, this does not mean that every opinion and way of life must be treated as equally valid. Rather, multiculturalism presupposes a joint expedition: we are all sitting in the same boat and have to find out together how to achieve further moral progress. There is quite simply no way around multiculturalism, which results automatically when millions of people (however 'ethnically' uniform they might seem) belong to the same society.

The categorical imperative as social glue

The famous Categorical Imperative, formulated by Immanuel Kant in order to express the most general principle of ethics, hits the nail on the head. As elsewhere, however, Kant's formulations are not immediately comprehensible, as he embeds them in a complicated philosophical system.

There are good reasons for this that I, as a philosopher, do not intend to question. My concern here is to offer an interpretation of the Categorical Imperative that is understandable for everyone. For that, we must look at two of Kant's formulations that are usually referred to respectively as the 'Formula of Universal Law' and the 'Formula of the End in Itself'.

> **Formula of Universal Law:** 'Act in such a way that the maxim of your will could at all times act as the principle of a basic law.'[20]
> **Formula of the End in Itself:** 'So act that you use humanity, whether in your own person or in the person of any other, always at the same time as an end, never merely as a means.'[21]

What Kant expresses here can be understood as the basis for successful socialization. One of the questions he answers with his Categorical Imperative can be formulated as follows: how can we coordinate our actions in such as a way that we can achieve what we want to achieve without causing harm to others who want to achieve different things, something we should not accept?

A concrete, sadly very commonplace example: the smartphone I carry with me consists of parts that are connected in a complicated way that is really fully understood only by a small number of specialists. This is what makes it possible for businesses to gain market advantages in the first place: manufacturing products that other companies cannot offer. But the parts that form my smartphone do not grow on trees; they are only available because there is a global production chain that involves many people. This includes the mining of rare earths by people working as wage slaves under miserable conditions and far below the acceptable minimum of freedom, nowhere near the minimum wage they would receive for their hard work here.

Therefore, the freedom I claim for myself to acquire a new smartphone as often as I can afford it harms other people in a way that is ultimately morally unacceptable. While the demand for smartphones also generates jobs in previously industrially underdeveloped regions, these jobs are considerably worse than those we should really be creating in order to give people in historically disadvantaged areas a scope of action that we would consider a self-evident human right in our own lives.

Many of our everyday consumer wishes are irreconcilable with elevation to a basic law, because they require that one group of people exploit several other groups of people in order to achieve their consumer goals – to say nothing of the meanwhile much debated ecological problems that we exacerbate through our methods of consumption. One does not reduce plastic only by doing away with plastic bags in super-markets; one also finds it on a huge scale in things like children's toys. So the question is whether the existence of Lego and similar products is morally justified (the answer is fairly clear …).

On closer inspection, the production chains of our contemporary overconsumption are thus incompatible with the Categorical Imperative, because we want many things (we make them the maxim of our will, as Kant puts it) that we can only gain by causing massive harm to other people. This harm, admittedly, is concealed or explained away with varying ease. In this way, moral progress is prevented, because something we have actually known for a long time is banished from the domain of public opinion-forming.

I have heard it argued more than once that one could bring about progress in so-called developing countries through industrialization and, admittedly, initially unjust working conditions. But why should developing countries have to pass through all the morally reprehen-sible stages of modernization found in modern Europe before finally being granted morally acceptable living conditions? This is a specious argument that only seemingly balances out current moral ills with future improvements. One could follow a better path of modernization than the so-called West by avoiding the pathologies of industrialization (child labour, brutal exploitation, unlimited environmental destruction or factory farming). There is no reason why Nigeria, Mexico or India could not realize modernity better than the Europeans demonstrated over the last two hundred years.

It is therefore our duty as Europeans to lead by example and pursue a global economic policy that meets cosmopolitan standards. If Germany or the EU became climate-neutral, but achieved this only at the price of a morally reprehensible acceptance of injustices in the Global South, this would ultimately have achieved nothing. The global crises of the twenty-first century cannot be solved purely in terms of nation states; answers can be found only if we build up a sustainable global economy driven by universal values.

Back to Kant, who already anticipated this point over two hundred years ago: the **basic idea of the Formula of Universal Law** is that the way of life that we set up for ourselves, both individually and collectively, falls into the good part of the spectrum of moral values only if it is reconcilable with *all people* sharing in good. A good that by nature excludes any group of people from its realization is only a pseudo-good. Hence there can be no such thing as Chinese, Russian, Judeo-Christian or Islamic values, since it is inherent in the idea of such local, particular values that some group of people (such as Europeans, unbelievers, polytheists, Muslims, Americans) will be excluded from the realization of these value concepts.

The **basic idea of the Formula of the End in Itself** expresses the same thought slightly differently. Here Kant introduces the concept of 'humanity in your person'. A person is the visible role played by the human being in a society. The word *persona* originally referred to a Roman theatre mask from which someone's voice is heard.[22] Our person is our publicly visible role, our behaviour as it is visible and palpable to others. Every person, Kant argues, contains humanity – that is, the universal attribute shared by us all: being a human.

We realize our humanity in different ways. One specific way of being human is referred to by Kant as a maxim. A **maxim** is the value concept that guides people's actions and represents what a person wants to be, or feels that they should be, in their life or their respective situation. Maxims are only morally permissible if they can be reconciled with the fact that other humans also form maxims. Thus Kant developed at least one criterion of exclusion for morally impermissible actions that constituted the foundation of his ambitious conception of society.

'A?': Don't contradict yourself!

Behind the Categorical Imperative (and the book you are currently reading) lies a rather complicated logical argument that Kant worked on for decades. The result of this argument can certainly be presented in an accessible way without getting into the finer ramifications to which it leads, and which I would like to spare the reader at this point.

The first assumption is that we can think and argue about moral issues meaningfully and rationally in the first place. Moral questions are thus not simply arbitrary postulations, expressions of a whim to do one thing or another. In short: there are various things we should do and various things we should not do. When we are faced with a concrete choice of doing one thing or another and ask ourselves if we should really do it, this assumption means that we are fundamentally capable of answering this question, however difficult it may be in any individual case.

Imagine that you are facing a morally relevant decision, though not necessarily anything tragic. For example, one thinks about whether to board the ICE (Intercity Express) train despite having a ticket only for the IC (Intercity). In one sense, it would be fraud to do so; at the same time, the alternative would involve missing a connecting train thanks to the German rail service's usual hitches. Is it therefore permissible, in this case, to cheat the rail service out of a few euros? Let us call this the rail question:

Should I cheat German Rail out of a few euros?

To understand Kant's argument that one must not cheat German Rail under any circumstances (which does not mean that they are allowed to cheat us, the customers, and save money at our expense to increase their profits), we must carry out a further abstraction. For this, we will refer to an action whose moral value is to be assessed as A. So we ask ourselves, 'A?' If the question 'A?' has an answer, it is either 'A' or 'not-A'.

This corresponds to that highest logical precept which applies to every development of an idea in some aspect: **the law of non-contradiction**, whose message is 'Do not contradict yourself!' More formally put, the following applies: non-(A and non-A)! Less formally: it is impossible for me both to perform A and to refrain from it.

If 'A?' in the rail example is the following:

Should I cheat German Rail out of a few euros?

then the answer is completely clear: no. Now at the latest, however, some of you will feel that moral questions cannot be so clear-cut. After all, German Rail demands extortionate prices but does not keep its promise of punctual passenger transport, so it is surely quite justified to board the ICE with an IC ticket if that will at least allow us to reach our destination more or less on time. As we all know, the opposite of 'no' is 'yes'. So anyone who thinks it is reasonable to cheat German Rail out of a few euros under certain circumstances will answer the question

Should I cheat German Rail out of a few euros?

in the affirmative.

Here, of course, I must consider your objections, since many of you with a grudge against German Rail will think that one should not cheat the company out of a few euros for no reason but only under certain circumstances. So let us meet in the middle and pose a seemingly less focused question:

Is it morally permitted to cheat German Rail out of a few euros under certain circumstances?

This question cannot be answered unless one knows what the circumstances are under which one would consider fraud. Let us fill this gap and pose a seemingly answerable question:

> Is it morally permitted to cheat German Rail out of a few euros if there are constant delays and I would miss my connecting train otherwise?

In this case, on the other hand, it is clear that the answer is no. The circumstances cannot change what is morally permissible or not; they can only change the action in question. This follows from the premise that one should not cheat the rail service, which was the point of the first question. If it is impermissible to cheat the rail service, then delays cannot change this.

One can see this from an analogous case: if it is impermissible for me to hit children, then it remains impermissible if they come home late. The fact that German Rail often falls short of our expectations does not entitle us to act in a morally reprehensible way. Because one should not cheat the rail service, the circumstances do not change this. Fraud remains fraud.

But the question is whether boarding the ICE with an IC ticket is actually fraud at all. One should therefore formulate a quite different rail question:

> Is it morally permitted to board an ICE train and occupy a seat without possessing a ticket that is fully valid according to the rules of German Rail, if there are constant delays and I would otherwise miss my connecting train?

The answer to this question could be yes, as one could imagine this not actually as an act of fraud but, rather, as the only way to gain the product (a more or less punctual arrival) one has paid for from one's contractual partner.

The trick here is the reasoning that, while one should never cheat German Rail, not everything that seems like fraud at first glance is actually fraud. The rail service owes its customers something too; there is no one-sided obligation to do everything in one's power to follow the rules stipulated by German Rail if these rules prove too efficient to define the contractual relationship between service and customer in a morally adequate way.

With this argumentation, one can also remove the bone of contention often associated with Kant's famously rigorous ban on lying. In his short text 'On a supposed right to lie because of philanthropic concerns', Kant argues that one should never lie, not even if one urgently needs to help a friend. It is an unconditional rule, then, valid under all circumstances: you must not lie![23]

To counter this, the following intuitively convincing scenario is often cited: in a totalitarian dictatorship, one hides a persecuted family in the basement and lies to the illegitimate state's police when they knock at the door and ask if one has seen the family in question. In this case, we would all say that it is morally necessary to lie in order to protect the family. This is often used as a textbook example to refute Kant's overly strict moral doctrine.

Yet this objection is mistaken. For the answer to the question

Should I lie to the police officer?

is clearly no. If it universally applies that one should not lie to anyone, this also applies to police officers.

However, this does not settle the matter of whether one is actually lying to the police of an illegitimate state by choosing not to answer their questions in the manner they would like. For the question

Should I save the family in my basement from the illegitimate state?

has an equally unequivocal answer: yes!

This seems to create an **ethical dilemma**, a situation in which one is supposed to follow two irreconcilable, contradictory demands for action – which is possible. One cannot avoid lying to the police officer in order to save the family. It does no good to soften the question of whether I can lie to the police officer, for example by assuming that one can lie to certain police officers under certain circumstances; this would upset the entire moral system, since it would mean abandoning the principle that one should not lie. For every major moral premise – including precepts such as 'Thou shalt not kill!', 'Do not torture children!', etc. – one can easily invent an apparent moral dilemma that ultimately justifies anything. For any immoral action, after all, one could set up conditions that would serve a good end, such that the whole moral system could be destroyed by following the rule that the end justifies the means. That is why it is precisely not the case that the end justifies the means.

What actually constitutes a lie? A **lie** consists in someone knowingly and intentionally presenting something false as true (or vice versa) in order to gain an advantage over the person to whom one lies. The aim of the lie is to mislead a person for personal advantage. If one says something untrue to protect a family hiding in the basement from a cruel, illegitimate state, this is not a lie, since the aim is not to gain an advantage but to ensure the safety of a family.

One might counter that one at least gains a strategic advantage over the police officer in order to protect the family, which harms the police officer by preventing him from achieving his goal. But the policeman's goal is one that should not be realized (because it is evil). Preventing evil is itself something good, so the strategic advantage one gains by not speaking the truth (or speaking an untruth) is a moral advantage in this case.

Even under the strict conditions of the Categorical Imperative, then, one can say something untrue in order to prevent evil and do good. The conditions in question consist in the fact that one is not actually lying in this case, since one does not gain any advantage at the expense of another person whose demand of us deserves to be honoured.

One can use a simple thought experiment to prove that there ultimately cannot be any moral dilemmas. Imagine that one had a time machine and could do away with the newborn Wilhelm II, the last German emperor (so far). In addition, one would know that this would prevent the atrocities of the twentieth century if one replaced the little Wilhelm II with the little, peace-loving Robert Habeck,[24] shall we say, who would transform the German Empire into a blossoming, green, progressive oasis that would gain the following of all peoples in the global community, resulting in a worldwide peace movement, worldwide democracy without borders, and so on. If one puts it in these terms, many people would find it harder to let the little Wilhelm II live (if they were Reichsbürger or other supporters of Wilhelm II they would turn the scenario around, leading to the same result).

It follows from this that there are too many (namely, infinitely many) ethical dilemmas if one can find a single one, meaning that there are any number of exceptions to every moral principle. If there are any number of exceptions to an instruction (such as a prime directive), however, it no longer has any value, and then the entire system of reflection on moral issues collapses.

For this reason, we must assume that the moral order, the realm of ends, can be coherently thought: we cannot be expected both to carry out an action and refrain from it. If something is morally necessary, nothing else can have the same force of necessity.

Self-evident moral truths and the descriptive problem of ethics

The logical argument I have just outlined, which lurks behind the Categorical Imperative, admittedly has a whole string of further questions attached to it. One particular problem we must face in the present context is this: how do we ascertain what we should do in a concrete situation if almost everything depends on how precisely we describe the concrete situation? Is any untrue utterance already a lie? Does boarding an ICE with an IC ticket already constitute fraud? Is flirting at the workplace already sexual harassment? Is fear of the coronavirus hidden racism towards the Chinese (as the Slovenian philosopher Slavoj Žižek surmised in *Die Welt* at the start of the viral pandemic)?[25]

Most of what we consider urgent moral questions arise in concrete situations and therefore cannot be solved at the drawing board through mere reflection. To judge whether a moral idea is true or false, we must first of all be clear about which category of value a course of action falls into. In situations where we face difficult decisions, we therefore struggle for clarity because the circumstances are too complex to reach a simple judgement.

Hence the common criticism that the advocates of moral realism and universalism are morally presumptuous. How is one supposed to know what to do in every complex action situation? Who decides who is right?

As we have often been mistaken in moral matters in the past, and have even set up systems of radical evil for the mass destruction of human beings, it is today considered impolite, and hence morally questionable, if someone argues that there are clear answers and truths even in the case of complex moral questions. Some might consider this a kind of fundamentalism or virtuous terror, believing that we should keep ethics vague for the sake of coexistence, and suggest that there is an area of moral approximation (such as our European values, whatever those might be …) that it is better not to clarify and finalize.

It becomes clear how untenable this vague, yet widespread notion is when one describes morally unambiguous situations. Anyone who thinks that we should not reach clear judgements because there is no such thing as moral truth or falsehood is willing to doubt the truth of the following principle:

Torturing children is evil.

Let us refer to principles such as this as self-evident moral truths. **Self-evident moral truths** are propositions that describe moral facts and whose truth value is clear to (almost) anyone without extensive reflection.

There are many self-evident moral truths. Here is an arbitrary list:

- Pushing wheelchair users down the subway steps is evil.
- Spreading vegan butter on grain rolls is morally neutral.
- Deliberately serving a grain roll spread with goose fat to a vegan is evil.
- Volunteering to help integrate refugee families who have fled from war is good.
- Investing money to advance climate action is good.
- Destroying the planet today so that future generations will suffer is evil.
- Leafing through a picture book with one's legs crossed is morally neutral.
- Consensual homosexual intercourse is morally neutral.

And so on. Perhaps there are readers of these lines who will question some of the items on my list and judge them differently. The South African philosopher Thaddeus Metz has compiled an interesting list of self-evident moral truths found in African philosophical traditions, especially among followers of the ethical system of thought known as *Ubuntu*. According to this list, the following are morally impermissible:

(A) killing innocent people for money
(B) having sex with someone without their consent

(C) cheating other people, except for the purpose of defending oneself or another person

(D) stealing non-essential items (that is, taking them from their rightful owner)

(E) abusing people's trust, for example by breaking a promise to gain a minor personal advantage

(F) giving people unequal opportunities based on their race

(G) making political decisions in open disagreement rather than seeking a consensual solution

(H) making retribution a fundamental and central aim of criminal justice rather than encouraging reconciliation

(I) accumulating wealth based on competition rather than collaboration

(J) distributing wealth primarily according to individual rights, not needs.[26]

The mere fact that someone (such as myself) considers something morally self-evident does not actually make it so; one can be mistaken about moral questions. That is why no catalogue of widely accepted moral judgements based on surveys or an examination of cultural scholarship automatically indicates that these judgements are correct. Unfortunately, self-evident moral truths can be overwritten by errors about non-moral facts through propaganda, lies, manipulation, self-deception, wishful thinking and other phenomena in the minds of individuals or entire societies.

There are complex systems of deception that blind us in moral matters. A simple example is a society organized in an openly racist way, as in the USA in the 1950s or contemporary India with its caste system, politically supported by a Hindu nationalist government. In such a society, many people (but clearly not all!) consider it morally self-evident that a group of people identified on the basis of external physiognomic features should have a worse position in the system and be limited in their scope of action in favour of an oppressor group. As outlined above (see pp. 72ff.), we sometimes treat our children in a similar way in Germany by excluding them from many activities that are unjustly reserved for adults. This does not mean that there are no morally relevant differences between children and adults; it means only that the systems distinguishing children from adults sometimes lead to morally negative discrimination and restrict children's rights.

If we find ourselves in a morally complex action situation, for example as the manager of a medium-sized business that deals with companies in states that do not accept moral standards we would take for granted, we are often unable to see the wood for the trees: it is not so easy to judge from the outside how exactly the Chinese dictatorship interferes in people's everyday lives, so European businesspeople cannot immediately see how deeply they are implicated in Chinese human rights abuses. The complexity of action situations gives the impression that moral questions are not objective – that is, not answerable by the standards of truth. But this is only because the questions are not formulated precisely enough to lead to morally solvable problems.

Let us take a difficult, morally controversial case: the issue of abortion. Up to what stage of a pregnancy is it morally permissible to have an abortion? Many of us know someone who has been faced with the decision of whether to have an abortion (or have even been in that situation ourselves). Those affected, especially the pregnant woman herself, often (though not automatically) experience an emotional roller-coaster; they are torn between bringing a child (which one imagines, and towards which one has presumably already developed feelings) into the world and not doing so. The circumstances of the pregnancy may be so terrible that the pregnant person feels morally torn between protecting her own body and soul and that of an as yet unborn being.

Strong opponents of abortion usually argue that a fertilized egg cell is already a form of human life and one should not kill any form of human life, leading to the conclusion that abortion should be viewed as murder and is thus clearly morally reprehensible, indeed evil.

Certainly it is the case that, from a certain point in time, an abortion is in fact murder – unless it is a matter of saving the mother's life because she and the child would undoubtedly die otherwise. I will not presume to stipulate here from which week of pregnancy an abortion constitutes murder; for our purposes, it is sufficient that there is a particular span of time in which a foetus is so far developed that it must clearly be considered a human being whose life must not be terminated.

It seems very clear from the findings of modern molecular biology, however, that neither a fertilized egg cell nor the organized cluster of cells that results soon after the implantation of the fertilized egg cell are human beings; they are only potential human beings. Not every cell cluster already constitutes a human being. It is not inherently immoral to prevent cell clusters from developing into cell systems, otherwise it would already be immoral to remove moles. So the question is whether we owe a cell cluster that can turn into a human being, and is already on the way to becoming a human being, a more significant moral respect than we owe the moral interests of the mother, which must also be taken into account.

The answer is that there is certainly a time span (let us say the first weeks after conception) in which an implanted cell cluster is not yet a human being, which means that an abortion within this time span is not murder and accordingly does not fall into the category of evil. Since the interests of an adult mother may carry greater moral weight than the not yet existent interests of a potential human being that will develop from a cell cluster (if one permits it), there is a range of situations in which an abortion is morally unproblematic.

Over many decades of our modern period, which is still young at a little over two hundred years, the legislature has defined a socially acceptable, democratically legitimized range of cases in which an abortion is not murder. This is an example of moral progress going hand in hand with scientific-technological, in this case medical progress. It is my intention here not to question the decisions made but, rather, to point out that, according to today's medical knowledge, there is a time span within which an abortion is not murder, meaning that one should give the pregnant woman concerned every possible form of moral, psychological and medical support in going through their abortion – which is mostly the case in Germany.

Things were different among the ancient Greeks, who developed biological theories about the emergence of species and individual life forms without knowing that human animals develop through cell division, which is largely regulated by genetic codes that came into existence in their current form over millions of years of evolution. Hence it was thought for millennia that humans already inhabit the womb as little human beings from the moment of fertilization, after which they grow in whatever way. If this were true, the moral situation of an abortion would be far more complex, since one would then definitely be killing a (very small) human being at any point in time. That is not the case, however, so we can proceed from the biological facts revealed by natural science.

This has ended the moral taboo on abortions. This does not, of course, mean that they are generally undertaken light-heartedly and without inner conflict. After all, there is a millennia-old tradition of thought that views all potential human life as actual human life, as well as the complex psychological and emotional states and situations of the people involved.

Anyone who reaches a moral judgement in order to assess an action and be in a position to choose between courses of action must first know what an action actually consists of, which is tied to a problem that is not easily solved. This **hard descriptive problem of ethics** consists in the fact that we can only find out what we should do in a concrete situation if we find the right description of the circumstances to give us the necessary moral insight.

This takes us deep into the philosophical theory of action as well as moral psychology, which is especially confronted with a problem formulated by the British philosopher Elisabeth Anscombe.[27] This results from the fact that any action can be described from different perspectives, for, whenever one does something, one is doing several things. Someone baking a cake separates egg yolks from egg whites, stirs ingredients in a bowl, turns the oven on, speaks on the telephone, consults a cookbook, and so on. So what does a person *really* do when they bake? If we do not know what *exactly* someone does, we cannot assess it morally either.

The moral category into which someone's actions fall clearly depends on how we describe an action. The assessment follows from the description once it is sufficiently clear what is happening. The impression that there are ethical dilemmas, as well as the widespread view that there are actually no clear facts in moral matters, comes from the fact that it is difficult, sometimes even impossible, to establish what someone has actually done and what their intentions were.

That is why the Arabist Thomas Bauer and the historian Andreas Rödder are right to insist that eliminating ambiguity can potentially lead to violence if it induces people to judge prematurely.[28] It is often important to assess a situation carefully and without haste before reaching a complex moral judgement, which is one of the reasons why court cases in which the stakes are high for those involved often proceed unbearably slowly. It is famously wise to sleep on a decision for one or more nights, or even to postpone it substantially, as a hastily generated attempted solution can lead to a dangerous loss of ambiguity. However, one should certainly not conclude from the principle of leniency and slow decision-making that nothing is morally unambiguous.

Why the federal chancellor is not the leader[29]

Actions have consequences that no one can see in their entirety. Any action, no matter how good, can have unexpected, disastrous results.

Let us take a recent example: the refugee policies associated with the name of Angela Merkel, especially in 2015, seem to have led indirectly to a surge in far-right extremism, a spread of xenophobia, and all manner of structural difficulties resulting from the need to integrate a large number of refugees in Germany, something that displeases many people for a variety of reasons. In so far as it was Merkel's intention to improve the sometimes terrible situations of people who had had to flee from their countries for the sake of their own and their families' safety, and to use Germany's prosperity and structural strengths for this purpose, her respective decisions and actions were clearly on the side of good.

Indirectly, however, her decisions and actions in this context have led to an increase in some people's cruelty and willingness to use violence, with personal threats to Merkel on social media and at demonstrations. Yet it would be absurd to argue from this (as the AfD politician Georg Pazderski did in various tweets relating to the Hanau attack) that Merkel's actions produced the right-wing terror of our time, and thus claim that her decision to help millions of people through intake and integration was morally reprehensible. What is morally reprehensible, indeed evil, is far-right terror, not the application of asylum law to help needy people.

One can describe the so-called refugee crisis and the chancellor's administrative actions from many perspectives, including geopolitical strategies for the Balkan route, negotiation processes with other EU states or party-political considerations, but naturally also the personal qualities and convictions of Angela Merkel as an individual. An overall analysis of the processes referred to as the 'refugee crisis' is impossible, as many factors inevitably remain hidden – and rightly so, since there is a right to privacy and state secrets, among other things. Our chancellor does not need to take part in a show trial to prove her good character. She deserves acknowledgement for her decisions, which are often very objective and balanced and have shown her to be a successful crisis manager in these days of the viral pandemic. This makes her neither a saint nor a heroine, simply a good chancellor (however much one might differ on specific issues with her moral or political assessments of situations). Merkel is not our leader but, rather, an individual who has attained the position of federal chancellor through a complex selection process (including her legitimate tactical manoeuvres to gain power as a professional politician) and, fortunately, has been notable not only for her awareness of power but often also for her intelligence and objectivity.

Even in a democratic law-based state, the goal cannot be to lay out explicitly all the preconditions for actions and decisions; this is fundamentally impossible. For neither Merkel's closest confidants nor she herself know all her intentions so well that we can really know the exact intentions behind her many major and minor decisions. No one knows themselves completely, not even the chancellor; and she, in turn, cannot remotely know about everything that happens in Germany, as this too is unknowable. We all act under conditions of uncertainty – for which we cannot be blamed, since we are always in a state of partial uncertainty.

Kant by no means ignored this; in fact, he argued that we cannot even be sure in our own case whether our motives cause us to have noble intentions when we do something that we – or others – may even consider a model of goodness. He writes:

> The real morality of actions (their merit and guilt), even that of our own conduct, therefore remains entirely hidden from us. Our imputations can be referred only to the empirical character. How much of it is to be ascribed to mere nature and innocent defects of temperament or to its happy constitution (*merita fortunae*) this no one can discover, and hence no one can judge it with complete justice.[30]

Kant himself presents an unnecessarily radical thesis here, for he argues that the morality of our actions remains 'entirely hidden' from us. This is because he considers our self-determination, our pure will, which is independent of all immoral motives, to be the exclusive carrier of morality. For Kant, everything depends on the motives behind someone's actions, and there is only one motive that truly corresponds to what we should do: that one does what one does solely because one should, without any other intention.

But how can one ascertain in any given situation why one reaches a particular decision? And how does one establish it after the fact? Kant does not help us here. In complex concrete action situations one always acts under conditions of uncertainty, which is part of the great responsibility borne by such figures as heads of state or government. One decisive difference between the chancellor and the self-proclaimed *Führer* [leader] is that, unlike him, she makes no claims to moral omniscience but, rather, acts as a citizen of the state system whose government she leads on the basis of certain democratic rules. We do not have a leader or a party that is always right – which is a good thing, since it is more in keeping with the facts.

The day of judgement, or, how we can recognize moral facts

We can recognize many moral facts quite well. There are even self-evident moral truths that people from all cultures can easily put in the right value category. Most of the time we are well aware of what is being morally demanded of us.

Unfortunately, however, this does not mean that we can simply approach ethics using common sense, for in many cases it is difficult to state and establish exactly what someone is actually doing or has actually done. And if one does not know what someone is actually doing, it is even harder to reach a moral judgement about what they are doing.

This leads to the impression that, in situations where we need to look responsibly for the morally right choice, we can never be completely sure of what to do. But that would be disastrous, for it would mean that our capacity for moral reflection abandons us when we need it.

To achieve greater clarity and escape from this impasse, one can start by distinguishing the ontology from the epistemology of values. The **ontology of values** deals with the question of how moral facts are constituted, what it means that they exist at all; it is concerned with the mode of being of values. The **epistemology of values**, by contrast, examines how we can recognize moral facts in complex action situations with reference to universal values.

In the first chapter I argued that values have a universalist and realistic ontology: they apply everywhere (at least for humans) and are partially independent of our value concepts, meaning that there are true and false moral opinions (about what someone should do in a concrete situation).

Even if you yourself are not yet convinced, you will surely admit that there are some things we should do for moral reasons and other things we should refrain from doing for moral reasons. According to universalism and realism, what we should or should not do is not simply the result of what someone thinks, even if it is an overwhelming democratic majority; majorities can commit moral errors just like minorities. Neither the democratic majority nor the democratic minority is morally privileged.

But this combination of theses – universalism and realism in the ontology of values – does not seem to solve the problem of how we can *recognize* moral facts. An additional component must therefore be introduced. Here a further sense of the philosophical term 'realism' comes into play, for realism means at least two things, as the British philosopher Crispin Wright points out at the very start of his important book *Truth and Objectivity*.[31]

Firstly, what makes one a realist with regard to a particular area of reflection is the belief that opinions about objects in that area are not true simply because one holds them. The objects are partially independent of our opinions, and they determine whether we are right in our opinions. Let us call this **ontic realism**. Moral facts are ontically objective; they do not come into existence because we as humans do something, such as producing systems of value concepts or employing our reason to reach a consensus that is acceptable to all parties. Moral facts genuinely exist, and they are effective factors in the lives of free spiritual beings.

Secondly, realism often entails the view that we can recognize those facts which exist partially independently of our opinion, and hence have good reason to believe that we have grasped some of these partially independent facts as they really are. Let us call this **epistemic realism**.

Now I would like to offer you an argument for an epistemic value realism, which means that we can (and often do) accurately grasp the universal, partially independently existing moral facts as they really are. However dark the times, complete moral darkness cannot reign as long as there are people who need to coordinate their actions in order to live together.

My argument rests on a thought experiment that I call the **Day of Judgement**. Imagine you wake up one day to find that you (as in the philosophically well-informed NBC series *The Good Place*) have died and are sitting in front of a door. The door opens, and (here I deviate from *The Good Place*) God is sitting opposite you. Somewhat baffled, having been an atheist all your life, you watch as God leafs through a thick, fiery book until he finds your name and utters a terrible judgement of damnation. What makes this judgement so surprising is that God condemns you for all sorts of things that more or less everyone you knew on earth considered morally commendable and noble. For example, you are accused of directing an inclusive kindergarten, caring selflessly for lepers, being a good father to your children, fighting climate change, rescuing koalas from the Australian bush fires, and so on. God praises you, on the other hand, for blasphemous newspaper articles, a fistfight you had in your youth, your small and big lies, and so forth. In short: God's damning judgement is absolutely incomprehensible, as it follows a logic that humans would expect only from the devil or a dangerous lunatic.

In this situation, one would be justified in asking God why exactly he is basing his judgement on criteria that contradict everything that was considered clearly good on Earth based on reading the scriptures, examining one's conscience as well as common opinion. How could it be that our actions are judged by moral standards that we simply cannot recognize? But that is exactly what would be the case if God's moral judgements deviated completely from those that we poor mortals could reach. If God's judgement were entirely incomprehensible to us, he could just as easily classify actions we consider morally irrelevant (such as stirring one's coffee counter-clockwise) as great transgressions on the Day of Judgement and present things we consider morally significant as morally meaningless.

This thought experiment is intended to show that moral facts are largely obvious; we can basically recognize, albeit often with some difficulty, what we should do – which does not mean we are never mistaken.

An almighty god who judged us by his own moral standards, standards that were completely unknown and unknowable to us, and took the corresponding punitive steps after our death, would be a terrible demon. That is why all world religions are revealed religions, which assume that

God (or the gods) sends us messages and prophets – however muddled these may seem – to tell us what we should do. God cannot lead us completely up the garden path in moral matters, since he would then not be a god but simply another demon. This is one of the thoughts that support the idea of God's goodness.

This does not mean, of course, that God exists and is all-bountiful. The thought experiment of the Day of Judgement is merely intended to show that it is nonsense to believe there are moral facts we simply cannot recognize. In addition, it demonstrates the absurdity of the assumption that the validity of moral judgements comes from a divine source.

This has no bearing on whether God exists or how exactly God, the gods and the divine relate to the universal order of values. We can, however, rule out the possibility that God, the gods and the divine twist the truth and the human knowledge of values. So there is no general conflict between ethics and religion; if there were, it would be to the disadvantage of religion, as we would have to reject it as an error for moral reasons. Our ethically guided thinking, our moral understanding, stands above religious traditions because we can assess these using ethical standards. In our democratic law-based state, this applies to all religions, which is why Christianity can no longer take the liberties it did only a few centuries ago. Fortunately, witch-burnings and exorcism are no longer a daily affair; they are morally reprehensible but were long part of religious tradition.

The moral universe of what we should and should not do must be partially transparent to us. It is impossible, then, for us to find ourselves in a situation in which we have no idea what would be the moral thing to do; we can simply never know *everything*. Fallibility does not mean complete ignorance of the facts, which would be disastrous for ethics. Fallibility means that we can be mistaken about complex moral issues. The ethical consequence of this is that we must be lenient towards ourselves and other people and not condemn their decisions too hastily. But this ethically necessary leniency does not mean that there are no objective moral facts; rather, it proves the exact opposite: because there are moral facts that hold the utmost importance in complex action situations, we should approach other people's judgements and way of life leniently and carefully.

With or without God in the kingdom of ends

Here at the latest, many of you will probably be wondering who 'defines' universal values if it is not God. But this question is based on false assumptions; asking who 'defines' or 'determines' universal values is like asking who 'defines' or 'determines' the fact that the Earth has a moon.

If there were no free spiritual beings, there would be no ethics. If there were no life at all in the universe, values would be insignificant. This does not mean that there are no values, since we are precisely not living in a universe without free spiritual beings. Because value concepts and values deal largely with us as humans as well as other living beings, values always relate also to us; this distinguishes them from natural constants. This does not mean, however, that values are not facts; it follows only that they are not mere facts of nature that can be uncovered with the methods of natural science.

Facts are not usually 'defined' or 'determined'; they are the standard by which the truth or untruth of our attitudes is measured. One can dispute facts (and be mistaken), but this does not make them disappear. If moral facts exist at all, if it is ever certain what we should do or refrain from doing at all costs, there is no one who 'defines' this fact, not even God.

Time and again in the history of humanity, however, new types of action have appeared that had not been considered morally in depth until then. One important example in our time is the development of social networks and the use of artificial intelligence in the context of digitalization. So far, there is no elaborated ethics of artificial intelligence. This does not mean we have to invent a new catalogue of values; rather, it signifies that we must recognize which new types of action fall into which moral categories.[32]

Let us adopt Kant's terminology again and refer to the moral universe, the field of moral facts, as the **kingdom of ends**.[33] The kingdom of ends can never be fully hidden from us. It essentially consists in the fact that our actions occur deliberately, because we resolve to reshape reality by determining the ends we wish to achieve. If I go out to buy strawberries, I follow a complex plan: I take my bicycle key, start pedalling, pay attention to the traffic rules, park my bicycle, find the strawberries, take them to the checkout and pay for them. This plan does not feel as complex it is because we have rehearsed such operations. It would not be feasible without determining an end that guides our actions and thus structures reality.

Whether or not God appears as the highest authority in the kingdom of ends is of no consequence for the structure of moral facts. For, if we should or should not do something, this cannot ultimately be because a god has imposed sanctions. That one should not torture children is not simply a decree from God to which one should adhere for fear of divine punishment – for tactical reasons – but, rather, a moral fact that applies with or without God. If someone abandons a religion and becomes an atheist, they do not change all their moral convictions as a result; rather, they can hold on to the fact that most of their moral judgements will survive this renunciation.

In a sense, the absence of God makes it even more unlikely that one will fail to recognize the kingdom of ends; for how, in a godless universe, could there be moral demands that are completely shut off from our understanding? This would be comparable to the existence of a layer of moral elementary particles, still undiscovered, that would explain why one should do some things and refrain from others, but which we can never see.

The influential American legal philosopher Ronald Dworkin made fun of this scenario, pointing out that there are surely no such things as 'morons', moral elementary particles that a future physics would one day be able to measure.[34] It would be equally absurd if there were a kingdom of ends that could be explored neither through natural science nor the humanities and which contained moral facts that concern us, yet which we could never know.

For all these reasons, moral facts can only be partially independent of us, as they must be fundamentally and largely knowable. Morality must be accessible to mortals, whether it is also justified by a god or not. Atheists and polytheists essentially recognize the same moral facts as theists.

This observation can be philosophically underpinned by means of a much discussed idea that comes from no less a thinker than Plato, the founder of systematic philosophical ethics. In his short but substantial early dialogue *Euthyphro*, Plato stages an encounter between his protagonist Socrates and Euthyphro, a pious fellow Athenian, in front of a court building in Athens. Socrates is already on trial at the time of the conversation, having been accused by a certain Meletus. As we know, Socrates is later sentenced to death for supposed theological deficits (he is alleged to have introduced new gods and corrupted the youth).

Typically, Socrates soon draws Euthyphro into a philosophical conversation whose goal is to clarify the relationship between piety and justice. Thus, in the context of classical polytheism, the two of them discuss the still unresolved question of where religious faith stands in relation to moral values. It is in this context that the so-called Euthyphro dilemma, a theorem repeatedly cited in contemporary metaethics, is introduced. The **Euthyphro dilemma** distinguishes between two seemingly diametrically opposed views on the relationship between God and moral value. The epitome of positive, moral values in Plato's language is justice (*dikaiosynē*) or, as he calls it in a more general sense, good (*to agathon*).

The two competing views in the Euthyphro dilemma are the following:

God considers certain actions good because he has knowledge of good. (Realism)

Certain actions are good because God determines it. (Anti-realism)

Which option one chooses has implications for one's view of justice and piety. The realist believes that faith in God (piety) at best contributes indirectly to moral understanding. God's superior capacity for knowledge at least guarantees that he will not make any moral mistakes; thus every moral fact that we recognize is automatically a moral fact that God recognizes, which is why we sometimes move closer to God in the practice of moral judgements. This was Plato's own view, which saw the meaning of life in trying to come as close as possible to God in order to become like him.

The anti-realist, on the other hand, holds the opposite view: they consider piety the only way to justify morality at all. Hence an action is only good because God determines the standards of moral goodness, which makes it decisive to find out what God has determined. The will of God is far more important than the details of an action, since God determines by decree (or whatever other method) what is considered good and bad. In contemporary ethics, God has simply been replaced by human reason or our subjective evaluations, but the argumentation is roughly the same, which the philosopher Ernst Tugendhat has shown convincingly and accessibly in his lectures on ethics.[35] Tugendhat is absolutely right when he points out that the things we consider correct in moral contemplation after weighing up different arguments cannot be justified with recourse to some higher authority (be it evolution, God or reason).

> Why should one justify something one already considers correct with recourse to something else, instead of simply understanding the supports on which this plausibility rests? Because of our background in traditionalist moral systems [which justify morality with traditions; M. G.] and because, as children, we grow up in an at least partly authoritarian understanding of morals, we tend to expect a simple justification from somewhere else (such as reason, etc.), which is analogous to relying on an authority for support.[36]

Plato already countered the anti-realist argument by saying that it implicitly or even explicitly paints God as a kind of villain. For if God determines good and evil through his mere will, and we cannot gain insight into good and evil independently of God's decisions, we are ultimately doomed to submit to God's will for no reason. From this perspective, anti-realism boils down to the blind adoration of an overpowering being that must be obeyed, whatever it commands. In this way, God is understood as a form of irrefutable heavenly dictator, a metaphysical tyrant.

Therefore, moral realism is more compatible with the assumption that God – should he exist – is not simply an almighty and hence dangerous being but also completely good. God cannot commit moral errors; whatever he does must flow from his knowledge of good, otherwise we would be justified in reproaching him. If, on the other hand, God determined standards for moral good for no reason, he could be reproached for this, since it would raise the question of why he communicates his standards in such a complicated way – for example, by appearing on a mountain in the desert at some point in human history in the form of a burning bush or by proclaiming the Ten Commandments.

As it is often argued in discussions that the Ten Commandments are a sensible catalogue for moral orientation, let us list them here as a reminder. According to the homepage of the German Protestant Church, they constitute the 'foundation of Christian ethics' in the following form and order:

(1) I am the Lord your God, who brought you out of Egypt, out of the land of slavery. You shall have no other gods beside me.
(2) You shall not misuse the name of the Lord your God.
(3) Honour the Sabbath day.
(4) Honour your father and mother.
(5) You shall not kill.
(6) You shall not commit adultery.
(7) You shall not steal.
(8) You shall not give false testimony against your neighbour.
(9) You shall not covet your neighbour's house.
(10) You shall not covet your neighbour's wife, or his manservant or maidservant, his ox or donkey, or anything that belongs to your neighbour.[37]

The Ten Commandments are certainly not a suitable foundation for any ethics (not even Christian ethics, which cannot exist anyway, since an ethics that is Christian would thus lose its universal validity). We would be right to find it morally offensive, for example, that a man's 'wife, manservant or maidservant' is treated as property; in this formulation, the tenth commandment goes against our modern view of gender equality. If we followed it, this would be moral regression. Moreover, few people seem to have noticed that servitude (the form of slavery referred to here) as such is already morally reprehensible, which would in turn make it morally recommended to liberate the manservant and maidservant from the bondage into which they were forced by the neighbour mentioned in the commandment. Indeed, we know that biblical texts raise no objections to slavery, which is a problem with many of the moral standards that are sometimes implicitly and sometimes explicitly applied in the diverse, extremely heterogeneous texts of the Bible.

In addition, Jesus announces a ranking of commandments in the New Testament and places two of them above the rest – though the second is not even in the Decalogue, the original list.

'The most important one', answered Jesus, 'is this: "Hear, O Israel, the Lord our God, the Lord is one. Love the Lord your God with all your heart and with all your soul and with all your mind and with all your strength" [Deuteronomy 6:4–5]. The second is this: "Love your neighbour as yourself" [Leviticus 19:18]. There is no commandment greater than these.'

My concern here is not to enter into a discussion on details of the holy scriptures and their interpretation, on the relationship between Judaism and Christianity (let alone Islam) or between the Old and the New Testament. The point of recalling the holy scriptures of the mono-theistic world religions is that God is sometimes presented as issuing rather unjustified and unexplained laws that, in addition to this, are irreconcilable with our contemporary value concepts, as well as (hopefully) those of the Protestant Church in Germany.

Love of God and love of one's neighbour are more plausible attitudes than following the Ten Commandments in their original form, though presumably the actual exhortations made by Jesus Christ in the New Testament are studiously ignored by the vast majority of observant Christians in favour of a few universally acceptable pieces of advice. In the Gospel of Luke, Jesus advises his followers to leave their families and devote themselves entirely to serving the kingdom of heaven:

'I tell you the truth', Jesus said to them, 'no one who has left home or wife or brothers or parents of children for the sake of the kingdom of God will fail to receive many times as much in this age and, in the age to come, eternal life.' (Luke 18:29–30)

As a whole, the New Testament reads like the proclamation of an apoca-lyptic religion: since the return of Jesus following his death by crucifixion and the Day of Judgement are near, there is little point in making earthly commitments (which might include moral obligations towards one's own family but also projects for the moral improvement of the legal system). And, indeed: if one really expects the Messiah to return soon, or believes that the entire history of humanity will culminate in an endgame staged by God that we are currently witnessing, moral claims change entirely. Whoever takes God's omnipotence to mean that he determines moral values at will, and can maybe even change them, accepts a very different form of morality compared to someone who supports our current political community, built on the constitution and the idea of human dignity.

This certainly does not mean that Judaism, Christianity or Islam are not in harmony with the constitution (or perhaps even in conflict with it) in all their institutional and existential forms. Over the millennia, the world religions have largely adapted to the real historical conditions of state formation and the organization of worldly power – though we should not forget that the Roman Catholic Church is governed from the Vatican, which is far from a modern, democratic law-based state; rather, it is an absolute monarchy in which, according to Article 1 of the Fundamental Law of Vatican City State, there is no separation of powers, for 'the Supreme Pontiff, Sovereign of Vatican City State, has the fullness of legislative, executive and judicial powers.'[38]

In their traditional forms, the world religions are all considerably older than the modern idea that moral progress could, should and even must be advanced in the form of a suitable state-based structure of institutions. One cannot do without this idea if one is to uphold the Enlightenment idea. Without the Enlightenment idea, there would be no modern democratic law-based state, whose complex differentiation into subsystems (first and foremost the separation of powers) ensures that there is no central power base from which someone can restrict and control all other people. For us, no one and nothing is *legibus absolutus*, independent of the law. The federal chancellor, the president of Germany, the ministers and the members of parliament do enjoy a limited form of immunity, but the mutual checks and balances of courts, legislature, legal scholars, civil society, and so forth mean that, at present, no one in Germany can seize absolute power. For that, one would have to turn the whole republic on its head – which is possible in principle but would face considerable strategic obstacles and would require coordination on a currently unimaginable scale.

The decisive factor is that realism, the idea that God – if he exists – prefers and rewards good simply because it is good, is reconcilable with all rationally justifiable forms of monotheism. Realism, however, is not dependent on theism. The moral facts exist in the kingdom of ends, whether it has a form of leader (God) or not. The existence of universal values neither implies God nor is it irreconcilable with him.

WHY THERE ARE MORAL FACTS BUT NOT ETHICAL DILEMMAS

Therefore, God does not play a relevant part in the grounding of morality. If he did (as the anti-realist imagines), this would contradict the notion of a good God. God as a moral tyrant to whom we must submit would doubtless be a frightful affair, and it would be of urgent tactical importance to do whatever such an almighty king of heaven demanded of us. The existence of this king of heaven would, however, call everything into question that one believes if one values the continuation of the democratic law-based state and the Enlightenment from which it emerged.

In short: if we want to stand up for moral convictions rationally, with good and universally valid reasons that can essentially be expressed in a way everyone can understand, we must base our conception of God on that of morality, not vice versa. This is theologically unproblematic to the extent that God is goodness itself, and hence it coincides with the most convincingly justified value concepts. (Though God is infallible in moral questions, one of the respects in which he differs from us mortals.) This is reconcilable with many interpretations of the holy texts of Judaism, Christianity and Islam, which are accordingly reconcilable with the democratic law-based state.

This undoubtedly also applies to atheism, however, which is no less morally acceptable than the world religions as long as it does not automatically oppose an acknowledgement of moral facts, the kingdom of ends. For some atheists believe that there is no kingdom of ends but, at best, altruistic behaviour with evolutionary causes. Yet this is no basis for universal values, only a non-binding recommendation to follow the wishes of the supposedly mostly 'selfish genes'.[39] The theory of evolution would then be irreconcilable with universal values, as it would have to take over the role of grounding morality. Fortunately, however, this is not necessary, since universal values have no need of support via the back door.

Beating children was never good, not even in 1880

Moral facts directly concern us humans and indirectly concern other living beings, as well as inanimate nature. Ethics deals with the question of what *we* should do; it is about *us* and our relationships with one another. Here, humans are spiritual beings. **Spirit** is the circumstance that we carry out much of what we do with a sense of who we are and who we want to be.[40] We all have a varyingly detailed image of humanity, as well as opinions about how people act towards other living beings and what the whole business of the universe – in which we include ourselves – actually means.

Moral facts display a spirit-dependent form of objectivity: because they are knowable by their nature, they address us humans directly as free spiritual beings. Thanks to our spirit we can recognize morally effective facts, which always also revolve around us.

We humans can see that factory farming is morally reprehensible, that a vegetarian way of life may be morally necessary in the face of the animals' suffering, that we have moral obligations towards other living beings, and much more. No other animal known to us has the slightest idea of complex moral situations – which does not give us a licence to mistreat animals whose capacity for moral cognition is below that of enlightened adult humans. On the contrary, animal and environmental ethics is a part of moral understanding. This does not, however, mean that other animals must themselves be equipped with moral understanding in order to deserve our protection.

A significant factor here is that we humans go with the times and accordingly develop, which creates new scopes of action. The problems of the twenty-first century resulting from such phenomena as globalization, digitalization and climate change did not exist when the first systems of philosophical ethics were conceived a few thousand years ago.

However, moral facts are not quite as historically variable as some might think. For they concern us, as spiritual beings, and are thus spirit-dependent, but they nonetheless exist objectively. That has a far-reaching consequence that plays a crucial part in moral realism and universalism. This consequence can be referred to as **modal robustness**:[41] if, in situation S, action A is morally necessary (or permissible, forbidden, etc.), A would have been equally necessary (or permissible, forbidden, etc.) in past cases of situation S.

This means that, even in the distant past, when early humans lived in cave-dwelling communities, sexual harassment was wrong. Similarly, it was already morally impermissible in 1880 to beat one's children for educational purposes. It may be that many in 1880 found it harder to understand that children are people just like them, and that it is therefore an act of senseless violence to beat them so that they will become obedient adults; but this does not mean that those who physically punished their children in 1880 were not committing a moral error. The error in the past was, among other things, that the non-moral, psycho-social facts of corporal punishment were often hidden, so that the moral judgement of the actors was limited because they proceeded from false convictions, some of them coming from religious tradition – though many parents who physically punished their children surely had guilty consciences that could only partly be suppressed through recourse to an unquestioned tradition.

Some moral errors are committed because the actors do not recognize the non-moral facts. For the longest period of their existence, humans had no idea how reproduction works at the molecular level and accordingly entertained all manner of (sometimes absurd) ideas about how humans produce other humans. These misconceptions had moral consequences, since they could lead to the opinion that a miscarriage had moral causes, for example, and the mother should be held morally accountable.

The same applies to illnesses. Many people today (though probably not the majority) treat purely somatic illnesses as the result of objectively identifiable causal factors that have little to do with the intellectual world of the afflicted. A brain tumour is caused by environmental toxins, not by the sufferer having too many sexual dreams about his neighbour. Unfortunately, it still occurs everywhere, even in rich modern industrial nations, that purely somatic illnesses are classified as moral deficits and sometimes severely penalized. Contemporary Hinduism, for example (unlike some of its precursors), is a somewhat anti-physical and anti-sexual religion as a result of colonization by the British and others, which leads some devout Hindus to beat their female offspring (who are considered metaphysically inferior anyway) when they experience their first menstruation. In many cultures that were born in pre-modern times but still exist today, menstruation is considered impure and a sign of moral deficits.

Of course, this is nonsense according to modern medical knowledge – though this is also true of globules and other homeopathic remedies to which some in our Western, enlightened society resort because they believe in the natural forces of self-healing that these supposedly encourage. What they overlook is that both the pharmaceutical industry and the conventional medicine on which it rests are, for better or worse (and there are undoubtedly dangerous and deplorable abuses in both), just as natural as enjoying a (potentially genetically modified) apple or bathing in a (supposedly) natural spring.

Moral facts are not natural facts. Nor are they unnatural or against nature; rather, they are the facts that classify courses of action according to the standards of good, neutral and evil. This classification is not in the eye of the beholder or a matter of taste but is objective in every relevant way.

THREE

Social Identity: Why Racism, Xenophobia and Misogyny Are Evil

Humans always belong to a variety of groups. For example, we are family members, employees, citizens, refugees, lobbyists, wine-drinkers, neighbours or strollers. The list of our group memberships is fairly long, and none of us has a full view of all our social connections. As the entire web of individual socioeconomic processes that sort people into groups, and which humans also consciously shape, society is too complex for anyone to see it in its totality. Some subsystems do control other subsystems (for example, politics controls the economy and vice versa), but no one controls everything because no one can even know how that would be possible.

We react to this intangible complexity as individuals. One reaction, which we will discuss in this chapter, is to develop simplified images of our social situation. These images are mostly false but have one or two details that correspond to the facts. This gives rise to social identities that, in the context of today's pervasive identity politics, are reinforced by social media.

In the following, I will argue that the social and cultural identities that are so important to many do not actually exist. They are distorted ideas of our own actions, a form of self-delusion connected to systems of delusion resulting from the fact that our modern life is pervaded by advertising, propaganda and ideology.

Because false, distorted self-images obscure the moral facts, the veil of thinking in identities must be lifted. The universalism of the new enlightenment therefore argues for the necessity of overcoming identity politics – without denying that we do indirectly owe elements of moral progress to it. People have always resisted the discrimination they face, which often involves violence and systematic oppression. But what we should conclude from these struggles and demands is that it is not ultimately a matter of preserving identities but, rather, of overcoming identities in so far as they dehumanize people.

Sorting humans into identity groups has no real explanatory value but only prevents those who stand up for local identities from seeing that they are indebted to universal values. Anyone who supports the struggle of a supposedly or genuinely oppressed minority against an imagined or real majority overlooks the fact that this perpetuates the same error which led to the oppression of the minority. No one who fights against unjust oppression should have the goal of unjustly oppressing the oppressors.

Habitus and stereotypes: all resources are scarce

Situations of crisis such as the COVID-19 pandemic bring home to us in dramatic fashion that all resources are limited. There is not an infinite supply of protective masks, caregivers, intensive-care beds or ventilators. But neither are there inexhaustible sources of energy (as we have known for a long time), endless smartphones, unlimited seats on the Intercity Express, in the restaurant, etc. So resources are scarce, which, in combination with dynamic population growth, leads to mounting crises.

The more valuable resources are, the more fiercely they will be fought over. Naturally, the exact economic value of material resources is not known to everyone; one aspect of their scarcity is that not everyone knows how to obtain them. Otherwise, the rush for the most valuable resources would be far too great and the distribution system would collapse.

Not all resources are materially or financially measurable in the same way as gold, smartphones or sources of energy. These material or financial resources can, as the French sociologist Pierre Bourdieu has shown, be distinguished from **symbolic resources**, which include a good reputation and academic standing, but also physical beauty, hereditary aspects of our intelligence, good upbringing and education, style of dress and the like – even good taste in art.

Symbolic resources correlate with material resources. Some can only be acquired if one has already reached a certain financial level (such as oenological expertise – excellent wines are expensive). Other symbolic resources are the basis for gaining material ones; this would include a good education or physical beauty (which implicitly or explicitly belong to the criteria for certain professions).

With our daily behaviour, each of us embodies a complex network of symbolic resources that are randomly or consciously acquired to different degrees. I would like to refer to this network with Bourdieu's term **habitus**.

Material and non-material resources are interwoven in complex ways. One can see how people with a certain habitus often have certain jobs, which is because (a) employers choose a particular type of employee and (b) the role one plays in a profession influences one's habitus. For our habitus changes constantly in the course of our life; we have a sort of habitus depot containing our symbolic resources, which develop according to a complex internal logic. To examine this internal logic, humanities scholars and social scientists develop methods that naturally make their own contribution to habitus and can lead to advantages. After all, an economist simply knows more about the stock market than a random layperson who is persuaded by their local bank to buy a dubious stock portfolio and knows how to implement this knowledge in society. A literary scholar has a better understanding of literature on account of their education, which might also lead to a better, or at least more informed, judgement of taste.

In general, one can view **politics** as a system that inevitably controls the distribution of resources in inadequate and unjust ways. The specifics of this control vary depending on the economic system and arrangement of subsystems and authorities in a society. Politicians therefore rely on a team of resource specialists with data that can be used to measure the existing distribution of resources and control the internal logic of their future distribution with varying predictability according to political guidelines.

So-called **identity politics** consists in establishing a connection between certain social patterns known as 'identities' and the distribution of material and symbolic resources in order to formulate political guidelines. The crisis in current identity politics, however, lies in the fact that a supposed identity that is invoked, unlike a habitus, does not really exist. A habitus can be sociologically examined, but an identity cannot. Behind the nebulous concept of identity politics lies a propagation of stereotypes that are fundamentally unsuitable to be true carriers of measurable distribution struggles and negotiations.

A **stereotype** is a description of action that distorts reality and is used to explain a person's actions with reference to their group membership.

Stereotypes influence our attitudes, and thus our actions, towards the persons who are perceived through the filter of the stereotype. There are no typical Germans, typical Bavarians, typical Berliners, typical Arabs, Catholics, transsexuals, men, women, West and East Germans, or whites and blacks whose strengths and weaknesses can be weighed up against one another. This is one of the main results of the developments in philosophy as well as the other humanities and social sciences, which only became academic disciplines in the modern age – that is, roughly from the mid-eighteenth century.[1]

People have gradually realized that our notions of what is normal and typical are impermissible simplifications of the social reality. We all know the phenomenon that we classify people as soon as we meet them for the first time (which happens every day in the street). This helps us make quite banal predictions about the likely course of everyday scenes. The old lady in the supermarket whom one lets past because she has only bought a few bananas, the impetuous cyclist who is clearly not following the traffic rules, the Italian pizzeria with a typical menu adapted to German tastes – our daily routine is full of standardized expectations that simplify our lives. They allow us to make varyingly accurate predictions about what will happen next, which only works because we all accept a system of stereotypes and go along with it to a certain extent. We therefore trust taxi or bus drivers, for example, because we assume that they will fulfil their role of bringing us to our destination as quickly and safely as possible as responsibly as we expect.

The organization of our everyday life hangs by a thread of typical scenes that are instilled in us through familiarization and upbringing. As adults, there comes a point when we can barely imagine how some processes could be different, which results in the notion that our daily lifeworld is like a piece of nature that proceeds according to immutable laws. If these processes are disturbed or, as in the coronavirus crisis, even completely overturned, this causes insecurity. This insecurity palpably teaches us all something about the structure of our daily lifeworld as described by the founder of the philosophical school of phenomenology, the philosopher and mathematician Edmund Husserl. This structure is contingent – it is an expression of historically grown, at times completely irrational expectations that we nonetheless take for granted, depending on our character.[2]

The irrational expectations of everyday life include social identities: one thinks of oneself as a Bavarian or northern Italian, as a Catholic, Hindu or homosexual metropolitan, as a fighter for leftist ideas of freedom and social justice or (for example in racially charged contexts) as white or black. All of these social identities are factually unfounded, scientifically impermissible simplifications of our complex social and natural situation as living beings on Planet Earth.

In the USA, people who are racialized as 'black' have a higher likelihood of being killed by police. This is one of many reprehensible racist imbalances. Racism exists, but the image in the racist's mind does not. This does not make the lives of those affected any easier, but it does mean that one can resist racism by referring to the facts: in reality, there are no human races. *This* should be the point of departure for critique and resistance.

We cannot comprehend either the socioeconomic conditions of resource distribution or our ecological niche well enough to predict the future. While economic crises and pandemics are to be expected at a general level, no one was specifically able to foresee the economic crisis of 2008 or the coronavirus pandemic. Even under quite ordinary conditions we are unable to make precise predictions, something we have all experienced with German Rail, whose timetables are not so much predictions of the arrival of trains as approximate guidelines.

The typical expectations of our everyday life come about not through the formation of theories in the natural sciences, humanities or social sciences but through ill-grounded, historically transmitted models that we rehearse in order to understand ourselves and our fellow humans. This works more or less well for as long as there are no interference factors revealing the holes in the system.

All fear of the unfamiliar is ultimately an expression of the deep-seated fear that our system of expectations might fail, especially because it is in constant change. There is no normal society in which everything functions the way it is supposed to, because the experience of social normality is always an expression of diverse mechanisms of deception and repression.

The ascriptions of (social) identity that are typical of the digital age because of the disseminative logic of news, including fake news, are untenable from the perspective of both the humanities and the social sciences. This applies especially to our main subject of moral action. No one acts in a good or evil way because they are a man, a woman, an East German, a Muslim, a Christian or a social democrat. At most, the ascriptions by others and by ourselves indirectly determine our behaviour if we allow our decisions to be affected by the mistaken opinion that our behaviour is an expression of our social identity. If, for example, a Brazilian who considers himself typically Brazilian meets a German who considers himself typically German, they will initially conduct their social interaction wearing their respective masks and confirm each other's prejudices: the Brazilian will appear as the passionate southerner, the German as a cool-headed rationalist; the one dances, the other fastidiously arranges everything around him – and so on. One can easily show that such stereotypes fall short of reality by comparing a passionately inclined German samba dancer to an introverted Brazilian. For every Brazilian who confirms a stereotype, one can find another who contradicts it. No Brazilian embodies all stereotypes, as the stereotypes vary: people in the USA will have a different image of a typical Brazilian compared to people in Japan.

Stereotypes are dangerous because they easily result in people morally miscategorizing their own actions and consequently reacting in wrong ways. If, for example, a thirty-year-old Green Party voter who has lived in Berlin and New York moves to Munich and encounters an eighty-year-old CSU [Bavarian Conservative] voter whose family has lived in Miesbach[3] for generations, she will probably make misjudgements if she expects certain behaviour based on that. Yes, the CSU voter will vote CSU, but this means little in and of itself. Perhaps he was especially active in the 'welcoming culture' during the 2015 refugee crisis and made donations; maybe he rebuilt his house according to ecological criteria in order to slow climate change. Conversely, it could be that the thirty-year-old Green Party voter, who is proud of her cosmopolitanism and thinks that she never judges people based on superficial, for example racist, criteria, actually condemns the CSU voter for that very reason and already adopts a stance of opposition upon their first encounter. Her attempt to do away with prejudices is directed all too one-sidedly at prejudice towards those whom she acknowledges as 'other', and she overlooks the fact that, for her, the CSU voter is also an other who deserves her moral respect. If someone is prejudiced towards CSU voters out of benevolence towards distant strangers and migrants who reach Germany, they are making the very mistake they seek to avoid, since they are automatically morally condemning someone who is a stranger to them.

It is often overlooked how many negative stereotypes about Europeans are common in the USA, something I have personally noticed during my teaching and research activities. I spent a few years as a young professor at the New School for Social Research in New York and lived in a Polish area of Brooklyn called Greenpoint. The rent was more reasonable than in many overpriced parts of New York, and there were also friendly people, good and affordable restaurants and many other advantages that resulted in a particularly large number of residents from many different European nations living in Greenpoint, whose real-estate market was firmly in the hands of Polish immigrants.

Now, there are a great many stereotypes and jokes about Poles (and Greeks) in the USA, and some American friends often gave me funny looks and asked why I would voluntarily live 'with the Poles'. This brought home the power of stereotypes to me, as well as the fact that even my highly academically trained friends are sometimes susceptible to thinking in stereotypes. So it must feel similar to that (only much worse) if one hails from a German 'problem area' such as Marxloh in the city of Duisburg, because some people associate certain neighbourhoods especially with a stereotypically identified problem, and this association clings to the people there. If one lives only temporarily in such a place and can afford to move away again, this is not problematic; growing up in a neighbourhood perceived as a 'problem area', however, will sooner or later result in experiences of negative discrimination in the form of classism.

The reality, however, is often the exact opposite of what classists believe: because there are certain prejudices towards certain groups of people who are identified via stereotypes, these people are deprived of both material and symbolic resources. Someone with a Turkish-sounding last name who says they come from Marxloh will have measurable disadvantages in many sectors of professional life, whatever abilities they might have independently of their social identification.

One of the primary aims of moral progress is to dismantle the system of stereotypes so that we can see and acknowledge every person as a human being. This is demonstrated to us in a drastic form by the global pandemic. Most people in Germany have never been in a situation like the coronavirus crisis before, personally experiencing a standstill of public life that was unimaginable to them. Not even the climate crisis has (so far) managed to interrupt the production chains of purely economi-cally understood globalization. Suddenly it becomes clear that a rapidly spreading viral infection connects us all as human beings – completely independently of gender, 'race', background, appearance, age, political opinion, income, religious affiliation, and so on. Thanks to COVID-19, humanity has suddenly been involuntarily united under the pressure of an invisible threat.

The coronavirus crisis has opened up the possibility of moral progress in dark times. 'Crisis', like 'critique', comes from the ancient Greek *krinein* ('distinguish' or 'choose'). Such a massive crisis reveals what our central values are and uncovers systemic connections that were not as vividly discernible before. And every crisis holds both chances and risks, which is illustrated wonderfully by the Mandarin word for crisis, 危机 [*wēijī*]. It consists of two characters; in isolation, the first means 'danger' and the second 'opportunity'.

Extreme situations require decisions that express our respective value concepts. Trump, Johnson, Bolsonaro, Orbán and Xi Jinping were already known as morally questionable before the crisis, and their political decisions in the coronavirus emergency were correspondingly amoral and antisocial. In Germany, by contrast, the solidarity in society as a whole that was at least palpable at the start of the coronavirus crisis resulted in part from the fact that the members of the government were not merely interested in looking good as crisis managers (which they are perfectly entitled to do) but took moral responsibility for their decisions, which led to a temporary increase in trust towards the government. The questions that became publicly visible were these: do we want to act as a community and protect the old and the weak by almost any means, or would we rather achieve herd immunity quickly at the cost of hundreds of thousands of deaths? Do we want to ensure the safety and survival of those fellow humans especially affected by the virus, or would we rather accommodate the profit interests of businesses and end the lockdowns as soon as possible? And how do we want to live together in the future, when all of this is somehow over?

What will be more important to us – keeping the infection rate as low as possible or ensuring that all children and young people have the same opportunities and go to school, knowing it will involve risks of infection? How do we deal with the fact that the elderly are especially at risk and require protection, while young families suffer because the children grow lonely at home and their parents cannot work, or only a little?

One way or another, we need ethically considered plans that allow us to maintain our moral standards of justice in a balanced way – which means that we cannot build society as a whole based purely on coronavirus statistics. In short, the coronavirus crisis confronts us with the ethically crucial question of who we are and who we want to be. The right-wing populists will not be any help; having risen to power not least through brazen lies and racism in many countries, they revealed once and for all in the age of the coronavirus that they have the potential to endanger humanity as a whole. This was especially visible in the USA, where Donald Trump showed his true face.

A pandemic, climate change, social injustice and exploitation in many parts of the world, the still very manifest potential for annihilation through nuclear weapons, and so on, cannot be overcome by unilateral national, let alone nationalist means. The temporary withdrawal to nation-state mode, in Europe too, was necessary to contain the first coronavirus wave, as the individual states needed access privileges to the flow of goods and free movement of people in order to interrupt the chains of infection, and the necessary laws for this are currently mostly tied to the constitutions of nation states.

We cannot reverse international trade, which already brought the plague to Europe in the past; this would be an unrealistic wish. We can only develop vaccines and effective drugs, as well as meaningful projects to contain and observe pandemics, through international cooperation. The future rules of this international cooperation will have to follow universal moral criteria, for, as humans, we cannot enter a competition against one another and against the rest of nature.

The nation state is based on borders that are of no consequence to viruses or climate change; from the perspective of viruses and other non-human life forms, nation states do not exist. Viruses do not distinguish between different kinds of people but, rather, demonstrate to us that, at the level of molecular biology, we belong to a single species, namely humanity, which is now infected by a shared fate.

Nation states are forms for organizing the distribution of resources; they allow us to maintain bureaucratic processes within borders. It is morally reprehensible to think in terms of nation-state borders, however, especially with the use of stereotypes that would fool us into believing in cultural identities such as German, French, Bavarian or Rhenish, which cause people to behave accordingly. These are illusions that always lead to groups of people being excluded and experiencing negative discrimination.

Lifting the veil of dehumanization: from identity politics to difference politics

Before we can behave morally towards others, we must remove the veil of stereotypes with which we conceal the faces of the others so as to expose them to our prejudices. This demand applies to everyone, including people who are themselves subject to prejudices and discrimination. Groups of people who experience stereotyping do not automatically consist of saints but usually spread stereotypes themselves. Those who refer to other groups in Germany as 'potatoes'[4] and only see themselves as victims that cannot be integrated are eagerly helping to build the wall that separates people from one another. But the ones who suffer the most discrimination and stereotyping in Germany are those with Turkish and Arab roots; *Kanake* is sadly still a common slur.[5] It is already an act of negative stereotyping and discrimination to refer to these people as of 'Turkish' or 'Arab' backgrounds, because it highlights something that should not matter and ultimately explains little. Certainly, some so-called *Biodeutsche* – that is, Germans whose ancestors have had German citizenship (or one of its antecedents) for many generations – unfortunately enjoy certain privileges; this is a moral and socioeconomic injustice. But there are naturally also lawyers of 'Turkish' origin from affluent families. No one acts as they do because they *are* from a 'Turkish background' or 'biologically German', but only – if at all – because they are treated as if their origins were socially significant. The social significance of origins is in the eye of the beholder; it does not correspond to any reality outside of our prejudices.

This makes negative discrimination especially dangerous: it is based on false notions of the other that are ostensibly confirmed by their behaviour. This impression stems from the fact that these false notions become socially effective and lead to counter-reactions that, coming after a long history of mutual distortions (to say nothing of the associated violence) are no longer easy to understand.

The antidote to identity politics is the **difference politics**, which recognizes that every person is the other of an other. Everyone is foreign to someone somewhere. There is no absolute homeland, no identity that is somehow superior to all others and can act as the reference point for absolute difference.

Being different is a symmetrical relationship: if person B is different from person A, then person A is also different from person B. We share foreignness with those who appear foreign to us.

But we must not stop at difference politics. While it serves the purpose of protecting us from the dangerous one-sidedness of identity politics, it does not transcend the framework of identities. It is simply a necessary invitation to dialogue that accompanies a principle of tolerance and leniency. Tolerance and leniency are not enough, however, because they still ensure that identities remain in place even though they only actually exist in people's minds as false images, like those of witches, wizards and demons. No one who was ever burnt at the stake was really a witch, a wizard or demon-possessed. The whole witch business was a gigantic delusion based on an ignorance of the facts.

There is currently a sociopolitical battle, at times fierce, over the subject of identities. These especially include ethnic background, race, sexual orientation and religious affiliation. Other significant factors in Germany are political opinion and a sense of origins along north–south and east–west lines that separates Hanseatics from Bavarians or Rhinelanders from Thuringians. Depending how closely one looks, of course, one can find further conflicting divisions within these categories: Düsseldorfers versus Cologners, meat-eaters versus vegans, hipsters versus yuppies, Bayern Munich versus Dortmund fans, and so on. It is hard to deny that much of what we consider important and gives our individual life stability and meaning is intertwined with the experience of identity. In some cases, the cultures of the individual federal states or particular regions (Baden versus Württemberg, North Rhine versus Westphalia), even differences between city districts (Friedrichshain versus Grunewald), are so deeply ingrained that we all sometimes feel the need to retreat to these experienced identities, possibly even to claim their superiority over their neighbours.

But this undeniable psychosocial reality is ethically questionable, to say the least. Strictly speaking, it is full of social errors and self-delusions that we urgently need to recognize and overcome. Of course there is a human need to belong. But one cannot consistently define oneself as a vegan from Schöneberg without implicitly or explicitly condemning the Wilmersdorf meat-eater's way of life. If she is only a vegan because she likes that way of life, she is not taking the real problem of meat consumption seriously.

To overcome misleading identity-based thinking, we must start with the *principal question of identity*, namely: *what does identity actually mean?* This question leads us deep into philosophical matters, as it has defined the entire history of philosophy for over 2,500 years in different variants.

In general, **identity** is a relationship that connects someone or something to themselves or itself. It is impossible to be identical to someone else; I am I, you are you – end of story. In matters of identity politics, however, it is naturally not simply a matter of whether someone is themselves, for the answer (at least at first glance) is simple. Rather, identity politics deals with seemingly very urgent, morally relevant questions: should we introduce a quota for eastern Germans so that there will be more eastern German managers in charge of businesses? Should we treat non-Christian refugees differently from Christian ones? Should we open all public toilets up to all genders, or is the existing practice of distinguishing between men's and women's toilets sufficient to do justice to the full range of sexual self-determination? Is it permissible to serve pork in kindergartens and schools, even though many children come from Muslim or Jewish backgrounds?

To bring clarity into this muddled situation, let us first of all distinguish between four types of identity.

1 Ontological Identity

What does it actually mean that each one of us is someone? Why am I myself and not someone else? Might I possibly have been someone else if my life had taken a different course? For example, if I had accepted a job offer in a different city instead of turning it down?

2 Metaphysical Identity

To what actually existing object am I, as a human being, identical? Am I a sophisticated speaking animal? An immortal soul that has come to inhabit a human body? A pattern of neuronal activity? A brain acting as the control centre in a body? A dream? A thought in the spirit of God? Or something completely different?

One cannot evade this problem by viewing it as a 'matter of definition', as something more or less arbitrary, for it is simply the reality that we are identical to something. If we were immortal souls whose virtue is tested by God in this life, this would surely be the most important information of all! If, on the other hand, we were merely a brief flaring up of neuronal processes, this would have equally decisive implications for an accomplished life, since we could then be sure that we can live only for one round, so to speak – precisely this one time. These metaphysical questions have not actually been resolved, which certainly does not make them unimportant, as the meaning of life just happens to depend on them.

3 Personal Identity

Am I the same person for my entire life? Am I the same person I was thirty years ago? Will I be the same person when I die, or will it be a different person who dies, someone I have become who wears my skin? Or am I maybe dying every moment, and my identity is only a momentary flickering anyway?

4 Social Identity

What does it mean for me that I am a father, the author of these lines, a university professor, German, Rhinelander, wine-drinker, neighbour, husband, philosopher, director of a research institute, and so forth? Each of these roles is tied to rights and duties, some of which are determined by sociological examination and coordinated with institutions of the democratic law-based state that define the spaces within which one can be a father, author, German, neighbour, wine-drinker, and so on.

These four kinds of identity (as well as others we can leave aside) merge in the heat of the public debate on identity politics. That is why social identity is metaphysically charged: for many people, it is a substitute religion.

There is a reason for the identity-political excitement that is connected to the origins of identity politics. The justification for placing racial, religious, sexual and ethno-geographical aspects at the centre of identity politics is based on past injustices, some of them severe, against certain groups of people on the basis of such divisions. In the not-so-distant past, and even in the present, atrocities and acts of cruelty have been committed against dark-skinned people, Jews, Christians, Muslims, women and transsexuals, as well as Germans, French, Russians, Chinese, and so on.

To justify and motivate such at times severe crimes against humanity, people have always used stereotypes, which takes us to the heart of the problem. You can easily see how strongly our thinking is influenced by stereotypes if you ask yourself what, in your view, characterizes a typical Spaniard. Perhaps it will cross your mind that the Spanish are very hot-blooded, speak loudly, eat paella, drink heavy red wines, have tanned skin, and so on. If you have spent a certain amount of time in Spain or know Spanish people, however, you will soon have realized that you have a very inadequate understanding of the Spanish if you look for the 'typical Spaniards' among them. It goes without saying that the same applies to the typical Bavarian, who – we assume – tends to wear certain traditional garb, drink *Weissbier* and eat *Weisswurst*,[6] speak in a deep baritone, curse with a strong accent and is a Catholic.

Naturally such stereotypes are also connected to certain roles. Many find it easy to imagine what a typical wife does and thinks or to explain what the inhabitants of Saxony want by imagining them as particularly rebellious East Germans. In addition, every country has its own stereotypes of other countries. The Portuguese have different stereotypes of the Spanish from ours, the Chinese have different ones of the Germans from Americans, and Italian stereotypes of Libyans are not the same as those found in France.

But I have already misled you somewhat, because the very things I have just said about countries and their stereotypes are themselves based on stereotypes. The notion that certain stereotypes are dominant in certain counties automatically leads to the emergence of new stereotypes. And that is part of the problem.

We owe the first theory of the connection between stereotypical clichés and public opinion to the American journalist and media critic Walter Lippmann. In his still relevant 1922 book *Public Opinion*, he shows that invocations of 'culture, tradition and the group mind'[7] are at best an expression of stereotypical patterns, by which he means prejudices and preconceptions that shape our expectations, and thus our perceptions.[8] He cites the following examples of national stereotypes, which seem bizarre to us today:

> ... the volatile Irish, and the logical French, and the disciplined Germans, and the ignorant Slavs, and the honest Chinese, and the untrustworthy Japanese, and so on and so on. All these are generalizations drawn from samples, but the samples are selected by a method that statistically is wholly unsound. ... The tendency of the casual mind is to pick out or stumble upon a sample which supports or defies its prejudices, and then to make it the representative of a whole class.[9]

It is no easy matter to shake off such prejudices, however, for prejudices always have elements of truth; but these are distorted, filtered and reinterpreted. There probably are more red wine drinkers and people inclined to hug in Spain than in Germany, where beer is more popular and there is less physical contact (which is why 'social distancing', the English phrase used in 'German' corona-speak, is more difficult for a large group of Spaniards than for a similar group of Germans, which meant that a lockdown was necessary in Spain to interrupt this cultural habit).

But generalized prejudiced thinking on the basis of such elements of truth is quickly refuted by reality. In March 2020, when the COVID-19 pandemic was already spreading visibly in Germany too, the first warm days saw Munich residents sitting almost skin-to-skin in the beer gardens and meadows, which was a decisive factor in the Bavarian infection rates. The proximity to Italy or Austria has little to do with this, for those who became infected in Italy were not only Italians and Austrians but also Germans. Chains of infection have nothing to do with nations; the virus does not discriminate according to nationality. In North Rhine-Westphalia it was the carnival that hastened the spread of the virus. So the Germans actually have far more physical contact than some people think, which is why the Bavarian government pulled the emergency brake by imposing a meeting ban and restricting outdoor activities. The stereotype of the standoffish beer-drinking German who avoids physical contact certainly does not describe what goes on at the Oktoberfest.

Even if it were partly true that the coronavirus led to particularly high fatalities in Italy, Spain and France because many Italian, Spanish and French people have a particular tendency for physical contact, this in no way means that the latter is reprehensible. General 'social distancing' is just as problematic and should only be an exceptional form of behaviour, otherwise racism, classism or misogyny threaten to be joined by a new, deplorable way of thinking that I have termed **hygienism**.[10]

'Hygiene' comes from the ancient Greek word for health (*hygieia*). The goal and meaning of human life cannot be to base our society purely on improving and guarding our health. Otherwise we would have to ban alcohol, unprotected sexual intercourse, French kissing and many other forms of affection, as well as chocolate, crisps and pizza. Judging others by hygienic standards puts us in a bad position, since not a single person who lives a meaningful life exclusively or even mostly attempts to live as healthily and as long as possible. Pure, maximum longevity is not the meaning of life, let alone the moral aim of a successful social order. A society that only revolves around health is bleak and totalitarian. The protagonist of the series *After Life*, played by Ricky Gervais, puts this in a nutshell when someone points out his excessive drinking: a healthy life is simply one that involves dying more slowly.

In reality, the steps taken to contain the spread of the coronavirus have also led to deaths: suicides, avoidable deaths resulting from delayed check-ups or medical practices with reduced working hours; the economic consequences, which will have a similarly negative effect, are not clear yet. So we are taking on board an uncontrolled and unplanned triage for the whole of society, and the only reason we fail to notice it is that it is morally necessary to protect the lives of those who are at risk from the novel coronavirus.

At the height of the COVID-19 pandemic in the spring of 2020, a number of European hospitals had to resort to **triage** (from the French word for 'selection'), a method developed in field hospitals to decide which patients should be treated first. For this, people are assigned to categories with the colours red, yellow, green, blue and black. Only those with red status are treated immediately; those with no chance of survival are given the colour blue and receive terminal care. The other colours are treated after the red patients. Triage situations lead to difficult medical decisions that will quickly overtax any responsibly minded doctor. For it is morally reprehensible to weigh up human lives against one another, yet nonetheless inevitable in emergencies where one has to coordinate life-saving actions somehow to ensure that not everyone dies and the greatest possible number survive. Triage is therefore also used in the case of earthquakes or large-scale accidents, as well as in accident and emergency departments all over the world.

The steps taken to contain the coronavirus are part of a triage in society as a whole that, for understandable reasons, made the health and safety of citizens the top priority for the distribution of resources for a time. This cannot be a permanent condition, however, otherwise we will propagate a new, highly dangerous form of stereotyping, namely hygienism.

Lippmann also presents his reflections on stereotypes in order to explain the emergence and manipulation of public opinion, which is why his train of thought is so relevant again today. The dynamics of public opinion, measured nowadays in 'likes', clicks and partly subliminal behavioural manipulations in the digital realm, are based on the fabrication and dissemination of stereotypes which ensure that, in our manifold daily micro-interactions of greeting, passing one another and exchanging things (money for bread rolls, etc.), we employ digitally spread patterns of behaviour. The internet is also primarily a machine with which one can measure and control the dissemination of stereotypes; this is the point of search machines, social media and the algorithmically regulated recommendation systems used by all major platforms. They have made our immense susceptibility to stereotypes one of the most successful business models of modernity.

Coronavirus: reality strikes back

National identities in particular have roughly the same ontological status, the same mode of being, as witches: they themselves do not actually exist, but one certainly imagines them. The imagined (and in this sense existent) witches are not, of course, identical to the people who are accused of witchery; but this does not prevent the images from being effective, and hence all too real.[11]

Gender identities such as male and female are only seemingly different from this. To be sure, there are non-moral (genetically determinable) facts that contribute to deciding which biological sex a human being has and how it is connected to biological reproduction. Certain social facts follow from this, for example that (so far) only biological women can bear children. This in no way means, however, that mothers have a fixed social role from which one can derive an identity that contrasts with that of fathers. The social roles of mothers and fathers do not follow from the biological, genetic contribution that they have made to biological reproduction.

The fact that thinking in identities rests on a variety of errors already makes it reprehensible. It confuses our reflection on ourselves and others, as it simply does not correspond adequately to the facts.

A social practice based on massive errors about non-moral facts cannot be morally acceptable, since the moral judgement of those involved in it is led astray by the smokescreens of identity discourse.

Unlike identities, the coronavirus is (unfortunately) not a figment of the imagination. It really does exist, and it is developing according to principles that are not yet fully medically understood. Given the complexity of possible and actual chains of infection, the uncertainty as to whether and when a vaccine will be developed and distributed, hitherto unclear data and limited possibilities for testing people, we can only work with models.

The models that explain the properties of the virus, its spreading, its lethality, the danger of infection, and so on, are fallible. Where they succeed, models are very good, helpful approximations of a reality that is not a model. It depends on reality, however, not on the models, whether the parameters of our models, and thus our computer simulations, are correct. If the model assumptions deviate too greatly from reality, the model supplies poor, false results and misleading recommendations for action.

I have referred to this reality elsewhere as **basic reality**.[12] Models themselves are real too; they are part of reality. Basic reality, on the other hand, is the part of reality that does not depend on the existence of models and, in particular, is not itself a model. The coronavirus spreads in basic reality; it is not a model.

Viruses are uncanny. The logic behind their transmission exceeds all boundaries: it is located on an invisible level and becomes visible to us only because of the symptoms of the disease and then the many fatalities. We can only examine the transmission logic via complex models and statistics, which means that we are currently exposed to a pandemic that is taking place without our being able to observe it directly. We do not even recognize all the symptoms; many who fall ill display too few of them or simply do not realize they have COVID-19.

The coronavirus defies the postmodern nonsense that reality is socially constructed and depends in general on our attitude towards it. The internal dynamics of the coronavirus are not a matter of attitude. We can attempt to contain it and develop a vaccine (which we naturally should), but we will never gain full control of the basic reality. New viruses will keep emerging, and each time humanity will be exposed to natural processes that are beyond our control.

In such situations, stereotypes develop a previously undreamt-of potency, proving that not only the virus but also our false notions of its nature are dangerous, including the absurd idea that it was produced in Chinese laboratories or even circulated by Bill Gates in order to sell his vaccine later on.

The coronavirus crisis also shows especially clearly what stereotypes exist and what sometimes dangerous and world-economically measurable consequences they have. First it hit the Chinese, who defended themselves with nationalist stereotypes about their alleged systemic superiority to 'the' West (which does not exist either, incidentally) and initially kept the incipient pandemic quiet to avoid showing any weakness. Next, some people no doubt thought that the Italians were hit especially hard because of their lack of organization. Then some people in the USA claimed that Europeans were maybe even more infectious than the Chinese, while they themselves were confronted with especially rapidly rising infection numbers. The virus mercilessly uncovers all the weak points in health systems and, in a country without universal healthcare or sick pay, the infected keep working or do not get tested at all so as to avoid being sent home. One should never forget that it is especially easy to become homeless in the USA, something that defines the streetscapes of many large cities there.

For the Trump administration, as well as many leading minds in US businesses (including those in Silicon Valley), our idea of a social market economy in which money must not ultimately win out over humanity is an enemy worldview. This already shows that the so-called West is also a stereotypical image, since there are identity-political divisions within this construct that separate the USA from continental Europe, but also from Australia or New Zealand.

While the viral pandemic gathered speed, the Chinese regime employed the usual strategies of its propaganda machine to create a growing suspicion that democracy is not up to the task of dealing with the twenty-first century. By necessity, the rest of the world resorted to the most drastic measures, such as closing borders, imposing curfews and declaring a state of emergency, which is not justified purely by the actually existing viral pandemic – for no political step is supported by a viral pandemic alone. After all, we could simply rely on endemic infection and herd immunity or kill the elderly to protect the health system. We rightly consider such a thing morally reprehensible, but this judgement cannot be reached by examining the virus. Virologists, epidemiologists and other medical professionals are neither ethicists nor politicians; they study the properties of viruses and their transmission, which does not initially have anything to do with ethics.

Nor does the coronavirus have anything whatsoever to do with state borders or systems of governance. We can indeed contain it via institutional measures and get it under control through medical research and reinforcing our health systems, which means that the state systems must be capable of functioning. But that is clearly the case in Germany as well as in China, Japan, Italy and the USA. It is sheer dangerous nonsense to believe that the coronavirus demonstrates the weakness of democracy or, in Germany's case, of federalism. German federalism is a particular way of determining and directing institutions and coordination processes. Our processes are designed in such a way that the possibility of setting up a control centre leading to a transformation of the Federal Republic into a dictatorship is very remote. The same is true of other democratic systems such as the USA, which cannot simply be turned into a dictatorship.

Alongside the very real dangers of the virus, one can unfortunately observe an equally real danger in the coronavirus crisis that is connected to the virus, namely the declaration of states of emergency. In general, a **state of emergency** is a suspension of value systems with the aim of getting a dangerous situation under control, and it justifies restricting certain historically acquired rights for preferably a short space of time. However, it is possible that a state of emergency will release forces that were already fighting this suspended value system under the surface before then. The more these forces spread in the state of emergency, the more likely it is that the legitimately restricted value system will be harmed.

It is no coincidence, then, that stereotypes and false ideas have been spreading since the first wave of infections and the resulting government steps, stereotypes that are used to harm democracy and its foundational values. This includes the electoral rhetoric of Trump, who seized the opportunity to do symbolic and material damage to continental Europe, and thus to the EU.

At the same time, it is pleasing that moral progress is still taking place in these dark times of the coronavirus crisis. It is clear that even many people who would not really be personally affected by the virus, because they are young and have no pre-existing conditions, are attempting to maintain social distancing and avoid infection so as to avoid endangering the lives of the elderly and immunocompromised. The production chains of global capitalism that were contaminating the planet until a few days ago have suddenly been radically broken – for moral reasons. Therefore, the state of emergency is also a chance for reflection and a possible trigger for a sea change. Whether we see the writing on the wall and finally come to our senses, or instead try to return to the old patterns, is still undecided. It is clear, however, that a return to supposed 'normality' would undoubtedly entangle us in far greater crises, including the climate crisis and the constantly growing social inequality. And let us not forget the systemic competition between the USA, the EU and China, which at times takes on warlike features and shows us once again that humanity must strive for global cooperation on the basis of universal values. Without that, the problems facing us in the twenty-first century cannot be overcome.

A different side of Thuringia: in Jena, racism is debunked

Racism is not only morally reprehensible in general; it is also based on many grave scientific errors. Uncovering these can lead to moral progress in the fight against racism. In Thuringia, for example, first-rate research is being carried out that can help with this.

If one currently uses the words 'Thuringia' and 'racism' in the same breath, many people unfortunately assume a general predominance of the so-called Wing [*Flügel*] of the AfD, which was treated by German domestic intelligence as a 'case for suspicion' [*Verdachtsfall*] and prominently represented by the regional AfD leader, Björn Höcke (who comes from Westphalia, not Thuringia), before it officially folded. This casts a regrettable light on Thuringia, which also includes Jena, the birthplace of German Idealism, which developed radically universalist concepts of being human.[13] This naturally includes Friedrich Schiller's version of a radical universalist ethics that can be realized through aesthetic education.

But moral progress in Thuringia is not merely a thing of the past. For the 112th annual congress of the German Zoological Society, which took place in Jena in 2019, zoologists and evolutionary biologists published the 'Jena Declaration' with the support of the Max Planck Society.[14] Its central message is already in the title: 'The concept of race is a result of racism, not the precondition for it.'

However, this result was only proved so irrefutably with the groundbreaking discovery in molecular biology that

> the vast majority of genetic differences between humans are not between geographical populations [such as a group of dark-skinned Africans in contrast to a group of white North Germans, M. G.] but within such groups. … Instead of definable boundaries, there are genetic gradients between groups of people. Among the 3.2 billion base pairs in the human genome, there is not a single fixed difference separating, for example, Africans from non-Africans. There is hence – to be quite clear – not only no gene that determines 'racial' differences but not even one single base pair. External attributes such as skin colour, which are used for typological classification or in everyday racism, are a highly superficial and easily mutable biological adaptation to the respective local circumstances. Skin colour alone has changed time and again

in the course of human migrations, growing darker or lighter according to local sun exposure or diet.[15]

The authors adduce a number of other biological and anthropological facts and, on this human science basis, concludes that, with the inapplicable concept of human races, the idea of 'ethnopluralism' especially common in the USA also becomes useless. 'Avoiding the concept of race should henceforth be part of scientific honesty.' Then it would make no sense to assign special rights to various ethnicities or races and develop the space of distributive justice accordingly, since there would quite simply be no adequately clear differences between ethnicities or races.

Here some theorists counter that there is indeed something called 'race', understood in a non-biological sense.[16] But this is nonsense: racism is always biologistic (i.e., pseudo-biologically justified), and the idea that one could make it more spiritual is an illusion. Of course there is a lived and experienced reality of 'African Americans' connected to how they are viewed and treated by others and by themselves for historical reasons. That is the practice of racism.

This practice is less biological in its approach today than in the past, since now no one can sterilize or enslave African Americans on the basis of the biological arguments that were once used to justify dehumanization. Different treatment has a morally reprehensible origin that we must not forget; but the goal should not be to turn racist nonsense into cultural stereotypes and perpetuate these under the banner of de facto non-existent cultures.

The impression of being among one's own kind, different from strangers, can be explained in ways that do not theoretically adopt the self-delusions of those concerned. Sometimes I too feel like a 'Rhinelander' and find the label amusing in my everyday banter with friends and, sometimes, also pleasant, because it gives me a sense of home. But this expresses only autobiographical experiences, not a definable nature of the Rhinelander. If one looks closely, Rhinelanders are far more varied than the stereotype suggests.

In short, from a sociophilosophical perspective, there are self-delusions about the course of one's own life and one's personality traits that may be experienced as a sense of home. Yet such a sense of home – however much one might enjoy revelling in it – is always rooted somehow in morally reprehensible practices in the past and the present. If I saw myself as a stereotypical Rhinelander, for example, what would that mean for someone whose parents moved to the Rhineland from abroad a generation ago? However amusing and emotionalized they may be, stereotypes always lead to exclusion and morally reprehensible ways of thinking. They are irreconcilable with moral progress. Training one's moral reflection includes becoming aware of one's own stereotypes and attempting to prevent them from affecting one's actions.

This eliminates the model of a kind of *friendly ghettoization* especially common in the USA. In cities such as New York, entire districts are still characterized by having mostly Chinese, Indian, Korean, Polish, Russian, Orthodox Jewish or rich white Protestant populations. The respective dining establishments offer ethnic cuisine and cultural events, so that one can practically 'try out' different cultures on every day of the week.

This is a problematic model of civilization, since it presupposes that the individual ethnicities, races or religious affiliations come together in a shared space to display their respective alterity in relation to one another and that they feel more at ease and safe among those who are supposedly the same. I do not mean to disparage the human need to belong; it is reprehensible, however, to seek to satisfy it by defining belonging in terms of ethnicity, race or the equally vague notion of a culture, since these objects do not actually exist. Communities that are held together by delusions and self-delusions are morally questionable as long as there is a tendency to develop illusory identities that see themselves in competition with other identities. Such a social structure inevitably leads to moral deficits.

There is no such thing as German culture; this immediately becomes apparent if one attempts to define it. If one names Luther, Bach, Beethoven and Goethe, one has overlooked Franz Kafka, Mario Adorf,[17] Hannah Arendt, Cem Özdemir[18] and Hadnet Tesfai.[19] If German culture existed, it would include the Berlin techno scene as well as punk, hip hop from the Ruhr region, Simon Rattle and the paintings of Albrecht Dürer. There is simply no well-defined collection of textbook examples of German culture from which one could derive a sense of belonging that is not deluded. The same applies to Chinese culture, Arab culture or whatever other culture one might imagine. What does exist are group formations that may be attributable partly to aesthetic taste and shared preferences, but partly also to other factors, which in the ethnic structures of the USA especially include waves of immigration.

Although the model of sometimes voluntary ethnic ghettoization is morally (and strategically) better than the attempt to isolate such groups from one another geographically via walls and barbed wire, it still has the flaw that it chooses to group people according to criteria that have virtually no connection to the reality of human life. The sense of 'home' that one carries as a migrant in order to come together with like-minded people while abroad is a delusion, and it is problematic because it morally divides us: the individuals thus united by an illusory home only imagine the foreign homelands of the others, and treat them correspondingly.

As we have seen, races do not actually exist; but racism certainly does. It already begins with the false notion that there are races. Racism as such is morally reprehensible (evil) because it divides people up into groups and assigns patterns of behaviour to individuals that are not real. Racists explain people's behaviour in terms of attributes that only indirectly affect their actions. Whoever falls victim to racist attacks must defend themselves, which motivates them to take actions that, in the eyes of the racist, confirm the stereotype. When a group is subject to negative discrimination through racism, anything it does to protect itself from attacks is treated by racists as a confirmation of its negative traits.

The solidarity that was palpable everywhere during the first phase of the coronavirus crisis led to the vast majority of people in Germany realizing that they were in the same boat and could experience first-hand how everyone was exposed to a common danger – which unites us. Unfortunately, this solidarity did not cross all borders, because stereotypes and a misguided sense of home often prevent us from thinking beyond our own narrow horizon. Strictly speaking, this new solidarity was not even present within our own borders, as individual states, districts, cities and demographic groups were (and still are) competing for resources; many people in Germany have found themselves in difficult socioeconomic situations and others will do so in the future. The homeless, the poor, children who were kept indoors and prevented by the state from meeting with their age-mates in public, single parents, single pensioners, anxious high-school seniors, and many others who suffered from our crisis management and will continue to do so for a while – who claps for them? And what would that achieve?

Extending our moral reflection to all people inhabiting a common territory would already be great progress, but we must not lose sight of the goal. This goal is the recognition of the decisive moral circumstance that we, as humans, are ultimately *all* in the same boat – and the seats of most Germans in the coronavirus crisis are certainly more comfortable than those of Indian itinerant labourers, without whom things would in turn be less comfortable for us. Given the challenges of the twenty-first century and a global population of over 7 billion people whose ways of life are interwoven, it is nonsense to believe that we could fall back on our sense of home as a source of values. Rather, in the long term, these feelings ignite war scenarios and lead to the self-extermination of humanity, because they motivate people to settle into highly dangerous delusions and self-delusions.

The *universal identity of being human* is expressed in that insurmountable difference without which we cannot be anyone. Humans always determine their concrete sequences of actions, their wishes, preferences, etc., in contradistinction to other people. It is mistaken to believe that there is one right, objectively existing distinction that divides people into different social identities that can be used as meaningful points of orientation. Social identities are a palpable and economically measurable expression of mutual attributions. This means that people already assess one another at first glance on the basis of their prejudices – that is, their opinions about others that have been developed without looking closely. These opinions have a long history that includes many errors. Moreover, many people profit from the dissemination of stereotypes: without prejudice and in part morally reprehensible stereotypes, for example, our advertising industry would have difficulties, since it leads us to believe in the existence of lifestyles and promises of happiness that are not real.

A good example of this are the pictures of purported singles on posters advertising online dating portals. One can be sure that dating portals are inhabited not by such stunningly good-looking, economically successful and relaxed people but by quite normal people who long for romantic relationships.

Unfortunately, the dissemination and production of such ideal notions of a successful life, which are intended to motivate consumerism, is usually based on lies, delusions and self-delusions of this kind. In his

Heidelberg seminars, one of my philosophy teachers, the political philosopher Rüdiger Bubner, liked to illustrate this idea with a dream about strolling along a deserted sandy beach with a perfectly styled partner after winning the lottery. As soon as one arrives at this beach, one finds that there are dangerous mosquitoes, it is unpleasantly windy, one gets food poisoning from the oysters at the beach restaurant, and the perfectly styled partner turns out to have insufferable opinions on most important issues.

This shows that the notions of winning the lottery and dropping out of society are illusory, because the happiness promised by the lottery win is merely an illusion of happiness. We long for freedom but have a tendency to confuse this with particular places or with owning something we have always wanted.

We always project our dreams of a successful life as well as our night-mares about a failed life onto other people and other places. This creates mechanisms of the imagination that structure our everyday life and keep us busy. This is the origin of the proverbial hamster wheel where we flail about aimlessly.

The problem is not that we dream and abandon ourselves to illusions – without illusions, dreams, works of art and similarly beautiful things, life would be joyless. The problem consists of the morally reprehensible ideas about the role of unknown, strange people in our dreams. The assumption that, as a German, I automatically feel closer to a Bavarian 'bio-German' fellow citizen than to the Spanish waiter serving us at the same hotel is a morally problematic illusion when it comes to our opinions about eurobonds and other economic bailouts.

In short, we ultimately imagine that we and other people are the same as we seem to one another in daily life. But this image corresponds only very partially to reality, which can be explained by the fact that our illusions are effective because we conform to them. Things become difficult when we encounter people who have other illusions and tell very different stories about a successful life. These counterpoints reveal our capacity for moral thought, and what counts is whether we manage to see this apparent divergence as a reason to dream differently. The ideal of a morally successful human community is to create morally acceptable illusions that do not lead us to split people into ethnicities, cultures and groups that treat one another as alien.

The moral processes of the twenty-first century revolve around the fact that the processes of ascribing social identity rest on dangerous (because in part implicitly or explicitly violent) stereotypes that are systematically reinforced via social media. Through its media-based attention economy, the digital age produces forms of identity politics that sort people into groups to which they do not belong on the basis of their nature; for by our nature we are actually all equal, being subject to the same processes of species survival and environmental adaptation that make us human animals – that is, animals of a particular biological species.

Racism is not limited to the past and present discrimination, persecution, abuse and murder of dark-skinned people. There is no adequately fair form of discrimination, only a momentary reparation for past injustice whereby one attempts to compensate particular people for suffering systematic negative discrimination. We must not lose sight of this when taking appropriate steps to overcome racism. These do not include identity politics, because it consolidates stereotypes as identities and shifts the focus to what we should actually be overcoming.

The value of truth (without a hall of mirrors)

On both wings of the politically radical spectrum, the right and the left, one finds a destruction of the value of truth. Overly hasty left-wing activism is justified with the argument that the minorities (supposedly) who deserve protection, for whom one can finally stand up after centuries of oppression, have already had to wait too long for moral and legal justice. Extreme right-wing activists, on the other hand, claim (in the USA, for example) that white men must be protected from the left forces that want to bring women, black people, and so on, to power. They invoke the democratic value of protecting oppressed minorities, falsely claiming that white men, of all people, are among the minorities who deserve protection. This misleading impression comes from the fact that recent decades have seen moral progress in the recognition of minorities who genuinely deserve protection, which has also led to redistributions of resources.

This is even used as a pretext to employ discursive and physical violence, as I experienced myself at a recent conference about the prospects of a more just future social order. The British philosopher

Nina Power, who considers herself a radical feminist and whose book *One-Dimensional Woman* received considerable attention, was attacked at a symposium by another participant, the Antifa activist and journalist Natasha Lennard.[20] She accused Power of being a 'TERF', a 'trans-exclusionary radical feminist' – a feminist who opposes the women's rights of transgender persons who feel they are women, even though they have external sexual characteristics that many would classify as 'male'.

My concern here is not to present a well-founded opinion on the issue of transsexuality and justice for people who, fortunately, are also recognized legally in Germany as 'diverse' (a case of moral progress) – a welcome first and major step towards a fully valid, human-scientifically secure acknowledgement of the fact that not all people are unambiguously female or male (however one defines these two categories).

What was notable and worrying about the exchange of blows between Power and Lennard was the fact that, in her lecture, Lennard argued explicitly that there is no such thing as truth and that 'fascism' cannot be defined. Rather, she stated, the meaning of 'fascism' is determined by the movement she represents, Antifa. The only reason she gave for claiming that she already considered Power a fascist was an online campaign against Power, which Lennard cited without any further evidence and which, as she did not seem to know, consisted mostly of fake news and even classified Power as a Satanist (which led Power to take legal steps in England). In advance of the conference, Lennard had attempted to bring about Power's disinvitation online, but she refused to give any reasons for this at the event. In the end, she even argued that there are no objectively better reasons, no truths, and that only activism against what she called 'fascism' exists – without being able to say what constitutes fascism or why she considered Power a fascist. Here, then, a person who takes a stand for equal rights (Power) – whatever one thinks of her theoretical achievements – encountered an activist who wanted to exclude her from the discourse without saying why.

Identity politics on both the left and the right is often thwarted by the fact that its moral claims do not correspond to the facts, which is sometimes pushed aside – on the left and the right – by denying a clearly proven truth or presenting untruths as truths, without employing processes for establishing the truth in order to reach a universally valid verdict. This occurs against the background of attacks on truth, facts, realism and universalism in the name of incoherent theories that often come from the postmodern spectrum. This produces the opposite of moral progress, despite often happening in the name of social, political or scientific progress.

A textbook example of the postmodern manoeuvre of abandoning truth for the sake of supposedly progressive politics can be found in the theoretical work of the American philosopher Richard Rorty, who has argued in a number of very prominent books that we should let go of the idea that our symbolically coded (linguistic, literary, narrative, cultural) belief systems are in any way a representation of an independently existing reality. Our thoughts and actions, according to Rorty, are not a 'mirror of the world', so there is no truth.[21] Instead of even speaking of truth, Rorty recommends producing a community of solidarity consisting of 'ironists' (as he calls them). The ironists do not believe in truth; they believe only in the fact that they share with other ironists the 'insight' that there is no truth. Thus processes of social and political negotiation are tied not to the goal of discovering the right way or the right value system but, rather, to decision-making processes that are contingent – they could take place in a variety of ways – and whose function is only to serve the cohesion of the community.

What many have so far failed to acknowledge adequately, unfortunately, is that the 'arguments' presented by Rorty to support his theses have been refuted by philosophers in various waves of critique. One example among many is Paul Boghossian's much discussed book *Fear of Knowledge*, which shows circumspectly and in detail that Rorty's version of relativism and constructivism is deeply incoherent and thus untenable.

We do not, however, need to deal with the philosophical theory of truth here in order to see where Rorty's version of postmodernism leads, since it is demonstrated every day in social media and on the stage of world politics. Because Rorty does not recognize any criteria for successful community formation independently of our feelings of cohesion, there is no reason not to connect a postmodernism thus understood (and thus ultimately misunderstood) to the New Right. 'Alternative facts', the 'post-factual age' or 'post-truth' are catchphrases with right-wing connotations that are used to replace the rational, institutional and publicly negotiable establishment of truth with irrational and incoherent emotional worlds. Today, postmodernism is not propagated by progressive French or

American intellectuals but, rather, instrumentalized by people such as Donald Trump, Nigel Farage, Viktor Orbán and Vladimir Putin, as well as many AfD politicians – who, in an act of meta-irony, have taken up the slogan 'courage to speak the truth' [*Mut zur Wahrheit*]; under this banner, they deny obvious facts and spread conspiracy theories. These ideologues use and reinforce a simplified image of the postmodern idea that truth is based on group membership, which ultimately serves only the law of the strongest.

We do not live in a hall of mirrors made of baseless opinions and beliefs, however; we live in reality. Our thoughts and actions are inseparably entwined with reality, if only because both are independently effective and take place in reality. One cannot escape reality. Our thoughts and actions are not in opposition to reality, like some mental screen on which little mental images and stories appear that have little or nothing to do with the world 'out there', as an ultimately mistaken interpretation of the canonic postmodern theorists would have it.

Nowadays, postmodernism has long ceased to be limited to progressive American literary theory departments, from where it has spread through society, especially in the USA. Rather, one now often hears postmodern 'arguments' made by evolutionary biologists, physicists, neuroscientists and, in particular, economists, which is a startling development. Things are hopeless indeed if even some natural scientists suppose that we cannot recognize reality because we are trapped in models and theories that only distort reality, never grasp it as it is. Then there would be no more arguments against (or for) Trump's project of making US economic performance the top priority; in fact, one would wonder what the point of a democratic law-based welfare state is at all.

We must not forget that the democratic law-based welfare state emerged from at times very bloody revolutions and political struggles over the last two hundred years in which people who were suffering because of the rapid industrialization fought for a more just society. Modern democracy, which is a very recent project in world-historical terms and did not produce stable forms of governance in Germany until after the Second World War, is based on the Enlightenment. The Enlightenment project is impossible without truth, moral realism and universalism. It is a grave error to believe that one could continue the project of a democratic law-based state without a commitment to the canon of Enlightenment values, which is laid down in our constitution.

Postmodernism leads to a new kind of 'self-imposed immaturity':[22] instead of using their 'understanding' 'without guidance from another', its purveyors rely on group mentality (Rorty misleadingly calls this 'solidarity'), believing that truth can be replaced by groupthink.

Here it is helpful to consider a famous metaphor used by Ludwig Wittgenstein, who saw it as the task of his philosophy to 'show the fly the way out of the fly-bottle'.[23] He recognized the widespread notion that our thinking is a form of inner process that cannot be compared to an outside world 'out there'. On the basis of this abstruse assumption, which has repeatedly been disproved in modern philosophy, recently in detail by Rorty's master student Robert Boyce Brandom, many people suppose that there cannot be such a thing as truth because we cannot establish an agreement between our symbolic systems of thought and reality.[24] Wittgenstein counters this with characteristic brevity in the following observation:

> When we say, *mean*, that such-and-such is the case, then, with what we mean, we do not stop anywhere short of the fact, but mean: *such-and-such – is – thus-and-so*. – But this paradox (which indeed has the form of a truism) can also be expressed in this way: one can *think* what is not the case.[25]

The head in which our thinking takes place is not impervious to reality. This is already clear from the fact that the head itself is something extremely real and a part of the supposed outside world. Indeed, truth consists not in the fact that something internal is connected to something external, a mental image with an event 'out there' and which mirrors the world 'out there', but rather in the fact that we 'say, *mean*, that such-and-such is the case', and that it is as we say. Statements and thoughts are not misleading images of an independent reality but, rather, suitable means to establish and communicate what is really the case.

That one can be mistaken does not mean that there is no truth. Quite the opposite! If one is mistaken, one fails to grasp the truth, from which it follows that the truth exists. Without truth there are neither errors nor lies, ideology, propaganda or manipulation.

A fact is a truth. Therefore, moral facts are moral truths about which one can be mistaken. In order to gain a clear view of this matter, which is so crucial for human coexistence, we must shatter the hall of mirrors – or simply find the way out – in order to stop mirroring ourselves and instead recognize that it is our common task to attempt in all conscience to do what is right and avoid what is wrong.

This certainly does not mean that it is easy to ascertain what we should do in any given situation. Practices of forgiveness, leniency and careful, tentative dialogue are contained in the portfolio of moral progress. The fact that there are moral facts does not entitle us to force our moral opinions on others without examining their reasons.

Here we can invoke a basic rule of philosophical hermeneutics, namely the doctrine of understanding formulated by the Heidelberg philosopher Hans-Georg Gadamer that 'the other may be right'.[26] Of course, this does not mean that we should seriously consider even the most bizarre recommendations for action; it signifies only that a fact-based conversation between several persons with seemingly radically different views on morally relevant decisions is subject to felicity conditions. Conversations can succeed or fail because they are ethically regulated. They open up new perspectives that were previously hidden from the interlocutors.

Rational dialogue is a laboratory for the formation of ethical convictions, which is why Plato, on whom Gadamer relies here, made his philosophical thought available to the public exclusively in the form of dialogues in which Sophocles, the master of rational dialogue, guides his interlocutors to test their opinions and establish whether they are capable of truth – that is, whether they are focused on discovering universally knowable and thus communicable facts. Opinions to which this does not apply are automatically ruled out as candidates for ethical guidelines, since ethics, as a discipline for establishing moral facts, seeks to ascertain what is good, neutral or evil for all people under certain conditions.

Whoever wishes to abandon the norm of truth and replace it with something else, elevating group membership above the quest for truth, is thus not only going against the basic rules of logic (such as the law of non-contradiction, which must be in force in any rational edifice of ideas) but also directly or indirectly undermining the moral order of values. Denying the possibility of an objective knowledge of facts, and hence truth, is not only an obvious error (because it is a false claim to knowledge that undermines itself); the attack on the possibility of objective knowledge and truth is also a moral error.

In some cases, verifiably false convictions about the foundations of the moral order of values are themselves moral errors.

The cultural relativism discussed and rejected in chapter 1 involves a number of errors about the order of values and leads to morally reprehensible systems of thought and action.

Stereotypes, Brexit and German nationalism

In recent years one has observed a constant production and reproduction of stereotypes taking place in every corner of the media in the wake of the Brexit referendum and its seemingly chaotic implementation. In the UK, stereotypes about European migrant workers based on stereotypes from the British working class were established and promoted. In the German media landscape, by contrast, there were stereotypes about Britons spreading fear and terror about the fatal consequences of leaving the EU.

It is certainly not my intention to take up the cause of any country leaving the EU, much less to play down the demagogic strategies of Brexit supporters and the British upper class. However, it is important to note that, in fact, barely anyone has an idea of what exact economic and general political consequences Brexit will have for all concerned, especially during the coronavirus pandemic. We can assume that some will no doubt profit from Brexit, though it remains to be seen how the additional profits of those enriching themselves will affect the Brexit losers (there will be both winners and losers on both sides of the divide).

Independently of these economic questions, the dissemination of stereotypes – including ones that are dangerous for certain groups of people – not only in the UK, but also in the rest of the EU (including Germany), has led to a new form of nationalism. Perhaps you will counter that there is no harm in a little nationalism, that there is nothing wrong with being proud of one's country, or such like. To bring light into the darkness of such concepts as 'nationalism' or 'patriotism', I will therefore define my terms more precisely.

Nationalism in its extreme form is the erroneous belief that one was born in the right country (within the borders of the right nation state) because one's country of origin is currently superior to all other countries in every relevant respect. Weaker forms of nationalism express themselves in the view that the country of which one is a citizen at least has some special strength. In this sense, one could be proud of German middle-tier businesses or the national football team (at least in 2014, or, depending on one's year of birth, also 1954 or 1990) and believe that Germany is truly unique in its economic or sporting strength, meaning that one was definitely fortunate to be born in the right place. A similarly minded American will prefer to rely on his country's military or worldwide dominance in basketball – though it is one of the stereotypes about Americans that they make a great deal of even the most trivial achievements and view them as indications of their leading position as a world power.

A still weaker form of nationalism is the belief that we are living today in a country that is upholding the democratic law-based state most stably in the face of the dangers to liberal democracy in Eastern Europe, the USA and elsewhere. On my travels, especially in the USA, I often hear that we Germans are now the centre of the free world because the connection between parliamentary democracy and a strong sense of values based on the concept of human dignity is still intact. This is a positive stereotype that must nonetheless be rejected, since Germany is by no means heaven on earth or the spearhead of the free world for all Germans.

Strictly speaking, no currently existing country is the spearhead of the free world. Every country has specific moral and legal deficits arising from its history. These deficits are covered up by nationalism. One example in Germany is the healthcare system. Many of us think that the German healthcare system is superior to that of the USA, which is known to us from television series such as *Breaking Bad* as unfair. The common view is that anyone with a severe illness, such as a form of cancer that is difficult to cure, will have to pay unimaginable sums in the USA. And the American system is supposedly accessible only to a few, is overpriced, inefficient, and so on, so one is glad to be German when one looks at the miserable conditions in the USA; the pictures of hospitals overwhelmed by coronavirus patients have reinforced this.

But this impression is in some ways deceptive. In particular, it conceals the sometimes alarming shortcomings of the German healthcare system. Anyone who lives outside of urban areas and is not privately insured receives considerably worse medical care than someone in a medium-sized city, while the large cities have problems of their own. We all know the long waits for important appointments, the many telephone calls one has to make to see a specialist, even in emergencies, and so on. Naturally there are deficits of every kind in the US system; I have no intention of suggesting otherwise. But these are by no means as extensive or far-reaching as people intuitively believe when they talk up our system in comparison to that of the USA.

However racist the USA may be, things are by no means better everywhere in Germany – recall the fictional Antje Kleinhaus (see p. 14 above). Unfortunately, everyday racism is widespread in Germany and is simply overlooked by most people. One aspect of this is that, in many parts of Germany, it is harder to rent an apartment if one has a Turkish or otherwise foreign-sounding surname than if one calls oneself Schmitz, Müller or Seehofer.

To cut a long story short: the impression that racism is not so widespread in Germany is false. It is enough to ask those who have been systematically, sometimes violently excluded, which applies not only to 'foreigners' or to Germans whose families have not been verifiably living in Germany for twenty generations. The very term 'German of X-origin' (such as 'Turkish-origin') is negatively discriminatory and is often used to justify disadvantaging those affected. That there is systematic racist discrimination in many areas of German life (though perhaps not all) becomes clear when one asks oneself some obvious questions: how many black or Muslim CEOs are there? How many non-white parliamentarians are there at the national and local level? This applies not only to dark-skinned people with African roots but also to people from Arab and Asian countries whose ancestors moved to Germany at some point.

The effectiveness of presumed communities

It is instructive for our time to fall back on a basic sociological operation that has, unfortunately, been mentioned only rarely in current debates about the concepts of people, nation, ethnic pluralism, race, identity, and the like. This basic operation comes from one of the founders of the disciplines of sociology and modern economics, Max Weber. He introduced it in his magnum opus *Economy and Society*, published posthumously and edited by his widow Marianne Weber[27] – who was, incidentally, herself an outstanding philosopher and national economist who made a considerable theoretical and political contribution to women's emancipation.

In his central work, Max Weber offers an impressive analysis of the 'ethnic group relations', which, already before the First and Second World Wars, showed that 'race', 'ethnicity', 'people' and 'nation' are socially effective, despite being 'unsuitable for a rigorous analysis'[28] (which would also mean that the rigorously mathematical discipline of economics, known as *Volkswirtschaftslehre* [theory of people's economy], should have its name changed). Weber points out that these collective terms are an expression of a merely 'presumed' commonality.[29] According to Weber, the 'belief in common ethnicity' [*ethnischer Gemeinschaftsglaube*][30] comes about primarily through 'the political community, no matter how artificially organized'.[31] Here Weber provides us with an instrument to explain the current trend towards a striking return of nationalist, racist or generally ethnic ways of thinking that indeed exist only as 'subjective belief', 'whether or not an objective blood relationship exists'.[32]

According to Weber, this misguided belief in commonality stems from a lack of **rationalization**. What he means by this is the planning of socioeconomic processes through essentially objectively transparent, bureaucratically documented procedures. In particular, rationalization differs from simply passing on traditional forms of behaviour and ways of life from generation to generation. Instead, it relies on our attempting to explain in appreciable terms why a habit should persist, or to abandon it if our reasons prove too weak. Modern industrialized and prosperous societies are based on this principle.

Without a constant rationalization, there can be no progress in modernity. If a morally reprehensible habit, such as the violent disadvantaging of a demographic group, comes under pressure and those who profit from the disadvantages have to justify themselves, they soon find themselves at a loss and start contradicting themselves. That is why people who benefit from massive injustice do not generally claim that they are objectively right; instead, they attempt to conceal the inequality by spreading myths and legends, for example by invoking the 'American dream' or time-honoured racist thought patterns. The discourse usually comes to an end when these thought patterns are questioned using scientific analyses; one does not usually convince far-right racists, climate sceptics or conspiracy theorists by pointing to objective facts or using better arguments, which often leads only to disregard or even violent outbursts.

Weber's diagnosis goes even deeper. He recognizes that the organization of those who rely on myths and legends about people, nation, blood community, and so forth, is actually based on rational principles, but that they reinterpret these by offering weak explanations for their own group membership that are simply poor because they rest on numerous verifiably false assumptions. While identity politics as a whole is reprehensible, its rational element consists in the fact that it attempts to justify group membership as a value. The error lies in basing this value on non-existent identities.

Weber expresses this in a characteristically precise fashion:

> This artificial origin of the belief in common ethnicity follows the familiar pattern of rational association turning into personal relationships. If rationally regulated action is not widespread, almost any association, even the most rational one, creates an overarching communal consciousness; this takes the form of a brotherhood on the basis of the belief in common ethnicity.[33]

Weber's words can be interpreted as follows: if immigrants who have met on an arduous journey and speak the same language arrive in a foreign country whose laws are unknown to them, it is rational for them subsequently to form groups to support one another in their unfamiliar surroundings. As the authorities and populace of the host country will view the immigrants as infiltrators in one way or another, it is sensible to join forces with people facing similar threats. This leads to the 'belief in common ethnicity', since people do not automatically recognize the rational basis of their actions. One function of sociology is to distinguish between *rational association* and such a partly illusory, certainly irrational *consciousness of common ethnicity*.

If one follows Weber's hypothesis, then nationalism, racism, invocations of peoplehood, tribal or even blood communities to justify ideas about the social order are spreading as resistance to the project of modernity, which seeks a rationally understandable distribution of goods, an optimization of processes with the aim of moving towards a solution to the global problems that affect all people. So it is not surprising that the nationalists have chosen figures such as the climate activist Greta Thunberg or publicly visible Green Party politicians in particular as targets. In this case, the evil of their actions not only lies specifically in the mostly verbal, but often physical attacks on people who work to help us overcome false thought patterns and recognize the decisive threat to humanity as a whole; it also lies in their suggestions of the wrong solutions for genuine problems (such as presenting the 'German' diesel motor as climate-friendly or wanting to protect the 'German' forest from wind turbines).

It is not only climate change, of course, that urgently requires a rational solution today; a fair distribution of resources and goods is equally important. Many of the gravest moral problems affecting us all in these times cannot be solved simply on the ground but demand activities across borders. Under the conditions of a global economic order that, paradoxically enough, is regionally controlled by nation states, the production chains of our consumer goods are full of morally reprehensible stages to which we, as consumers, still do not pay sufficient attention. These include factory farming, animal testing for purely scientific research, the production of cheap clothing, unsustainable building methods, and a good deal more. Much of what we do every day is systemically connected to immense suffering among humans and other life forms.

Resorting to myths and legends tied to nation, race or local cultures generally serves to relieve us of our own responsibility. This relief exacerbates the problems, because we refuse to seek a rational form of association that would involve examining not only the large, but especially also the small morally questionable transactions in which we are involved. For the large problems are the result of many individual actions that ultimately produce the systems threatening us, threatening humanity as a whole.

The society of populism

As members of human communities, we occupy ourselves day in, day out, with understanding and at times predicting the actions of our members. Each of us constantly asks ourselves what another person is expecting or thinking at a given moment, what they will do or say next. What we like most is to occupy ourselves with other people, which is useful because it distracts us from the question of what we ourselves actually expect, think, say and do. Since the others are also busy understanding us and predicting what we might do, however, we are somehow thrown back on ourselves in every human communication, as if the gaze that others direct at us were a kind of mirror.

Let us put ourselves in a banal everyday situation. Imagine you enter the local post office with the intention of buying a stamp for a letter to send directly. You stand in a queue and observe how the person currently being served is having a laboriously slow conversation with the postal worker about the various possibilities for sending a parcel. Everyone is listening to the conversation but pretending not to hear it. 'One's supposed to be discreet, after all!' You respond to this situation depending on your mood and interests: if you are in a particular hurry, you may feel a growing impulse to get annoyed and take action. Then one might clear one's throat, shift one's weight back and forth between one's feet, and maybe even try to push ahead in the queue by directly addressing the person in front. But one might also keep especially calm, to prove to oneself that one has one's impulses under control and understands the needs of one's fellow citizens.

Either way, you are forming an almost theatrical image of the situation. On your mental stage, the different acts are given particular roles: the typical old lady who can't just get on with it; the self-important businessman who's always pushing; the gum-chewing teenager who wants to buy a lighter; the mother with two infants who carefully signals that someone in her situation deserves to be let past; and the overenthusiastic employee who gives far too many details about different delivery options and slows everything down.

We have sophisticated ideas of roles and imagined sequences of actions that we have acquired over the course of our lives through the contributions of other people (parents, educators, friends, colleagues, writers, lovers, scientists, software engineers, etc.) and rehearsed in everyday life. The others do the same. Then, in an actual action situation, we incorporate our stage programme and it encounters those of the others. We assume that we have all arrived in the same play, and the name for this assumption is 'society'. **Society** is the totality of social exchanges that, in the eyes of the actors involved, ensures that there is ultimately a single play to whose realization they are all contributing with their respective actions.

In sociology one speaks of **complexity**, which means that society comes about and is maintained only by the fact that its individual actors, whom I call 'persons', have imagined ideas of what society is. But this means that society does not exist independently of our ideas about what it is and how it works. From this perspective, society exists only in the heads (or imaginations) of the players.[34]

Society is complex; it does not exist without the incalculable web of imagined ideas that is woven anew in every action situation, no matter how banal.

Society is constantly changing – sometimes quickly, sometimes slowly. How it changes depends fundamentally on what the persons do and how they assert themselves – that is, how they present themselves.

It is quite impossible to bring society to a halt by finally doing away with this complexity and setting up clear conditions. One can illustrate this using the everyday situation at the post office. The different persons present there all have their own imagined ideas of who they are and who they want to be, and these encounter the imagined ideas of the others. There is no possibility of clarifying the social situation independently of this. It is therefore impossible to predict which play will be performed at the post office.

Social ties can be exchanged for completely different ones at any time, a circumstance one calls **contingency**. For example, there could be a bank robbery at the post office, which would shatter the expectations of all present but occurs in every society – in that sense it would be normal, albeit bad for those affected. Moreover, society does not take place outside of nature, so someone might have a heart attack, for example, which would likewise clash with the rules at the post office. One can see from this that there is no 'normal' course of events during a visit to the post office. Every **social transaction** – every observable action that people take in a shared situation – can be predicted and controlled only in very approximate terms.

What is decisive about this reflection is that it shows there is no normality that applies to the whole of society. There is no overall social status quo, neither one to preserve nor one to change – only a web of social transactions that is incalculably complex for every person. Neither the federal chancellor nor the Bundestag, the secret services, Google, the economists, the socialists or the freemasons, not even the neoliberal global business elites and the pope, are capable of seeing through society, predicting it and controlling it accordingly.

A manifest problem of our time is that the completely abstruse notion of an overall social normality is directly and indirectly evoked by parties, social networks, associations and other sociopolitically active groups in order to justify courses of action. Let us refer to this problem by what is now its common name: *populism*. It is especially fitting to speak of **populism** when the imagined, but currently non-existent overall social normality is associated with 'the people' [*Volk*] (Lat. *populus*). Populism believes that there is a normal people on one side and an interference factor on the other. One example is the widespread German notion of some essentially German society associated – especially since the Second World War – with Christianity, sometimes extended to include Judaism. So it is German if the church bells toll on Sundays, if one can eat schnitzel, pork knuckle and *Currywurst*, if the city centre looks like those of Heidelberg or Munich, if one drinks beer, if one is a member of the rifle club or carnival society, if one occasionally wears traditional garb, and so on. There are also the 'high culture' variations on this, which invoke Goethe, Hölderlin and Wagner, somewhat reluctantly Beethoven, but also Nietzsche, Heidegger and lately Peter Sloterdijk (whom some AfD 'thinkers' unfortunately cite as one of their own). Sometimes German Idealism is added to this canon (paradigmatically represented by the names Kant, Fichte, Schelling and Hegel) so that one can feel like a member of the 'nation of poets and thinkers'.[35] A former fellow student with this form of populist mentality recently told me that he revered the great German physicists, naming Heisenberg and Planck, but not the thoroughly German, Ulm-born Einstein. When I asked why, he replied that Einstein was Jewish as well as Swiss.

To be clear: each of the figures named (including Nietzsche and Heidegger) can be credited with artistic, scientific and philosophical achievements that are outstanding in world history. There is scarcely an author who writes more seductively in German than Nietzsche, Hölderlin penned major poems, Wagner was a compositional genius, and some of Sloterdijk's writings are stylistic masterpieces. The texts of German Idealism are in any case among the greatest philosophical work ever done.[36] Even Heidegger, a dyed-in-the-wool Nazi, cannot simply be left aside, for – unlike Alfred Rosenberg, Adolf Hitler or Joseph Goebbels – he left behind major philosophical writings that influenced Hannah Arendt, in my view the most important political theorist of the twentieth century, as well as many other progressive minds, including such diverse thinkers as Jürgen Habermas, Hans Jonas and Jacques Derrida.

The problem of populism is its production of an imaginary, distorted picture of normality. It skips intermediate stages and overlooks details, such as the question of whether Islam belongs to Germany. There are Muslims on the territory of the modern German state as well as Jews, Christians and atheists, and this has been the case for many centuries. Fun fact: before Protestantism even existed, before the Reformation, there were already Muslims in North America (mostly as slaves). Naturally there was also Hispanic immigration before the Anglo-Americans, as the Spaniards (and not the Anglo-Saxons) explored the majority of the 'New World' – to say nothing of the fact that there were already people on the American continent before the Catholic Spanish and their Muslim slaves.

The 'normal Germany' wished for by populists never existed. Nor is there such a thing as *the* elites that set themselves apart from the people, even if there are obviously very rich and influential people who use their power and their control of the media landscape to manipulate less rich, less well-trained and less influential persons. There is no true 'normal German' – or, more precisely: there is a muddled notion of the normal German, but it is never clearly articulated by those who cling to it, otherwise they would find that they themselves are not a homogeneous group. Not even the paradigmatically populist representatives of the AfD are homogeneous: Björn Höcke and Alice Weidel have far less in common than some would like to admit, which would become apparent if the AfD had to nominate a candidate for chancellor or were part of a government. The same applies to the CSU, the Left Party, the Green Party, the SPD and every other party: there are certain basic patterns that give a party its character, but this does not mean there is a homogeneous party opinion. Thilo Sarrazin is (still) in the SPD alongside Gerhard Schröder and Kevin Kühnert; Boris Palmer is (still) in the Green Party alongside Annalena Baerbock.[37] Not even the Nazi Party was homogeneous; rather, it was internally divided and split into camps that plotted against one another, as the National Socialist dictatorship was anything but a normal state of affairs that pleased the great majority of people. In this, the parties reflect only the nature of society in general. The people as a yardstick for normality quite simply do not exist, and never have. The same applies to so-called ordinary people, the working class and similar constructions.

The term 'populism' has many meanings, of course, and it is quite unclear what exactly this political catchword means each time it is used. What is clear is that some are in favour of it and others are against it – though none of them are really sure what exactly they are supporting or opposing. There is an urgent need for a clarification of this word, which has meanwhile generated an extensive body of political science, sociological and philosophical work that we do not need to discuss in detail here.[38]

The idea that there is some overall social normality that is usually imagined to have been realized in the recent or distant past, and in which every person can play a well-defined part, is verifiably wrong.

In my view, this is a central aspect and defect of populism: populism does not understand society. It views it as something that objectively exists and is independent of how individual actors behave and constantly change and reinterpret their roles, which populism would like to fix in a certain form. One can recognize populism in the fact that it sketches and disseminates mostly clumsy and vague role models that are meant to relieve us from the burden of interpreting our own roles.

One example is the family. There is a variety of populism that believes in a kind of normal family (mum, dad, two to four children, a home of one's own with a garden and carport) that must be protected and supported because it constitutes the heart of society, the cell of sexual reproduction or whatever. Such argumentation overlooks a great many things. Firstly, there are countless ways in which such families can be dysfunctional. Every small family has problems of some kind. But there are naturally also singles, homosexuals, die-hard bachelors, large families, patchwork families, orphans, refugee families and many other forms in which humans live together.

Human life, with all its risks and different stages, cannot be straightened out by trying to impose some contingent family structure as a guideline, which is to overlook everything that we know from psychology and sociology about people and how they live together. There is simply no such thing as overall social normality. This does not mean that we should not particularly protect and support certain family formats because they need protection and targeted support; but that is a different issue.

The contradictions of left-wing identity politics

In the light of the many processes of moral progress currently taking place (#MeToo, Fridays for Future, the at times very successful integration of Syrian refugees in Germany, and much more), the real threat of a new right-wing extremism that is an expression of a spreading racism is particularly striking.

Because of this, the word 'populism' is often wrongly associated with right-leaning and regressive party programmes. But the counter-measures of left-wing pluralist identity politics, which seeks to give voice to minorities simply because they are minorities, are equally incoherent. As stated above (pp. 157ff.), not every minority deserves our moral respect.

Unfortunately, the left uses the same types of relativist manoeuvres in the culture war of identities that are familiar from the right-wing populist denial of reality: both sides stand up for the protection of identities without any adequate, universally valid reasons. The one side protects mostly affluent white Anglo-American citizens and their industrial and financial foundations, while the other protects the whole rainbow of identities that it considers important, but not the white Anglo-American citizens. They see these as the enemy, the representatives of a dangerous patriarchy.

Yet both sides are concerned primarily with defending certain identities against others, not with supporting arguments in a way that makes it clear to all which groups of people are systematically excluded when they should be heard. The state of today's North American identity politics is based on cultural relativism, which developed on both the left and the right from postmodern edifices of ideas. The political discourse is staged as a culture war: either races (as in the Trump camp) or economic classes (as in Bernie Sanders's camp) are incited against one another. The relativist contradictions have likewise been evident on both sides – when, for example, Cornel West made the following arguments at a Sanders event in New Hampshire: 'I don't care what colour you are. I don't care what your national identity is. I don't care what region you are from. You're a human being. We got a deep Jewish brother named Bernie Sanders who's bringing us together!' Why, one wonders, is it significant that Sanders is Jewish? This is a questionable identification in a context in which neo-fascism (of which West accuses Trump) is being played off against universalism.

West continues towards disastrous self-contradiction when he proclaims in a preacher's voice: 'A neo-fascist believes in the rule of big military and big money, dividing people up by their colour, by their class, by their sexual orientation, by their religion and non-religion, to ensure we're at each other's throats, rather than confronting the elites at the top.' In just a few steps, this argumentation revokes the universalism previously proclaimed and instead calls for a war of the supposed masses against the business elite; thus West divides people up into conflicting groups in the same way as his opponent, the alleged neo-fascist Trump. In this deeply incoherent way of thinking, the difference between right and left consists almost entirely in how one plays off groups of people against one another; thus both sides of this absolute political battle accept the rule of the law of the strongest rather than seeking an overarching dissolution of the conflict line to achieve a structural involvement of *all*.

This example displays an almost uncanny *coincidentia oppositorum*, the confluence of radical opposites on an all-important point of commonality. Right- and left-wing identity politics mobilize groups against one another, undermining the foundations of universalism so that they can pursue their respective interests in the political arena without regard for the interests of those they reject, and in some cases violently exclude. It is only seemingly more progressive to attack the rich or the 'elites at the top' in the name of the more economically vulnerable masses than

– like Trump – to serve the interests of the USA in world politics and the interests of rich industrialists through tax concessions and other measures. The rich deserve the same moral respect and consideration in the processes of the democratic law-based state as the poor. The universal foundations of freedom, equality and solidarity do not mean that a majority which is disadvantaged in relation to a minority automatically has the right to establish systems of disadvantage for the rich minority. That taxation for the extremely rich has hitherto been unjust, especially as it is easier for them to conceal their financial flows from the authorities, is another matter – though it is a matter not of waging war on the rich but of achieving a universally just, sustainable distribution of resources.

Let there be no misunderstanding: the extreme economic inequality that is especially rampant in such countries as the USA, Brazil, Argentina, Chile, China or India, which accumulates veritably unimaginable wealth in a tiny section at the top, a wealth that is not put to use through suitable state measures to free people from poverty, hardship and despair, is morally reprehensible. That is why the idea of a social market economy is morally superior to the American-style unfettered capitalism often labelled as 'neoliberalism'. An economic system that is implemented by the state in such a way that millions of people are systematically forced into poverty, and cannot escape it through their own actions, reveals moral ills that must be overcome.

This is not achieved through political battles unless the combatants show their moral cards as universalist arguments and justify them accordingly. A fairer taxation of the extremely rich, for example, is undoubtedly necessary, but this does not mean one has to fight against them.

Brazil is an especially impressive example, as it thrived primarily due to the existence of family scholarships (*bolsa familia*) for a little over a decade, thanks to Luiz Inácio Lula da Silva, who was the country's president from 2002 to 2010. After some clumsy economic steps taken by his successor Dilma Vana Rousseff, some of them tainted by corruption, 2013 marked the beginning of a gigantic political intrigue that ultimately brought to power Jair Messias Bolsonaro, a man of profoundly anti-democratic thoughts and actions, who put his main rival Lula in prison with the support of Sergio Moro, his minister of justice and public security. Instead of introducing a set of social measures that builds on the positive experiences of the Lula period, Bolsonaro relies on an aggressive economic policy that exploits the natural resources of the Brazilian rainforest ruthlessly, without regard for the indigenous population of the Amazon region, in order to make quick and dirty deals that enrich only a small, already affluent section of the population. Meanwhile, the destitute inhabitants of the favelas are kept under control with brutal military methods and the slim middle class is sucked dry.

These and similar examples of a ruthless capitalism devoid of moral understanding are clearly reprehensible. Yet this in no way means that capitalism as such is reprehensible, as long as one does not define what exactly the terms 'capitalism' and 'neoliberalism' actually mean and why the creation of added value, capital and property under the conditions of a market economy is inherently morally reprehensible (or, as Karl Marx and Friedrich Engels argued, automatically leads to the self-destruction of the economic system, with disastrous consequences).

Whoever attacks the elites while arguing the case for universalism is contradicting themselves, for then what is being propagated is not universalism but, rather, a statistical pseudo-universalism of the crowd preferred by leftist politicians such as West. In this respect, left- and right-wing identity politics are equally dishonest and wrong and are historically indebted to the same patterns of argumentation based on the postmodern abandonment of truth, facts and knowledge. This remains the case even if such politicians as Sanders rightly appeal far more than Donald Trump to the readers of my book (and to myself). This should have no bearing on my argumentation, as it is not a matter of mobilizing sympathies for the African-American Cornel West and the Jewish Bernie Sanders against the old white Protestant men. Old white Protestant men like Donald Trump, or indeed – to name a more positive example – the head of the Council of the German Protest Church, Heinrich Bedford-Strohm, initially deserve the same moral respect as other segments of the population.

Everyone is the other: from identity politics to difference politics (and beyond)

Our capacity for moral understanding is based on our being human. This being human has at least two interwoven, non-identical aspects. On the one hand, humans are animals: our organism has a particular structure that can be examined using the methods of evolutionary biology and human medicine. Our organism consists of cells organized in clusters whose processes are coordinated in the organism as a whole. We have only a rudimentary understanding of how the many systems that form our organism (the cardiovascular system, the central nervous system, our digestion, and so on) are all connected; neither biology nor medicine are anywhere close to knowing everything about the human organism. However, what we definitely know thanks to the great revolutions in molecular biology since the mid-twentieth century is that, as organisms, we are actually subject to the same principles as other animal species. I refer to this side of animality as our **survival form**.[39]

The human survival form is universal: it unites all human animals. The minimum conclusion from this is the validity of a *biological universalism*, which stipulates that we are all equal before nature. The consequences of this for the cultural and intellectual sphere should not be underestimated. Because of our biological nature, all 'neurotypical' people – which means the vast majority of newborn children – can learn any language as their native tongue. A child just born in China could easily become an outstanding poet in Arabic or German. Superficial phenotypic attributes such as hair colour, skin type, eye colour or body size have no direct effects on the dynamic wiring of the central nervous system (the 'brain', as we call it). The brain is very malleable; one speaks of **plasticity**, which is a foundation for the basic human ability to settle within any cultural or intellectual surroundings.

Biological universalism has direct moral effects, since it falsifies racist stereotypes from the outset. Germans do not have any genetic predisposition to musicality, profundity or precision, any more than Arabs have a genetic predisposition to Islam or Swabians to cleanliness. Swabian children do not automatically become thrifty Christians, nor are Bavarian children predestined from birth to consume *Weisswurst* and *Weissbier*.

However, it is wrong to conclude from this that humans are merely an animal in the sense of a particular species whose conditions of production and reproduction can be explored by molecular biology. Humans differ from bacteria, vertebrates and other mammals in so many ways that one can adduce numerous criteria to show that we are not only gradually but fundamentally different from other animals.

Only humans have cinema, airlines, internet access, business finance, literature, social media, automobiles, factory farming and, most importantly, an understanding of the fact that they are animals of a particular kind.

But there is a specific human trait that represents the other side of our being human, and to which I will refer with the traditional philosophical term 'spirit'.[40] Generally speaking, **spirit** is the capacity to lead a life according to a notion of who we are and who we want to be. We humans locate ourselves at some point of the universe, history, the animal kingdom, culture, the social order, and so on, and whatever we do always stands in relation to this location.

Presumably, lions do not think about whether they should become vegetarians or whether they could migrate to a different region with particularly tasty gazelles. Nor do lions practise astrophysics, and they probably have no idea that they exist within a gigantic universe. They have never heard of quantum theory or Greek tragedy. In short, lions do not have leonology, but humans have anthropology.

Anyone who denies that we humans are categorially different from all other known life forms on our planet on account of our knowledge and the associated achievements is thus denying obvious facts. The human being is not simply one animal among others but, rather, an animal whose cognitive faculties exceed those of the entire animal kingdom: no other animal practises science or makes linguistically coded, historically cumulative knowledge claims. And no other animal is capable of higher morality, and thus systematic changes of behaviour in the light of moral insight. Lions do not become vegans, as they do not realize that this is better for the climate, and hence for living beings as a whole.

This does not give us the right to treat other animals in cruel or degrading ways, of course, though some organisms (such as bacteria or locusts that appear as infestations) force us to do precisely that.[41] Here I am concerned not with the scope of animal ethics but, rather, with the fact that we humans, unlike the other animals, are on the whole spiritual beings. Everyone uses their capacity to locate themselves in reality in different ways. We each determine ourselves in our own way, which is also connected to the socioeconomic contexts to which we belong. A virologist perceives reality differently from a concert pianist or a North Korean dictator.

So there are a variety of self-perceptions. They are all closely connected to our **existential identity**, our respective individual idea of the meaning of life. Someone who is genuinely religious, for example (whatever world religion they follow), believes that the purpose of this earthly life is to attain a higher form of salvation for the existence after it. True lived religion does not consist merely of following rituals such as going to services, making sacrifices to the gods or donating for the needy; it demands a great deal more of us, namely to do everything humanly possible to attain the goal of salvation.

Existential identities bring us into contact with the sacred. Unfortunately, pure economic and technological progress is sacred to some and the consumption of luxury goods to others. There is no one to whom nothing is sacred, no one with no implicit or explicit conception of their salvation. To Donald Trump, his fortune, his hotels, his golf clubs and his family are sacred; he could no doubt say what he considers the purpose of his life if one had the opportunity for a genuine tête-à-tête with him.

The general freedom to lead one's life in accordance with a conception of oneself, of who we are and want to be as humans and individuals, is an **anthropological constant**. It distinguishes humans as spiritual beings and unites us with all other humans to form a moral community. This constant, this being human itself, leads to moral rights and duties: the kingdom of ends. The English philosopher Bernard Williams sums this up in his brilliant essay *Morality: An Introduction to Ethics*:

> If there were some title or role with which standards were necessarily connected and which, by necessity, a man could not fail to have nor dissociate himself from, then there would be some standards which a man would have to recognize as determinants of his life, at least on pain of failing to have any consciousness at all of what he was. There is certainly one 'title' – for good reason, we can scarcely speak here of a 'role' – which is necessarily inalienable, and that is the title of 'man' itself.[42]

Because universal, being human, which consists of both biological and spiritual levels, is the foundation of our capacity for moral judgement, it is highly dangerous that superficial stereotypes which are verifiably false in sociological terms are currently resulting in the invention and dissemination of social identities that distract from the existence of human universals, which, in addition to our biological nature, include our existential, inalienable need for the meaning of life. The meaning of life is not simply naked survival but reveals itself to us only once we have created the conditions in which we can do more than merely survive.

This is one of the many reasons why people flee from situations in which naked survival is the only concern left; they would rather face dangers that are unimaginable for many of us, travelling thousands of kilometres with their families and then attempting to reach the Greek islands or Italy in dinghies, despite knowing that they will immediately be confronted with the systemic violence of the European border authorities.

Our manifold social and existential identities are distorted expressions of a universal identity: that of being human. This follows from a philosophical reflection:

> Everyone defines the meaning of life somewhat differently, since people have different levels of knowledge, different perspectives, experiences, feelings, relationships, as well as a different position in the dynamic fabric of society. Each person is thus different from every other. But this very fact is something that unites us all – an anthropological constant – because we all define ourselves differently, but, in doing so, we use exactly the same faculty, namely the faculty of self-definition – that is, spirit.

We could not be different from others if we did not have a great deal in common with them. The core of our universal humanity, our being human, goes far beyond the biological universals. People experience joy and sorrow in similar situations, feel sympathy with others, fall in love, enjoy listening to music (whatever kind), like to distract themselves from mere survival, engage in sports, intoxicate themselves with various substances and have more or less well-founded convictions about the position of humans in the cosmos, convictions that would not exist without art, religion and science. Humans are much more similar than the optics of misleading identity politics would suggest.

The first step towards moral progress beyond identity politics is therefore **difference politics**. This consists in not only tolerating the diversity of existential identities – which is already indispensable merely for the division of labour – but in fundamentally understanding that everyone is different. Difference politics places us all in relation to universal being-human and exceeds the boundaries of the self-identification by which we set ourselves apart from others.

There is no absolutely normal, absolutely exemplary life, no objectifiable standard for a good life. No one has to be literally like Buddha, Jesus, Steve Jobs, Mother Teresa, Mao Zedong or Gandhi (or whomever one chooses as one's hero). If everyone actually did what Jesus did, we would have long died out, since Jesus himself rejected any family life out of the belief that the end times had come and people should prepare themselves for the kingdom of heaven. The same applies to other saints and founders of religions, including worldly 'religions' that see the meaning of life in chains of material value creation (something on which Steve Jobs and Mao Zedong completely agree).

Difference politics does not believe that some minorities who have suffered injustice in the past should therefore be morally privileged now; rather, it views every moral claim in context. It attempts to eliminate inequalities and advance universal equalizing mechanisms in the framework of cosmopolitics. To be sure, it is a sign of social injustice that we still have a massive gender pay gap in Germany. It is an obvious moral flaw in our distribution system that women, on average, are paid less than men for the same work. But one does not solve this simply by giving women better jobs and higher salaries than men for a while. One can achieve an important equalization via quotas – a first, justified step that uses the methods of identity politics. The next step, difference politics, consists in taking into account what we know about the lives of women in order to create a distribution system that is fair in its totality.

Let us make this seemingly abstract thought more concrete: many women (though obviously not all) become mothers in the course of their lives. And as long as we desire the continued existence of humanity, this should not be avoided. Obviously, the fabrication of offspring in futuristic clinics where children are bred in laboratories is not a morally justifiable strategy for solving the gender-specific wage gap. So it will remain the case that many women will be mothers. This means that we must take into account the psychological and biological aspects of motherhood in suitable socioeconomic ways. More concretely still:

when women apply for jobs (whether they are already mothers or not), we should at least give them financial security for a certain number of years in which they can live out their maternal role as they see fit for themselves and their families, without any adverse effects on their career options and pensions. As long as there is no financial coverage for state-guaranteed worry-free and perfect childcare (from 8 am to 6 pm) for all, we should even pay women higher salaries than men, because they are systematically disadvantaged in their pension expectancy owing to pregnancy and childcare.

The same applies to fathers, of course, if they take paternity leave, reduce their working hours or are single parents. The rules are different for fathers in some areas, however, because they do not become pregnant and have different (by no means less valuable, simply different) bonds with their children, some of them biologically and some socio-economically explicable. We can take this into account to the advantage of mothers, who would therefore need slightly modified rights because there is quite simply a biological side to pregnancy.

In short, if one considers the relevant facts of motherhood and the hitherto inadequate state childcare in Germany, we should actually pay women higher salaries than men at present. This must not influence the selection process, however, so applications should be completely anonymized (and thus gender-neutral) to prevent employers from making cynical calculations based on the new wage structure.

Another case of difference politics became clear again in the corona-virus crisis: the professions supporting our whole social system (medical staff, public administration, food supply, digital and analogue infra-structure, and so on) are often worse paid than those that are not only completely superfluous but may even be dangerous. These include Formula One drivers or biological weapons manufacturers.

The point is not that everyone should be paid the same or receive an unconditional basic income (although I personally consider it a good idea, but that is another matter). Equality means not that everyone should receive exactly the same for the same or similar work, but that we take a look at otherness and, on the basis of this, carry out redistributions based on universal criteria that relate to all people.

The first and most urgent goal of difference politics, however, is to overcome racism, xenophobia, misogyny and similar phenomena. For many of the morally unacceptable inequalities I have mentioned are expressions of dangerous and verifiably misguided ways of thinking. There are not only biological viruses; there are also moral viruses that infiltrate our thought processes with misguided patterns.

To recognize these and fight them appropriately, we need other experts than natural scientists, economists, technicians and professional politicians: in the course of the urgently needed new enlightenment, we require a new orientation and positioning of the humanities in order to explore the complex, historically variable forms of human otherness. This otherness must be represented in the public sphere, so that we are all constantly aware that social normality can never consist in some fictional national unity, which may even coincide with races, genes and gender, attaining political dominance. Moral progress in dark times thus also means the right of all people to ethical education and participation in public debates with a sound basis in contemporary philosophy and humanities, as we will see (see below, pp. 239ff.).

Indifference politics: on the way to colour-blindness

If one asks oneself what steps a society can take for the realization of ethical goals – that is, for moral progress – it is indispensable to formulate one's goals as clearly as possible. Without these, one cannot make any fallible knowledge claims in ethics.

One approach to overcoming racism is often termed 'colour-blindness'. This would be a condition in which people no longer identified other people's skin type as a special attribute by which to divide people into groups. That this is possible is demonstrated by the fictional example of the Earlanders. The Earlanders classify people based on the length of their earlobes and develop forms of identity politics that determine the distribution of resources in Earland. Not being Earlanders, we find this rather absurd. Analogously, the goal of moral progress in the area of racism must be to overcome completely the impression that there are morally relevant difference between people that can be measured in terms of race, always bearing in mind that races do not actually exist. There is racism, but no races – just as there were witch hunts, but no witches.[43] Unfortunately, race is even registered in official documents in the USA, and so I learned at some point that I am classified as 'Caucasian', which in official US bureaucracy denotes a different race from 'Hispanic'. White Spaniards thus belong to a different race from equally white Norwegians. All of that is completely scientifically untenable and absurd. It is no help to be aware that the meaning of the word 'race' in contemporary English [with its strong sociological component] does not have exactly the same meaning as *Rasse* in German [which is primarily biological]; this does not change the fact that neither of them exists.

The US system of classification already contributes substantially to racism, because it discriminates on the basis of racial notions (whether positively or negatively). This is comparable to asking if someone is a witch for official papers, even if the intention is to use this information as a way of somehow compensating for past cruelty towards witches through positive discrimination. The non-moral facts prove that there are no races, and the moral facts about what one should or not do cannot contradict them. Consequently, there can be no moral facts concerning a fair treatment of races, since there are no races that would deserve moral respect – neither white nor black nor any other colour.

At this point, the question often arises of how we can achieve colour-blindness; after all, people with particular skin types have experienced, and continue to experience, systemic and at times severe negative discrimination and disadvantage. I myself have given numerous seminars at various universities in the USA, and less than 1 per cent of participants were African American – even at progressive institutions such as Berkeley, New York University and the especially well-conceived New School for Research in New York. So the question is this: how can one correct this imbalance without setting up special programmes that employ positive discrimination and support to ensure that people of colour are involved fairly in the distribution of symbolic and material resources?

At this stage of the discussion one sometimes hears the argument that there are entire commemorative cultures as well as culinary, musical and many other forms of traditions that were connected via racial classifications in the past and deserve to be recognized in their individuality. In some conversations, US colleagues classified as African American have tried to convince me that positive discrimination is the right way, as they saw a danger that the resistance suppressed in the past, without which there might never have been any moral progress in this area, would simply be forgotten.

There is a response to this important objection. It is the task of *historiography* to consider and adequately honour those oppressed in the past, their cultural products and their resistance. This commemorative culture is crucial for the consolidation of moral progress.

This is demonstrated by the German case of the Holocaust. We must never forget it, as it is probably the most grievous example of radical evil. Underlining the contribution of those who were oppressed and murdered is therefore decisive for moral progress. Without Jewish intellectual life, there would never have been an Enlightenment; consider such thinkers as Moses Mendelssohn or the brilliant philosopher Salomon Maimon, who contributed decisively to German Idealism, to say nothing of Baruch de Spinoza, one of the most important philosophers of all time, without whose writings the modern Enlightenment would have been inconceivable. It is well known that Muslims also made great contributions to European high culture (including the Enlightenment). All of this is documented in literary works, such as Gotthold Ephraim Lessing's plays *The Jews* and *Nathan the Wise*. Great Muslim thinkers such as Ibn Rushd (Averroes) or Ibn Sina (Avicenna), to name only the most famous, advanced philosophy and science no less than Aristotle, whose writings they fortunately passed on. In so doing, they advanced logic and ethics and enriched them with their own arguments and thought processes – to give at least a tiny idea of the complex history of Islamic history and silence. The notion that Islam is somehow a particularly anti-enlightened, even anti-scientific, religion is completely untenable. It is equally important to give full recognition to the pre-colonial African thought traditions, which were aggressively wiped out by the brutal European colonialists because they were deemed 'primitive'.

Certainly, commemorative culture and historiography can easily be employed in the wrong way to produce complex stereotypes through careful selection. As mentioned above, there were already Muslims in North America before Protestantism was even invented, which makes it absurd for there to be a common belief that the USA was a Protestant project in any relevant sense. This is a crassly one-sided emphasis on one part of factual history, and it must be corrected in order to make it clear that cultural otherness was always already present, and thus to do away with the misleading fiction of a pure primal state using historical evidence and a corresponding new commemorative culture.

Nonetheless, this important and justified aim should not make us lose sight of the goal of colour-blindness. People who were massively affected in the past by systemic negative discrimination because they were assigned to a (non-existent) race do not consequently have a moral right to maintain racism in order to balance out that past damage and to make visible the ongoing damage caused by malign habits of thinking and action (especially neo-Nazi ideology). The better way is to discredit and ultimately remove the false interpretive framework, the entire thought pattern of racism, through research and the political implementation thereof. For example, there should be neither black nor white identity politics, as both are equally wrong and have caused damage in various contexts. The same applies for other forms, such as the active Hindu racism towards very fair-skinned and very dark-skinned people, as these have low or non-existent positions in the racist caste system.[44] The very idea that racism is automatically directed at dark-skinned people misses the heart of the matter and induces people to take steps that are unsuitable for genuinely overcoming it. Racism and xenophobia, but also phenomena such as misogyny, are thought patterns that lead to morally reprehensible, indeed evil actions.

If we look once more at black–white racism, we see that Germany is currently faring no better than the USA – simply differently. The public sphere in which our society stages its self-identity is decidedly white and full of clichés that are presented as historical normality. Newsreaders, the absolute majority of German celebrities, as well as the guests on talk shows that play an important part in shaping public opinion in Germany are almost always white. This passes on and cements role models and norms, even when there are no bad intentions at work.

The important thing is to understand and acknowledge how effective the symbolic representation of social conditions is. The image of society that we form both consciously and unconsciously, the many individual actions and their social interconnections, contributes to shaping society. In the symbolic order of things, thought patterns emerge that we must analyse and examine critically. Sociocritical analyses, especially those concerning our own immediate surroundings, are indispensable for moral progress.

FOUR

Moral Progress in the Twenty-First Century

Moral progress generally consists in recognizing and revealing moral facts that have been partly concealed. There are no moral facts that are completely concealed or fundamentally unknowable; because ethics is concerned with ourselves as human beings, with what *we* should or should not do, it is always possible to bring good and evil to light.

Self-evident moral truths are the basis for the uncovering of moral facts. These result partly from our human, social way of life and partly from historical experiences. Because of the complexity of our systems of action, we are always fallible in the application of our knowledge of values: we can make wrong moral judgements. There is therefore no guarantee that we will always stay on the path of moral progress towards a better future.

Reality always goes beyond everything we currently know about it. It is never completely knowable. This means that some non-moral facts always remain hidden from us, which is an important source of errors in moral reflection. For if we knew all non-moral facts and were able to employ our well-practised moral compass for self-evident moral truths, it would be possible to act in morally reprehensible ways only if we had malign intentions.

The possibility of moral progress is closely tied to moral realism; progress can be understood as a form of discovery, which includes bringing forth new moral ideas. The problem with this view is that it can invite **historical relativism**: because what we consider morally necessary may not have been morally necessary at some point, we cannot morally reproach those who acted and thought differently in the past. In the eyes of the historical relativist, the fact that the ancient Greeks subjected women and children to systematic and regular sexual harassment without the majority seeing anything wrong with it points simply to a form of cultural difference, not an error.

But this view is irreconcilable with an ontology of values, which works on the premise that it is in the nature of sexual harassment that – on closer inspection of all the circumstances, at the latest – is morally reprehensible in all cases as a form of violence and oppression. This was no different in the past but was systematically concealed by power structures that prevented the weaker party from fundamentally changing conditions through resistance, or even simply condemning the abuse.

As the discovery of moral facts is always also about ourselves as free spiritual beings, moral progress takes place not in the medium of quantitative natural-science or social-science modelling but at the level of our self-knowledge.

Moral progress can never be achieved through algorithms, computer simulations or some experiments, because these methods partially distort the human spirit.[1]

It is one of the errors of our time, a systemic weakness of twentieth- and twenty-first-century ideology, to believe that we could fully grasp ourselves in the medium of natural-science and social-science modelling. This error causes us to lose our moral compass and no longer know what we should and should not do, because we lose sight of the relevant source of knowledge: our moral insight and self-knowledge, which developed in the medium of intellectual history.

The science-oriented ideology of our time, which holds that all knowledge ultimately has the form of natural-science models and can be represented in quantitative relations, contributes substantially to darkening our horizon; from this perspective, one cannot understand how objective and simultaneously spirit-independent moral facts, facts that we cannot recognize through natural-science modelling and empirical studies, can even exist.

Another reason why we live in dark times in which the project of the Enlightenment and the democratic law-based state are endangered is that social media, artificial intelligence and other digital distortions of human spirit are rampant, sometimes actively and purposefully undermining the truth, facts, knowledge and ethics.

On the basis of scientific-technological progress, our highly modern society of knowledge in the twenty-first century has produced systems that block our moral progress by eroding our faith in truth, knowledge, reality and our conscience through fake news, digital surveillance, propaganda and cyberwars. This is the paradox of our time, and it is therefore urgently necessary to place a suitable conception of the human being at the centre of moral reflection so that we can correct this imbalance.

Many moral facts have always been completely obvious; there have always been self-evident moral truths that are almost never questioned, and not even noticed most of the time. There have also, however, always been individual people and groups of people who profited from dismissing those facts as wrong or simply ignoring them. Self-evident moral truths – for example, that enslavement is reprehensible and racism is vile – can be systematically concealed by dehumanizing people and thus presenting violence and cruelty as justified. This is a central function of political propaganda, manipulation, ideology and other forms of what is known in ideology theory as 'false consciousness'.[2]

In our current world-historical situation, this function is carried out especially by the social networks and search engines, whose algorithms are designed to keep us glued to our screens. They make us systematically dependent, practically addicted to information and news of any kind; it is secondary whether this information and news is actually truthful. All that matters is for us simultaneously to consume and produce data in order to improve the algorithms of the tech monopolies: the more data we make available to the social networks through our use of them, the better they can feed our addiction to getting more. Click by click, like by like, we produce an invisible digital drug.

In the course of its massive expansion over the last thirty years, the internet has developed into a machine for hurling ideology around: it spreads a great deal of ideological distortions and half-truths that keep us, the consumers, constantly busy. The danger of this process is that self-evident moral truths, such as the value of respect towards people we do not (yet) know, are rendered null and void online. This is proved by the comment sections of every social medium as well as those of traditional press portals. The willingness to insult strangers without any attempt to understand them is considerably greater than in the classic reader's letter format; this is simply because, online, there is no time lag or filter between the impulse to express one's opinion and the possibility of immediately publicizing it.

The internet – along with economic globalization, which accelerated in parallel with the former's expansion – has contributed massively to darkening our spirit. To a certain extent, we have, step by step, lost our ability to orient ourselves towards an ethical conception of the human being. It is no coincidence that the hope of human progress spreading across the world through the movement of goods after the end of the Cold War was disappointed; for one cannot further human progress – which always means moral progress too – by using chains of exploitation for the production of banal consumer goods for wealthy nations.

In addition, there have been numerous wars since the 1990s under the pretext of supposed democratization. This includes the two Gulf wars in particular, as well as other targeted interventions by the superpower USA that have cast the Middle East and North Africa into turmoil. Such objectively unjustifiable actions, which have been carried out by every single US president of the last thirty years (including Barack Obama), are accompanied by lies and half-truths. Their function is to make morally reprehensible attacks on the sovereignty of other countries (especially murder via drones and digital warfare) seem justified.

The darkening of humanity's moral horizon is thus by no means only the work of Russian hackers or Chinese propaganda, though both no doubt also play an increasingly important part. It has been advanced primarily and deliberately over decades by US digital monopolies and research centres whose business models are closely interwoven with brain research, behavioural economics and computer science in order to make the largest possible number of users addicted – a profitable enterprise.[3]

Naturally Chinese platforms have meanwhile become equally skilled at this and, on top of that, are supported by a dictatorial regime. Nonetheless, we should not forget that Russians and Chinese are not only hackers but often also victims of state campaigns and sometimes brutal interventions. Here too, then, it is not a case of two opposing, homogeneous groups and cultures – if we failed to see this, we would quickly revert to the idea that there is some form of culture war between value systems after all.

The threat of new cyberwars and digital surveillance dictatorships, as real as it unfortunately is, does not preclude the possibility of moral progress in the twenty-first century. In the last thirty years, environmental ethics and the ethics of artificial intelligence have developed just as much as scientific-medical research into the survival conditions of humans and other species. We are gaining more and more knowledge about our sphere of action, which conveys to us the responsibility that we bear for ourselves, other people, other beings and also non-animal nature. History, then, neither develops automatically in the direction of overall progress nor its opposite. Because each of us is an actor, what the future looks like depends on all of us.

If we are to shape history responsibly, however, we must work systematically to ensure that the highest priority of our institutions (which includes the state and its educational facilities) is for us to achieve moral progress together.

> *The* new enlightenment *therefore demands that we place the idea of moral progress at the top of our overall social goal structure and shape the subsystems of science, business, politics and civil society in this light.*

This naturally also applies to art, culture and religion, which have been a decisive factor in overcoming misguided ways of thinking and conceiving of better social conditions for millennia.[4]

Slavery and Sarrazin

One drastic example of the world-historical implementation of moral progress is the almost universal abolition of slavery, which has always been morally reprehensible. It has always been evil to abduct people against their will from their homes, to sell them and subject them to the interests of a small group of slaveholders who could, as necessary, physically punish them or even let them die if they did not obey.

The fact that self-evident moral truths and moral progress exist does not mean that we *automatically* better ourselves; it means only that we *can* do so. To an extent, who we are and who we want to be is in our hands. Hans Jonas sums this up pointedly: 'Man is the maker of his life *qua* human, bending circumstances to his will and needs, and is never helpless, except against death.'[5] Neither progress nor regression occurs automatically; both depend on whether we have a form of society at our disposal that is geared towards cooperation, coexistence and peaceful stability. Every form of society arises from the many actions of individuals; it is not somehow imposed from above (by economic and political elites, for example). Similarly, social processes – such as digitalization – do not take place automatically but are a result and expression of many individual actions and decisions, including everything that each of us does daily.

In modernity, long phases of brutal slavery, resulting especially from the European colonization of non-European areas, eventually gave way to moral progress through the official abolition of slavery. This moral progress did not mean that no one had ever noticed that slavery is morally reprehensible; all one had to do was ask the slaves. On the other side too, that of the slaveholders, there were phases of insight into the reprehensible nature of their own actions, which is why the entire system of slavery could only be maintained by dehumanizing the enslaved with pseudo-theories – especially race theory.

At the same time – especially in the eighteenth century, but also earlier – there were efforts to bring about a recognition of the (obvious) humanity of slaves. This wave of incipient moral progress among the slaveholders was connected to the emergence of new Protestant communities in the USA but also with the French Revolution and the daily resistance of slaves, which frequently erupted into revolts (which were usually crushed brutally).[6]

On the oppressing side of asymmetrical power – that is, the side of those who profited directly or indirectly from slavery – emerged modern racism: the belief that humans can be divided into races that, owing to certain biologically measurable, essentially phenotypically visible characteristics, exhibit particular traits and behaviour. After centuries of racist pseudo-science, we now know that there are no different races among humans (see above, pp. 134ff.). Even in times of brutal racism, however, many were aware of this fact; there were always people who recognized that humans cannot actually be divided into races, let alone be morally or economically evaluated on the basis of this classification. We are ignoring these voices if we think that slavery and racism (which both unfortunately still exist, only no longer in the legally and politically legitimated form that existed in the USA or South Africa) were morally acceptable in the past simply because people did not know any better at the time.

In order to oppress people brutally or even exterminate them systematically, one must always dehumanize them, or at least severely denigrate them using pseudo-arguments based on verifiably false assumptions and distorted scientific data. This applies as much to slaveholders as to the National Socialists and today's neo-Nazis as to the scientifically easily disprovable theories about intelligence, culture, heredity and religion disseminated by Thilo Sarrazin, which place him in the tradition of the eugenic theories formulated by the British naturalist Sir Francis Galton (a cousin of Charles Darwin). His research on intelligence led, among other things, to the sterilization of tens of thousands of women (roughly 20,000 in California alone) because they were supposedly not intelligent enough to give birth to intelligent children.[7] In the same spirit as Galton, Sarrazin – to take only one example and refute it – claims the following:

> Everything suggests that the significantly below-average educational perfor-
> mance of Muslims in Europe is culturally conditioned, and ultimately rooted
> in the religion and the cultural environment shaped by it. Unfortunately, this
> backwardness is an irrefutable fact.[8]

Like most of Sarrazin's controversial statements, this claim is easily refuted. In the twelfth century CE, when parts of Europe (especially today's southern Spain) were under Muslim rule, the educational performance of Muslims in Europe led to such outstanding intellectual achievements as modern mathematics. We use *Arabic* numerals, not Roman ones, and the key term in current technological progress is 'algorithm', which was coined by a mathematician from what is now Iran who taught and researched in Baghdad centuries ago.

At any rate, Islam (whatever that actually means) is not anti-educational. Even in states that are certainly backward in democratic terms, such as today's Saudi Arabia or the United Arab Emirates, there are impressive achievements in research and finance as well as architectural mega-projects, all of which are advanced intellectual achievements. And this contradicts Sarrazin's false claim that 'the standard of universities in the Islamic world'[9] is low in mathematics and natural sciences, for without universities in the Islamic world – which currently include NYU Abu Dhabi and the Sorbonne Abu Dhabi as well as Turkish universities, where some outstanding cutting-edge research is carried out in all fields – modern mathematics and natural science would not exist at all, which can surely be considered an exceptional historical achievement.

Moral progress is still possible in dark times, for no time, no matter how terrible, is so dark that moral facts can be completely obscured. There have certainly been unjust systems, one paradigmatic example being the Third Reich, whose Nazi rulers deliberately did everything in their power to destroy understanding of moral facts, enabling them to dehumanize groups of people (most of all Jews) completely and then exterminate them.

Things were no better with Japanese racism, of course, which fired the starting gun for the Second World War in Asia and was initially aimed mostly at Chinese and Koreans. In the light of the atrocities of the last century, many parts of humanity (albeit certainly not all) decided after that war to allow moral progress and implement it in the various forms of a democratic law-based state.

(Supposedly) different conceptions of humans do not justify anything, least of all slavery

Unfortunately, these achievements of moral progress are qualified in the present day. Some fall back on the weapons of cultural relativism to discredit the idea of universal values. There is a regrettable tradition of this in Germany, and the work of Nietzsche, Schmitt and Heidegger forms an especially important part of it; their sometimes glaring ethical errors are still treated uncritically, even though they have long been rendered philosophically obsolete by better arguments and newer research in ethics and political philosophy.

A recent example of the moral aberrations of cultural relativism is provided by the Freiburg Nietzsche scholar Andreas Urs Sommer, in his book *Values: Why We Need Them, Even Though They Do Not Exist.*[10] Following his model Nietzsche, he presents an argument that can scarcely be called indirect to justify the slavery of the past. After (unsuccessfully) arguing that values do not exist, he turns against human dignity. He states that, 'for the largest part of its history, humanity knew neither the phenomenon nor the concept of "human rights"':

> Their supposed universality and absoluteness are not historical universality or absoluteness, not a fact, but something that *ought* to be. Not even a hard-line human rights universalist would claim that human rights, like the three laws

of thermodynamics, had always applied but were only discovered in the course of history.[11]

These lines are riddled with errors; it is worth pointing them out in order to illustrate how philosophical critique works. For philosophy, and hence ethics, is not simply a matter of opposing opinions; philosophy is an academic discipline that aims to find the truth by rational means. If a line of reasoning proves faulty upon closer inspection, if it proves incoherent or even contradictory, it can be laid aside until the philosopher who formulated it reworks it in order to take the objections into account. This is how philosophy progresses. As an academic discipline, it is marked by both progression and regression; even the natural sciences do not simply experience cumulative successes but move through their respective histories in complex cycles of progression and regression, which are examined in the discipline of the history of science.

Returning to the paradigmatic errors in Sommer's statements about human rights, let us begin with the claim that the universality and absoluteness of human rights are something that *ought* to be. He probably means to say that human rights are not something that was always measurable in the universe with the right instrument or even the naked eye. Rather, there is a view that humans *ought* to be viewed in accordance with human rights. According to Sommer, then, the famous statement in Article 1.1 of the German constitution that

> Human dignity is inviolable. To respect and protect it is the duty of all state authority.

is not a descriptive statement about the fact that humans have an inviolable dignity in some timeless sense; rather, it is a call to treat people in a particular way, as laid out concretely in the following human rights norms in the constitution.

This thought might have been worth considering, but Sommer commits a grave error in concluding from it that the 'supposed universality and absoluteness [of human rights] are not historical universality or absoluteness, not a fact, but something that *ought* to be.' He overlooks the point that what ought to be can be universal and absolute, that its validity extends across all cultures and times; this is why we can accuse the slave-traders of antiquity of behaving in a morally reprehensible fashion, even if they actually thought they were doing something good. The fact that something is a demand, an ought, does not mean that this ought should not apply universally.

The constitution deals not with any *supposed* universality or absoluteness, as Sommer writes, but with a form that is certainly real and effective, at least to the extent that it must be protected and respected.

This does not mean that one learns of moral facts by the methods of thermodynamics or natural science in general. Moral facts are recognized historically – that is, by humans who find themselves in action situations. The fact that something cannot be explored by means of natural science certainly does not mean that it does not exist. Not every advancement of knowledge consists in a discovery of physical facts; there is also mathematical progress, after all, or indeed moral progress.

In dark times it becomes obvious what we should do, but often too late; this is why moral progress can be hard won and painful. Slavery cannot be justified by the fact that it was defended by some in the past, such as Aristotle or Nietzsche. Sommer therefore takes the typical relativist detour by claiming that one cannot refute Aristotle's conception of humans; the latter's moral reflections were simply different from ours, but not worse.

> Human rights are based on a different conception of humans from the one that predominated for the largest part of human history, and the latter should not necessarily be considered an unenlightened or fundamentally inadequate conception: to Aristotle, for example, it was self-evident that some people were 'natural slaves' who belonged to others and participated in reason, in the logos, only if they could do so through someone else. If there are natural freemen and slaves, it is out of the question to ascribe something such as human rights to them equally, least of all the main categories listed in the Universal Declaration of Human Rights: dignity, freedom, equality and solidarity. Now, it is easy to say that Aristotle's conception of humans is simply pre-Enlightenment and antiquated, but it is visibly harder to explain to what extent this conception of humans is untrue or wrong in the same way that we would claim about much of Aristotle's physics.[12]

This is nonsense, for it is extremely easy to explain why Aristotle's supposed conception of humans is untrue and wrong. It is enough to point out that natural slaves have never existed and never will. Some people were and are enslaved, and we do not know when slavery will finally disappear for good.[13] It is utter humbug to believe that those who are enslaved were somehow made slaves by nature prior to that;[14] Aristotle is wrong here. And it was by no means self-evident to Aristotle that some people are natural slaves – that is why he argued the case with such vehemence and attempted to justify the prevailing slavery. If his conception of humans implies that some people are natural slaves (which, on closer exegetic examination, is questionable), it would simply be wrong, at least in this respect.

My understanding of the basic errors in the argumentation of cultural relativism to support slavery after the fact emerged from a conversation with the literary scholar and trauma researcher Ulrich C. Baer, who teaches at New York University:

> If we asked them, those who were and are enslaved would surely not be of the opinion that they were natural slaves. Rather, many of them would agree that slavery is morally impermissible, indeed evil, because it violently attacks the core of their humanness.

That is why there were always slave revolts, even in antiquity: precisely because not everyone believed that slavery was a natural and thus justified matter. This was merely the ideology of morally reprehensible slaveholders, which Aristotle (himself a slaveholder) shared in some of his writings. Slavery, especially since the introduction of a global slave market in the sixteenth century, functioned through a systematic 'status degradation, i.e., racism'[15] that served to 'push aside what was actually obvious',[16] as Michael Zeuske, one of the leading slavery scholars, puts it.

Of course, slavery in a case such as the USA, where one can study this phenomenon especially well because it is historically closer to us and hence better documented (through photographs, press, etc.) than pre-modern forms of slavery, was not overcome because the slaveholders suddenly realized that their conception of humans was wrong. Without slave revolts and the ultimate impossibility of ignoring the suffering inflicted by humans on other humans in the system of slavery, this historical moral progress, namely the realization that slavery was always morally impermissible – in the past as well as the present – would never have come about.

However hard Aristotle or some other classical writer might have worked to justify slavery, this is no proof that there was a different conception of humans at that time and that human rights did not apply in the past. If one reads *Mein Kampf* or Goebbels's journals, one can see that, even as late as the German Reich that existed from 1933 to 1945, the system was guided by a different conception of humans; this does not mean that the genocide systematically carried out in the Nazi death camps was somehow justified for a certain time, simply because the Nazis had a different conception of humans that cannot easily be refuted. For, according to relativism, this would have been the valid and thus rightful conception for that time – which is patent nonsense.

The ideology of slaveholders is based on the premise that they have to dehumanize people by viewing them, like Aristotle, as 'living possessions'.[17] In modernity, racism took over this function when slaveholders classified their slaves as black and sought to identify inferior forms of humanness in this supposed black race. Likewise, the Nazis dehumanized Jews and Indian Brahmins dehumanized outcasts (which has unfortunately still not been overcome entirely). But the slaveholders certainly recognized one another's human rights; they were *perverted universalists* and therefore had to classify some humans as non-human – a morally reprehensible contradiction.

Moral progress and regression in the time of the coronavirus

The coronavirus crisis is multi-layered. It was triggered by a viral pandemic – that is, the spread of a novel virus that is not yet sufficiently understood for researchers to assess exactly how dangerous it is to humanity. For this reason, some drastic steps were taken to restrict public life and thus protect human lives.

Before the virus, all people are equal – in the sense that, from its perspective, we are a cell cluster in which it can reproduce. The virus is passed on from one person to the next and does not discriminate.

Because of this, the first weeks of the pandemic saw unprecedented forms of solidarity. Suddenly it became clear that it is merely an excuse when people say that morally ambitious but economically costly and risky politics is impossible. Moral politics is not a luxury; it is the only form of politics that does justice to people and makes them the central focus.

To protect human lives, our hectic society, constantly on the verge of burnout, was brought to a halt and transformed into a gigantic home office. Nonetheless, the lockdown was initially largely accepted, leading to a clear case of moral progress before our eyes: the vast majority of people were willing to protect especially at-risk groups by supporting the contact bans and staying at home in order to interrupt the infection chains.

How lasting this moral progress will be has yet to be determined. For it also depends on how we can shape a more sustainable future that does not set us back to the fatal errors of compulsive consumption and the associated burnout capitalism.[18] If we adhere to the (empirically false) idea of an individual geared exclusively towards maximizing profit as a compulsive consumer, we cannot even understand moral progress. For then we assume that our primary aim is profit, which makes moral action seem naïve or even impossible.

One thing is certain, at any rate: the virus, invisible to the naked eye, made the structures of our society visible through its uncanny presence – especially in terms of how relevant public transport and intensive-care units are, how families function, how the state and its representatives act, and so on. In those days, each of us experienced in one way or another that interpersonal contact is irreplaceable. A crisis is always a thought laboratory too. In the face of the massive threat of the coronavirus, which exceeds all the shocks we have experienced in affluent societies in the last decades, the contours of our society, who we are and who we want to be become unmistakably apparent.

An important reason for reacting to the spread of the virus with a lockdown was, and is, the threat of overtaxing our health system, and thus also doctors and care workers. Now, at the latest, we are seeing how morally reprehensible the underfunding and the inordinate profit-oriented nature of the health system are, because they can force us to apply the criteria of triage in peacetime (on triage, see pp. 145f. above).[19]

Because of that, among other things, it was justified for the German government and the individual states to introduce a lockdown mode in order to avoid the triage situation that had already come about elsewhere (especially in northern Italy). Furthermore, it would have been irreconcilable with the founding values of our society to take on board hundreds of thousands of deaths in order to keep the economy running; from the decision-making perspective of the government, the prioritization of human life was not only morally justified but absolutely necessary.

In choosing this path, however, a different kind of triage was accepted; there are already manifold forms of collateral health damage from the lockdown, such as the postponement of non-essential operations and examinations as well as certain preventative measures. In the eyes of the decision-makers, the risk of triage in overtaxed health systems trumped the other risks for individuals and groups that were taken on board to interrupt infection chains. The aim was to avoid at all costs a situation in which intensive-care beds and ventilators would not be available for all those who urgently needed them.

The first phase of the lockdown was thus driven by moral understanding. Unfortunately, this was accompanied by the moral regression of a retreat to nation-state territories along with nationalist hubris. The resulting state of emergency was used differently in each country to realize political goals that had not been in reach before the coronavirus. This does not apply only to Hungary, Poland or the USA, where the state of emergency was used out of pure cynicism to expand government powers.

But Germany is no ideology-free space either, a place where governments simply do the right thing as advised by experts. Rather, this impression is part of the ideological architecture in Germany, which allows political decisions to be made that are supported in public by seeking expert opinions. The state is entitled to keep decision-making processes and internal debates partly secret, which is not only legal but also legitimate. Unfortunately, many people believe that this constitutes a conspiracy of the elites against the people, which is not the case. It does not follow from the partial concealment of politically complex negotiation processes that those in government are acting against the interests of the people. In a democracy, rather, they are themselves part of the people, elected representatives of the people who are not above the law.

Naturally the question of how to react to occurrences of infection also involves political calculation, which is no cause for reproach. Politicians are not obliged only to follow the advice of medical experts; they are not externally controlled but decide which facts are important to achieve the larger goals of society. Politicians are experts themselves, and of course they will have an eye on their own strategies for optimizing their party's profile as well as their own career paths. This is legitimate and corresponds to the rules of play in parliamentary democracy, especially as one should note, in spite of all dissent, that the public debate about the coronavirus in Germany is diverse, multi-perspectival and genuinely guided by moral understanding.

It would be a mistake, incidentally, to believe that our governments could be controlled by virologists. In the best case, the role of experts in the political domain consists in advising governments that need to align complex systems and take into account different perspectives.

The political and always also tactical dimension of the coronavirus crisis must be examined in the same way as moral progress as well as the welcome government decisions, which were based on moral and scientific insight. Otherwise we allow ourselves to be blinded by moral progress and our new sense of solidarity and do not see that massive processes of regression (such as the closing of borders within Europe and the nationalist competition between health systems) are occurring at the same time, to say nothing of the notions of world conspiracies rampant on the political fringes.

If one closes off a region with a very high rate of coronavirus infections, this is sensible in order to save lives – assuming that those who are closed off receive the necessary medical care and can be transported elsewhere if necessary, for example by rescue helicopter. But such considerations have nothing to do with the borders of nation states. It is not as if a 'German' life is more worthy of protection than an 'Italian' one. As one can see in all countries, the number of sick varies greatly by region. Should one then reintroduce border controls within Germany for Bavaria and Baden-Württemberg, for example, or maintain those between Brandenburg and Mecklenburg-Vorpommern permanently? And why not between Baden and Württemberg? One could keep breaking this down further, which shows how absurd it is and why closing borders has nothing to do with virology or other medical expertise.

Moral progress is **progress *sui generis***. That means it is not based on any other form of progress, especially not purely scientific, technological or economic progress. That is precisely what the coronavirus crisis has impressively demonstrated. The reduction of moral progress and ethics to scientific-technological modelling in research systems governed by targeted economic competition has contributed indirectly, but considerably, to the coronavirus crisis. The novel coronavirus fell on fertile social ground where it could flourish. Without the transport routes of purely economic globalization, without business travellers and the mass tourism of cruise ships, the viral pandemic would never have spread at this speed and in this form.

If the coronavirus crisis can only be overcome by unleashing a global, nationalistically organized systems competition around the discovery of a vaccine and the interruption of infection chains by sometimes morally questionable means, the aftermath of the crisis will see us sliding straight into the next crisis, which might be even worse. For nationalist rivalry and brutal market competition lead to presumably poorly tested vaccines and are already subjecting scientific research to unhealthy time pressure.

The good news is that any crisis that affects everyone holds the potential for an improvement of social conditions. A visible example of this was the wave of solidarity that motivated many people to save lives through voluntary social distancing. The temporary collapse of the global production chains of a completely overheated turbo-capitalism that had been rapidly destroying the quality of people's lives for decades led to a moment of reflection. We can now experience first-hand that we have gone too far with our compulsive consumption and hectic affluence.

Until recently, our life consisted mostly of working enough to afford consumer goods that indirectly endanger our survival (including plastic toys, smartphones, automobiles, etc., depending on income). In times of leisure and relaxation, the best we can come up with is practising mass tourism, bustling about on overcrowded Italian resorts at the height of summer, squeezing between hundreds of people to see the *Mona Lisa* and take a photo without acknowledging the actual work, and so on.

In addition, we spend our free time using social media and digital entertainment, and this has increased during the coronavirus-induced lockdown. So this not only creates opportunities for progress but has already triggered moral regressions such as an even greater pervasion of our daily lives by social media and digital companies.

Social media companies, already far too powerful as a result of monopolization, are now enriching themselves even more: never before have we voluntarily surrendered so much data to them without being paid for it; we are on the cusp of installing tracing apps on American operating systems, which – whether we like it or not – can easily lead to data mining and other methods of soft cyber-dictatorship. We express our worries, fears, hopes and political opinions on social media, which has made the coronavirus crisis a goldmine for digital exploitation, as we will all soon discover. And while the retail sector, bookshops, cafes, restaurants, theatres, universities and opera houses are closed, Netflix, Amazon, Zoom, Skype, and so on, rake in huge profits because, in Germany, we gave these US giants almost complete control of our economy for weeks, resulting in the loss of urgently needed tax revenue.

That people retreated to their own four walls during the lockdown can in part be taken as a sign of moral progress: we acknowledged the moral necessity of interrupting infection chains in order to protect ourselves and others. In effect, we accepted an overall social quarantine for the protection of human life. We thus acted according to an understanding of a moral fact that I call the '**virological imperative**' (VI):[20]

In a verified pandemic, act as if your social contacts were guided exclusively by the prognoses of the best virological models.

The virological imperative calls upon us to reduce the complexity of reality massively so as to prevent an impending, only imprecisely identifiable risk to the health of many people. This is the foundation for some of the most far-reaching hygienic measures in recent times. Based on the globally predominant political recognition of this imperative, the state intervened in our lives in a way that was unimaginable until recently and forced us, sometimes more and sometimes less gently, to retreat to the private sphere. In so far as the isolation chosen by many and the implementation of the virological imperative by governments were based on moral understanding, this wave of solidarity can be taken as an indicator of profound moral progress in dark times.

Put drastically, the lockdown also changed us into a digital proletariat in the space of a few days. For one thing, as mentioned above, we do unpaid work for US digital monopolists; in corona-German, this fatal ill is known as 'home office', one of the euphemisms that has meanwhile become standard. In addition, what the home office (a euphemism for this ill) means for many affected families (especially single parents) is that there is no longer any privacy or leisure time. People work around the clock, and the main beneficiaries of this work, as noted, are the US companies that live off licence sales and data streams.

Moral progress always presupposes an understanding of non-moral facts. The course of an illness, the statistics, the state of the health system, and so on, are non-moral facts that we must take into account for the moral evaluation of our courses of action. The aforementioned solidarity was based on social motivations that brought forth moral progress.

The situation is not entirely rosy, however. Since moral progress consists in recognizing and uncovering sometimes hidden moral facts, one can conversely assume that **moral regression** consists in concealing and failing to recognize sometimes obvious facts. Because of the virological imperative's one-dimensionality, the moral progress associated with it conceals other, in part equally or even more important facts, both moral and non-moral.

The logic of a virus's spread demonstrated in computer simulations is not a representation of reality. A model- and computer-assisted prognosis is a statement about how probable each future outcome is. But the future has not yet arrived, which is why virological models do not offer any unquestionable factual insights, any knowledge of what is the case. For many, however, it seems as if we might predict the future through prognoses based on statistics and probability calculations. **Prognosticism** is an ideology that believes the future will come about automatically if one simply quantifies all social factors and feeds the data into models developed in the natural and social sciences.

But that is a mistake, for the future depends fundamentally on how we shape it as individuals capable of moral understanding, as free spiritual beings. Ideally, prognoses are made in order to develop possible scenarios and establish which ones we should avoid and which we should bring about. We should not, however, believe that they can truly predict our actions or even make them superfluous. Furthermore, because its complexity can never be fully grasped, nature foils any prognosis of the human future.

We must learn to acknowledge that the society of knowledge is not a society of omniscience; under the complex conditions of our survival as animals on Planet Earth and the equally or even more complex conditions of the historically variable life of humans as spiritual beings, there cannot be any complete certainty or security. Life is risk – no diagnosis or prognosis will ever change that.

Models take on reality only through their application to data sets. The larger and better the data sets (for example, those obtained through coronavirus tests), the better the models' conditions of application. Yet even if one had perfect data sets and had tested the entire population, one would still have applied only a single model: the virological one. And the reality to which we belong in both sickness and health can never be captured by one single model. Other models – including models of the current situation from the humanities and social sciences – compete with the virological model and likewise make prognoses. Models of emergencies from political theory, for example, predict that emergency laws and warlike conditions, some accepted voluntarily and others imposed by the state, automatically change our understanding of the state and thus the state itself.

Before our eyes, the neoliberal understanding of the state, in which the state maintains preferably weak rules in order that the economy can remain at a high level so that we can shape our lives individually, is turning into the early modern conception of the state represented especially by Thomas Hobbes. The political scientist David Runciman, who teaches at the University of Cambridge, pointed out this parallel in an article for *The Guardian*: in nationwide situations of life and death, for example, when the health of all its citizens is at stake, the state proves its strength, and thus also its ruthlessness.[21] In effect, governments can decide over life and death; this is the famous doctrine of the state's monopoly on the use of force. According to Hobbes, state authority alone is legitimate, as it guarantees that reliable social rules exist at all and can be sanctioned beyond the circle of small groups (such as families or clans).

This creates a risk potential for our current liberal and democratic conception of the state: in extreme cases defined by the government bodies, the state is entitled to curtail our freedoms in order to ensure its functionality. Every social emergency – and that includes a pandemic – can be used by the state in order to expand its monopoly on the use of force and secure lasting control of the formation of opinion among the citizens. In democracies this can be abused to consolidate and expand the power of ruling parties; this is happening in especially brazen fashion in Hungary, where Orbán seized the opportunity to acquire options for long-term rule. He rules via emergency law, without parliamentary controls.

It thus depends on the moral understanding of political actors and citizens whether liberal democracy survives, and how. Our democracy has so far proved itself in the time of the coronavirus, which has led to an increase in the trust of citizens in their elected representatives.

However, the entirely justified virological imperative, which is meant to protect us and our health system from the worst, must not cause us to neglect other models. If we disregard the critical analysis of state actions provided by the media, universities or think tanks, for example, we conceal non-moral and moral facts that should also be taken into account if we are to overcome the coronavirus crisis. If now, under the pretext of the virological imperative, a subtle, yet totalitarian surveillance regime (as demonstrated by China) were to spread further, the coronavirus would have dealt a blow to liberal democracy and its Enlightenment-based value system. This would amount to a fatal moral regression.

It does not follow from political science's models of the state of emergency, however, that we are in effect experiencing the self-abolition of democracy. Like every model, they develop consequences under hypothetical conditions: if only the emergency rules applied for an extended period, as examined by such political theorists as Thomas Hobbes, Carl Schmitt, Jacques Derrida and Giorgio Agamben, this would gradually lead to the self-abolition of the foundations of the democratic law-based state.[22] Analogously, if the virus spreads in the way described by the computer simulations, we will experience a particular number of infections. Yet reality is not a dystopian novel in which a state of emergency subjects all humans to regime change (as conspiracy theorists believe), nor do we, as individuals and historical actors, behave as described by a computer simulation (as some virologists believe).

If we only consult models of one kind – those suitable for the discovery and examination of scientifically measurable facts – but ignore others, this increases the likelihood that non-physically measurable facts will develop in an unfavourable direction. This would inevitably lead to a moral regression that would take place in the guise of a moral progress driven exclusively by natural science and would thus be overly one-sided.

Neither moral progress nor moral regression takes place automatically. There is one decisive reason for this: morally weighty decisions are made by spiritual beings, paradigmatically by humans. As spiritual beings, we do not automatically do what is right or wrong, good or bad. Even if one tries always to do what is morally right, and in this sense to live a good life, one can be mistaken about the non-moral and moral facts and ultimately make moral misjudgements. History is written by humans; it is an expression of our complex free decisions as well as manifold social systems, habits and biological factors in human life.

That is precisely why it is morally necessary to view a situation of great moral complexity such as the coronavirus pandemic from numerous perspectives, since the reality in which our decisions matter is never monocausal; it is not like the unfolding of a single programme that can be reconstructed using suitable computer simulations. We cannot remotely predict reality; we can only envision particular systems that we isolate from reality to study them as if they were not part of larger contexts.

The self-appraisal of our cognitive faculty and the transdisciplinary exchange of knowledge claims and insights beyond every conceivable discipline is an integral part of the new enlightenment, which strives to develop universal values for the twenty-first century. To that end, we must overcome the stubborn one-sidedness of the mistaken belief that scientific-technological progress alone is sufficient for human and moral progress.

This notion, which I refer to as the **scientistic reduction**, involuntarily causes moral harm, for it disregards both non-moral facts that cannot be physically measured and dealt with through engineering and the moral facts *sui generis*, which cannot be established without ethics.

The limits of economism

A widespread form of scientistic reduction consists in overestimating the explanatory power of economics. What makes this especially fatal is that large parts of it either rest on a crude confusion between moral and economic values or subordinate moral values to economic ones. **Neoliberalism** is a school of economic thought that essentially relies on the assumption that one automatically achieves human progress by leaving as many decisions as possible to the market and its financially measurable competitive logic.[23]

The coronavirus pandemic has revealed many contradictions in the predominant market logic of the last thirty years, which is tightly interwoven with neoliberal thinking and its implication in purely economically understood globalization. By its own criteria, neoliberal market logic failed first in the 2008 financial crisis and then, on a much larger scale, in the 2020 coronavirus crisis: now, for example, there will probably be more state funding going towards saving our economy than it would have cost to exempt the health system from the logic of profit. And if one takes into account the environmental damage caused by neoliberally controlled, purely economic globalization of the last thirty years, one even arrives at a negative balance – that is, the destruction of the ecosystem and its consequently necessary technological replacement cost us more value than we are actually producing.[24]

We have known at least since the 1970s that the horrendous wastage of natural as well as man-made resources is not sustainable and will, in the long run, very probably lead to the self-extinction of humanity – or at least to disasters far more terrible than the coronavirus pandemic. This fact of a future jeopardized by wrong thinking was advanced largely without regard for the factors of sustainability and general human wellbeing, relying instead on growth indicators.

This form of economic management should not, I must underline, be equated with capitalism as such; rather, it results from a particular interpretation of the human being, the state and the economy whose details rest on at times questionable, even falsified assumptions. These include especially the assumption that every individual involved in exchange transactions is automatically driven by greed and self-interest, so that every morally tinged, mutual relationship between market actors should be understood as an encounter between egotists. This model, known as *Homo oeconomicus*, still plays an important part in the teaching of economics to this day, even though it has long been recognized as one-sided. This also includes the false assumption that humans are greed-driven compulsive consumers.

Unfettered neoliberal capitalism is a roaring, but frequently stalling motor that accordingly needs frequent interventions by the strong state to get started again. One of the major tasks for post-coronavirus society, philosophically speaking, will therefore be finally to escape the logic of capitalism versus communism that has shaped modernity for almost two hundred years. The market economy is not per se antithetical to a good life and does not automatically lead to exploitation and social inequality. For there are various contrary regulatory mechanisms, which include not only the state and its territorially defined sovereignty over resources but also the rest of society and thus each one of us. There is no need for exchange transactions to be driven by a cold egotism where each party tries to cheat the other. That this is often the case is a wrong that can be righted – and it must be, if we are to tackle the great challenges of our century with any prospect of success.

A moral form of economic management, a humane market economy, is possible.

Neither Adam Smith nor Karl Marx offer suitable models to analyse today's social conditions or the possibility of socioeconomically measuring and regulating them. The markets and the systems they describe only remotely resemble our socioeconomic reality; they knew neither anthropogenic climate change nor globalization nor the democratic law-based state. The systems they analyse are no longer ours, which means that any attempt to apply them to our own time can succeed only to a limited extent. We should neither replace the state's influence on the distribution of resources with market logic at all costs (which corresponds to the neoliberal doctrine of undermining the state) nor do the opposite, namely to aim for comprehensive nationalization or even a planned economy in which the creativity of markets has no chance to develop. Neither of these obsolete extremes is capable of meeting the technological and ecological challenges of our times, and both work with philosophically outdated conceptions of humans and the world that, unfortunately, still at times influence modelling in economics.

The ancient Greek word *oikonomia* means 'law of the house'. It originally described the allocation of household roles in ancient city states (especially Athens), where women had no political influence and there were naturally also slaves. And let us not forget how late universal women's suffrage was introduced: 1918 in Germany, and not until 1971 in Switzerland.

For millennia, economics has followed norms and value concepts that are no longer relevant to their time, including the still popular *Homo oeconomicus* as a (flawed) model of human rationality. What is overlooked is that economic science is never neutral but, rather, based on mostly subjectivist value theories that, on closer inspection, are ethically and anthropologically untenable. There is no such thing as a completely value-free examination of the space of values, and this applies to both economic and moral values: economists are remunerated for their research and ethicists reach moral judgements themselves when they research moral value. For values are spirit-dependent by nature: they exist in concrete situations of thought and action that concern us and our attitudes. The political economist Maja Göpel puts this in a nutshell:

> ... every reshaping of a worldly phenomenon into a number is exactly that: a value decision. And every value decision influences what we pay attention to and what factors we take into consideration, both in decisions and in our assessment of politics and its fairness, for politics always plays a part in fixing prices.[25]

According to the fallacious model of *Homo oeconomicus*, people strive primarily for economically quantifiable utility values – a striving to which they ultimately subordinate everything else in the struggle for survival.[26] This was used to develop mathematically precise theories whose function is to determine the preferences of different actors, thus enabling them to develop prognostic instruments for predicting and controlling markets.

Empirically, however, these models of human behaviour are thwarted by the fact that, even in situations of economic competition, people make decisions guided by considerations of mutuality and fairness. The behavioural economics literature in this field is substantial, and there are numerous economic theory constructions that economically refute the neoliberal ideas of unfettered markets and radically shrinking the state, instead arguing the case for sustainability and forms of distributive justice geared towards social equality.[27] In game theory, it was already discovered decades ago that people still make moral judgements even in competitive situations, that they are concerned not only with profit but also with fairness – which initially struck economists as irrational.[28]

Unfortunately, this knowledge has not yet reached everyone. Far too many areas of our life are still primarily economized – that is, they are controlled by economic assumptions that have little to do with people's actual lives. Hannah Arendt showed in her highly recommended book *The Human Condition* how the modern economization of our entire society endangers the public exchange of ethical-philosophical arguments, and thus the very idea of the public sphere.

An extreme example of how the neoliberal economy follows a naïve family model can be found in Margaret Thatcher, who, as British prime minister, and together with US president Ronald Reagan, contributed significantly to economizing as many sectors of society as possible through political interventions, which is why she has been a figurehead of unfettered neoliberalism since the late 1970s. In a famous interview from 1987, she stated:

> … who is society? There is no such thing! There are individual men and women and there are families and no government can do anything except through people and people look to themselves first. It is our duty to look after ourselves and then also to help look after our neighbour.[29]

Elsewhere she explains even more explicitly why she relies on the family, specifically invoking a stereotypical family model as the basis for economizing all relationships: 'Any woman who understands the problems of running a home will be nearer to understanding the problems of running a country.'[30] This is no slip of the tongue but the expression of a socio-ontological assumption. **Social ontology** examines the conditions under which a group of people acts in a coordinated fashion, using this to explore the foundations of socialization. Neoliberalism is based on **socio-ontological atomism**: the assumption that, in reality, no cooperation goes beyond the accumulation of individual preferences in the competition for scarce resources. Unfortunately, this fundamental philosophical error forms the basis for many outdated state-philosophical and socio-philosophical ideas and wreaks great socioeconomic havoc, something that has been pointed out in an incisive analysis by the Oxford philosopher of digital society Luciano Floridi.[31]

Economic deliberations are always shaped partly by non-economic value judgements, which is why the models of economics include some hair-raising absurdities such as *Homo oeconomicus*. Behavioural economics is no better off, since it often has to assume that people are ultimately always victims of bias, of sometimes evolutionarily explicable misjudgements and premature judgements; this means that behavioural economics considers us irrational, and hence manipulable.[32]

What the behavioural economists thus classify as irrational, however, is our rationality, which developed through evolution because we are social creatures, and is the origin of our higher morality.

Our rationality is not economic calculation based on profit and added value; such a self-definition of human reason overlooks ethics and logic and is therefore – unsurprisingly – unethical and illogical in its consequences, i.e., incoherent.

The rationales for our contemporary value concepts are certainly not derived purely from the natural sciences, much less from economics. Neither Smith nor Marx had any notion of sexual liberation or gender equality based on the emancipation of women from role models that oppressed women for millennia (and which we are far from having left behind entirely).

Depth psychology, especially psychoanalysis, was crucial for progress in the field of emancipation, as were modern literature and art, which, especially from the eighteenth century onwards, familiarized us with the range of sexual desire. The emancipation of women to become legal equals in civil life would have been impossible without the self-exploration of the human spirit and the sentient body in the humanities, philosophy and culture.

It is one of the bizarre misjudgements of our time, then, that moral values can somehow be derived from economic values, a misconception that is often wrongly attributed to Adam Smith.[33] Moral understanding cannot be gained from competitive situations between actors vying for resources. At best, one can ascertain through behavioural economics experiments – such as those undertaken by my renowned colleague Armin Falk at the University of Bonn, for example – that people still adhere to moral principles in competitive situations. It has been shown in experiments that people often behave more morally than one might expect if one assumed that humans are egotists by nature (which is verifiably false).

The conclusion I wish to draw from this experimentally well-grounded reflection is that ethics is the foundational discipline that develops guidelines for the conditions under which one should apply models of economic competition in the first place. This presupposes large-scale transdisciplinary research if we are to set up a more sustainable form of economic management that puts humans at the centre – as they really are.

Neither economic nor any other prognostic models are ever better than the assumptions from which they emerge. Assuming there are mistakes in philosophy, ethics and the humanities that are taken as a basis for economic modelling, this means that our economy is characterized by a one-sided, possibly false conception of humans, which can lead to grave errors that become especially manifest in crises.

If we cling to the conception of humans as compulsive consumers, then the axiom 'growth creates material wealth, which is all people want', cannot change. The consequences for humans and the environment are well known.

A morally acceptable form of economic management can only succeed if the discipline of philosophical ethics, which is independent of economic concerns, takes into account human science-based insights from all areas of science, but also life experience, art, religion and everyday wisdom. For ethics deals with the whole human being, which other disciplines split up into their respective subsystems for examination.

It is a fundamental mistake, however, and one that is unfortunately still firmly rooted in the ideology of the twenty-first century, to believe that humans are identical to any one of these subsystems (biology, psychology, economics, etc.) and thus decipherable with the gaze of a guiding discipline that governs all others. This is what, since Gilbert Ryle, philosophers have termed a **category mistake**.[34]

A category mistake consists in classifying a complex phenomenon one-sidedly, and thus incorrectly: people behave in an empirically, sociologically observable fashion. In doing so, they also express value concepts to which, as empirical analysis quickly shows, they themselves do not always adhere. From this perspective, humans appear to be partly irrational. This does mean, however, that their value concepts are wrong or ineffective. The category mistake I mean here lies in concluding from the observation of human behaviour that there are no real universal values, only more or less statistically ascertainable value conceptions coinciding with the preferences of the respective actors. I refer to this category mistake as 'economism'. It is especially dangerous because it exerts a strong influence on our everyday socioeconomic reality. It attributes moral values to economic ones, which it in turn attempts, by means of behavioural economics, to reduce to biological patterns of behaviour in the human animal.

Economism assumes that behavioural economics is the paradigmatic behavioural science for groups of people who are in competition based on market principles. As it has been shown that competition in the animal kingdom – among both non-human animals and humans – sometimes follows moral principles, it is still assumed that one can ascertain what people should do through economic modelling. That is precisely the mistake.

Economism owes its semblance of plausibility to the fact that it smuggles moral judgements into its models, then passes them off as the results of experimental observation. Recent work in behavioural economics points out that people (and other living beings) are guided by fairness and reciprocity, that there is also a *Homo cooperativus*. It has become clear, at any rate, that people in their social reality do not strive purely for individual profit at any social cost. This idea can only be expressed, however, if one has the concept of moral thought and action at one's disposal. This concept is not derived from the empirical observation of people but, rather, precedes any behavioural-economic theorizing, however sophisticated.

Thus genuine moral value judgements come before the social sciences, and hence sociology and political science.[35] It is (fortunately) simply false that economists, sociologists and political scientists judge from a morally neutral position and, fortunately, establish at some point that it is in the biological nature of humans to cooperate altruistically and to judge in a similar way to the economist conducting the experiment.

Moral understanding simply cannot be gained purely by ascertaining non-moral facts. For example, it does not follow from any one economic model that massive socioeconomic inequality has morally reprehensible consequences, since one cannot measure what is or is not morally reprehensible by economic methods. From the perspective of economics alone, then, it is not obvious that massive socioeconomic inequality leads to moral deficits, which in turn ruin the economy.[36] For how can it be beneficial for the maintenance of a liberal democracy such as the USA that only high earners can even think of running for president? The USA has long been displaying practices of plutocracy – that is, a system of government whose leaders are pre-selected according to wealth. The gulf between the millions of poor in the USA who cannot even afford health insurance and the rich who rule them is so huge that the system of resource distribution within the country has clearly taken on reprehensible dimensions.

This moral fact cannot be recognized via economic criteria alone. How much wealth each person possesses in relation to another is a purely quantitative question. The fact that this economically measurable and partially explicable inequality has moral dimensions remains hidden from the economist and, indeed, need not interest them as long as they are simply working on determining the parameters of general economic growth in order to support statements about the percentage of an economy's growth or shrinkage. But these figures, which determine such matters as stock market value or whether to declare a recession, have consequences that become morally and psychosocially apparent in human reality; the financial crisis of 2008 made this especially clear.

Since the coronavirus crisis of 2020 at the latest, our modern form of society can simply no longer afford to neglect moral aspects – which include ecology – because the economic promise that scientific-technological progress would somehow automatically (guided by the 'invisible hand' of the markets) lead to an improvement in our living conditions has verifiably and repeatedly failed.[37] For this thinking has led to our ecological crisis, which is more dangerous than any other known crisis.

It is unquestionably true that modern accelerated scientific-technological progress and its economic implementation have improved survival conditions for many people. It has countless victims to answer for, however, for without these processes there would obviously never have been an arms race or the material and human carnage of the last centuries. Let us also not forget that, with the 'Great Leap Forward' in China, Mao Zedong caused many millions to die of starvation in order to industrialize his country and catch up with the West.

The purpose of these critical references to well-known facts is not to recommend an abolition of the market economy but, rather, to point out that a reordering of the social market economy is called for. Neoliberal economic philosophy and its implementation on the experimental field of pure economic globalization have failed not only because the previous global production chains exploit both people and their surroundings in an unacceptable fashion but also because our system-relevant infrastructure (such as transportation and our health system) has been excessively privatized. If we recall the time before the coronavirus, we must not forget that there were increasing infrastructure problems in Germany (such as the rail service or unacceptable waiting times for medical appointments). Even in economic terms, the neoliberal philosophy of economics was thwarted by the facts, for it slides from one crash into the next at psychosocially damaging speed before consuming astronomical sums in tax revenue to get back what it burned up. This cannot seriously be a recipe for good, responsible and sustainable economic management.

In short, it is possible to replace the calculus of neoliberal modelling with a new version of social market economy geared towards sustainability whose goal is to advance a good and sustainable life without causing a decline in prosperity.[38] We simply have to recognize that prosperity does not consist in working exorbitantly and striving to acquire consumer goods, risking a burnout that we seek to counteract with pollutive mass tourism. This loop, which many people have experienced for years as a kind of 'hamster wheel', is not prosperity but a morally and psychically harmful life. Prosperity is not the senseless and excessive accumulation of money and goods; this instead causes stress, which has contributed for decades to overloading our health system and already does economic damage for this simple reason alone. Together with the accompanying environmental destruction, high speed capitalism ultimately does more economic damage than it creates value. This should be reason enough to rethink.

Biological universalism and the viral pandemic

Like the financial crisis of 2008, the coronavirus crisis, as mentioned above, has revealed many systemic weaknesses in unfettered global capitalism, whose market logic and negotiation processes lie beyond the democratic law-based state's direct access; accordingly, since the digital revolution, many major corporations have been following business models that directly or indirectly threaten the survival of democratic law-based states as well as Germany's social market economy.

As noted above, the word 'crisis' comes from the ancient Greek *krisis*, one of whose meanings resembles 'decision'. Crises bring about decisions and thus reveal structures in which they are made. In this way, they make new courses of action visible that we previously believed impossible or did not imagine at all. Hans Jonas captures this when he observes: 'We know the thing at stake only when we know that it is at stake.'[39]

The coronavirus crisis makes it clearer than ever who we are and opens up spaces for new kinds of decisions about who we want to be. The present time of a crisis always contains a new future in embryonic form.

The coronavirus crisis thus confronts us with the aim of a **biological universalism**: as humans, we are all members of a species that is used by the virus without distinction of person to multiply inside our cells. We cannot solve the moral problems that have been brought to light by the virus without starting a new chapter of moral progress.

The excuse that democratic politics cannot possibly make and implement morally ambitious yet economically difficult decisions can be considered refuted since late March 2020.

All of a sudden, it became possible to disable the global economic order of neoliberalism. Emmanuel Macron, who had previously advocated establishing more neoliberal structures in France, made it unmistakably clear in his television addresses in March 2020 that one cannot leave everything – least of all the health system – to the market. And even Boris Johnson, presumably shaken by his own serious bout of COVID-19, expressly renounced Thatcher's neoliberal dictum that there is no such thing as society, stating in a video message from late March 2020 in direct and deliberate contradiction of her words: 'We are going to do it, we are going to do it together. One thing I think the coronavirus crisis has already proved is that there really is such a thing as society.'[40] The markets cannot reflect the moral aim of defending ourselves from the novel virus together at all costs, since this is not a case of *competition* but *cooperation*. The crucial difference between *economic competition* and *moral cooperation* is that moral cooperation addresses everyone and calls on them to overcome all boundaries (be they national or mental, such as imagined boundaries between cultures, generations or races). Anyone who plays groups of people off against one other in this situation and relies on economic competition, for example, is committing a moral crime before the eyes of digitally interconnected humanity. This includes the political lies of Donald Trump, who tried to blame the Chinese for the virus and thus 'nationalize' it, so to speak, as much as Xi Jinping's fairy tale that the virus originated in the USA and was implanted in China. But it also applies to the common opinion in Germany that our Italian and Spanish friends suffered higher fatalities owing to the virus because Mediterraneans are simply more chaotic and less well organized than Germans. Similarly, it was an act of nationalist hubris to believe that we Germans have the best health system in the world, which leads to unfounded optimism and a false sense of security. These are all examples of morally reprehensible ways of thinking, and hence of ills that are being revealed by the coronavirus crisis.

The good news is that every crisis offers a chance to improve social conditions. In this case, one can see from the aforementioned morally reprehensible ways of thinking how dangerous it would now be to fall back on nationalist isolationism. Without mutual global support for people through medical expertise, ventilators, goods, economic umbrellas, and so on, we would be helpless to fight the novel virus and would soon be digging mass graves, even in Germany.

That is why the Slovenian philosopher Slavoj Žižek is right to point out that the coronavirus pandemic will be the end of an era that has led since the fall of the Berlin Wall to unfettered economic globalization.

Since a suggestion by Paul J. Crutzen and Eugene Stoermer, our epoch has been known as the **Anthropocene**, a period that is characterized primarily by the creative power and presence of humans.[41] We humans are indeed interconnected in manifold ways, and this global interconnection cannot be reversed by introducing border controls. Germany cannot suddenly turn into a pre-modern autochthonous system that lives off its own resources like an ancient city state. The same applies to all other European states. And even if the USA were fundamentally capable of isolating itself completely, it still has neighbours, and its economic dominance depends both on its military superpower and its cultural soft power. The great task facing post-coronavirus societies is to overcome the contradiction between humanity's global interconnectedness and nation-state organization so that we are capable of jointly developing universal values for the twenty-first century and new forms of cooperation that are not based on the logic of the market, let alone of war.

For a metaphysical pandemic

There can be no overall human progress without moral progress. In the dawning age of a new enlightenment, human progress consists in a cooperation between scientific, technological and moral progress with ethically defensible aims. The coronavirus simply makes something even more obvious that has long been the case: that we need a new idea of global enlightenment.

> *The twenty-first century will be the era of the pandemic of the new enlightenment as a consequence of globalization.*

Here one can use and reinterpret a term introduced by Peter Sloterdijk: what we need is not communism but **co-immunism**.[42] We must all vaccinate ourselves together against the spiritual poison that divides us into national cultures, races, age groups and classes and incites competition between us.

Since the beginning of the coronavirus pandemic, we have protected the sick and the elderly in our society. For this purpose we locked our children up, kept educational facilities closed, and generally created a medically justified but politically dangerous state of emergency. And we are investing trillions of euros to get the economy going again in the time ahead.

If we go back to business as usual after the pandemic, however, we face the threat of far worse crises: viruses whose spread we will once again be unable to prevent; escalating economic wars between the USA and

China, with the EU positioned helplessly in the middle; the spread of racism and nationalism, for example in the battle against migrants who flee to us because we have provided their executioners with the desired weapons or knowhow. And what we must not forget at any cost is the climate crisis, which is a far greater threat to humanity than any virus.

The world order before the coronavirus was not *normal* but *lethal.* This leads to certain demands. Now that there are new starts in many areas, could we not invest billions to change our mobility? Could we not rely consistently on digitalization in order to have pointless meetings online, rather than jetting around the world (which for business managers often involves private jets)? Have we finally understood that it is disastrously superstitious to believe that business, science and technology alone could solve all the problems of modern life?

The problem is not scientific-technological progress itself but, rather, its immoral use. It is up to all of us to change our behaviour and question our way of thinking. In a democratic society, people always vote with their feet too: how we act as individuals has consequences for the framework of political resource distribution and vice versa. We are not ruled by an omnipotent clique that imposes morally bad priorities on us, for there is no elite 'at the top' that is separate from us, as imagined by the populist inventors of conspiracy fantasists on both the left and the right. No, all of us contribute to the current state of society through our own behaviour. In a parliamentary democracy, governments react to the debate as presented by public opinion; they cannot govern by top-down decree. Politics and civil society are joined in a loop of mutual influence.

The threatening scene of the twenty-first century sends out an appeal to all people, not only us Europeans: we need a new enlightenment. Every person must be ethically educated so that we recognize the gigantic danger of a moral blindness that makes us rely almost exclusively on natural science, technology and neoliberal market logic. The current solidarity during the pandemic will ultimately remain only a brief moral highlight unless we fundamentally change direction. We must recognize that the infection chains of global capitalism, which destroys our nature and causes moral stupidity in the citizens of the nation states, turning us into full-time tourists and consumers, will ultimately kill far more people than all viruses combined. Why is it that a medical-virological realization causes solidarity, yet the philosophical insight that the only way out of suicidal globalization is a world order beyond an agglomeration of warring nation states driven by a cynical, quantitative economic logic does not?

The ancient Greek word *pandēmios* means 'concerning all nations, all people'. After the virological pandemic we need a **metaphysical pan-demic** – a gathering of all nations under the all-encompassing canopy of the sky, which we will never escape. We are and remain on the Earth, whether we like it or not; we are and we will remain mortal and fragile. So let us finally become citizens of the world rather than states, cosmopolitans rather than egotistical consumers. The alternative is our annihilation.

Morality ≠ altruism

The population's solidary acceptance of drastic, yet morally necessary security measures in the coronavirus pandemic is, as stated above, a clear case of moral progress in dark times. For ethics deals, among other things, with moral reflection, which asks how we can place the needs of others above our own interests and at what times and under what conditions this is necessary. This is known as altruistic action – in short, altruism.

Yet in the heat of the moment, we should not overlook the fact that there is more to ethics and morality than subordinating our own interests to the needs of others. In a completely altruistic society, after all, no one would have interests of their own any longer. And why should the interests of others automatically count for more than one's own?

As stated above, this is opposed by a fundamental moral insight: everyone is the other (of another). By applying this simple, but often suppressed idea to action situations, we are capable of uncovering moral facts, for the ethical toolbox includes the highly advanced human ability to put oneself mentally in the position of others and to be guided by the question of how a particular action affects them. This ability has led to the formulation of the famous Golden Rule, which appears in various cultural contexts and expresses the idea that fundamentally, when it comes to the question of what one should or should not do, there can be at least some element of tactical self-interest in not harming any other person. We know this rule as a piece of everyday wisdom: do unto others as you would have them do unto you. According to this idea, one should not harm others because one might be the other oneself.

Indeed, we would be incapable of understanding complex moral facts if we could not put ourselves mentally in the position of others. Many people conclude from this that morally guided action is essentially altruistic. From this perspective, **altruism** (from the Latin *alter*, 'the other') means acting for the benefit of others, whereas **egotism** means acting for one's own benefit. Altruistic actions for the sake of other people is an expression of our ability to see beyond our own interests and put them aside in order to help people and other living beings – even if it puts us in danger. My Bonn colleague Christoph Horn took this as a basis for the suggestion of a 'working definition of morality'[43] that one can largely embrace:

> Morality refers to a system of normative demands of an actor that commits them to put aside or suspend the perspective of their *own* advantage under certain circumstances in favour of pursuing *other people's* goods or interests. Morality is the more or less far-reaching, relatively palpable demand for temporary self-limitation that impacts the state of our own interests based on the wellbeing of other persons.[44]

This working definition covers many cases of moral action. If, for example, a lifeguard dives into an ice-cold river to save a less able swimmer, they are putting their own interests (not being cold, not placing themselves in danger) second for the sake of another person. This does not mean, however, that morality and altruism are identical, for it would be a mistake to think that we can act morally only by subordinating our own interests to those of ours; this logic overlooks the fact that our own interests are at least as morally relevant as those of the others. For we ourselves are also the others! Solidarity cannot mean always sacrificing oneself for others if they do not equally sacrifice themselves.

That is why, on a side note, European solidarity in the coronavirus crisis does not automatically mean that richer states in Europe that have been affected less by the virus owe compensation to other states. Rather, what we owe one another is mutual support. In the absence of this, calls for solidarity and altruism are only seemingly morally justified and are thus hypocritical.

The realization that each person is the other of an other, which means that one also has moral attitudes towards oneself (because my future self certainly differs from my current one), corresponds to the 'idea of moral grounds' that Horn summarizes as follows: 'Morally acceptable grounds must be actor-neutral, i.e., equally important for all those involved in the respective actions.'[45] Anyone who engages in moral reflections in order to find the morally right course of action, and thus do the right thing, must take their own position into account as *equally valid*. As everyone is the other (of an other), no particular other takes moral precedence. It follows from this that morality cannot be justified solely with recourse to altruism.

Genuine moral reflection, and thus ethics as a discipline, operates beyond egotism and altruism; neither of these is a moral category.

This important point is a consequence of moral universalism: what we should or should not do always concerns (at least) all those who are affected by an action, whether in a direct or an indirect but recognizable fashion.[46] We therefore have moral duties towards ourselves, because each of us must be taken into consideration in action situations. Otherwise, morality would ultimately demand that we always sacrifice ourselves as much as possible for others, which would lead to the nonsensical outcome that there would be no one left to support others, as shown by the American moral philosopher Susan R. Wolf in an influential essay about 'moral saints'.[47]

The equation of morality and altruism is often made because it has the (supposed) advantage of offering an evolutionary explanation for the birth of morality. For altruistic behaviour is also common outside of humanity, and one might think that it can be beneficial for a species if some members sacrifice themselves for others.

However, as we have seen (see pp. 87ff. above), the fact that some animals (including humans) regularly do something does not constitute any moral reason to keep doing it. Much of what the pleasant, comfortable everyday life of our species entails is morally reprehensible, such as brutal factory farming and environmentally destructive mass tourism. Nature is not our moral taskmaster: we are not swarms of locusts or bees, whose behaviour is controlled by entirely biologically conditioned social instincts. Our evolutionarily explicable stimulus-response patterns can at most encourage moral reflection, but they cannot replace it.

Moral grounds cannot be justified by offering an evolutionary explanation of their inception.

It is notable that no less a figure than Charles Darwin made this argument. In his text *The Descent of Man: Selection in Relation to Sex*, Darwin consistently distinguishes between social instincts, which can be observed in evolutionary terms and explained with reference to selection, and moral behaviour. In his view, humans are the only morally capable creatures; he supports this with the fact that we have intellectual faculties that have not developed in a comparable form in other creatures.

> A moral being is one who is capable of comparing his past and future actions or motives, and of approving or disapproving of them. We have no reason to suppose that any of the lower animals have this capacity; therefore, when a Newfoundland dog drags a child out of the water, or a monkey faces danger to rescue its comrade, or takes charge of an orphan monkey, we do not call its conduct moral. But in the case of man, who alone can with certainty be ranked as a moral being, actions of a certain class are called moral, whether performed deliberately, after a struggle with opposing motives, or impulsively through instinct, or from the effects of slowly-gained habit.[48]

I am not using this passage because I agree with Darwin. The book in which he develops this thesis contains many scientific errors and moral misjudgements, including extremely racist prejudices that Darwin adopts from the accounts of others instead of impartially examining for himself how the supposed 'savages' think and act. It is not only the 'lower animals' that Darwin considers immoral – that is, socially organized but incapable of moral understanding – but also the 'savages'. He supports this with ethnological reports of his time, all of which abound with morally reprehensible prejudices and attempts to justify genocides of indigenous populations that Darwin himself saw as morally impover-ished clans.[49] Darwin's purportedly neutral descriptions of the behaviour of people he found culturally alien express a manifold and at times disastrously nationalist hubris and self-distortion that he justified with a biologically grounded race theory. Darwin's writings are not an especially suitable source of moral insight, to say the least.

It is not my intention here to discredit the theory of evolution, which has naturally progressed considerably in scientific terms since Darwin's time and still offers the best explanation known to us for the origin of species and the development of organic forms. But evolutionary theory does not remotely explain everything about the human life form. In its constantly developing, scientifically mature form, it does not provide any explanation, let alone justification, for moral action. It is a category mistake to think that moral reflection can be wholly derived from biology.

Obviously it is true that moral reflection develops in nature, since we are living beings and thus part of nature. In so far as nature is an object of natural science, these clearly have something to say about how moral reflection fits into nature. However, one can approach this question productively only if one acknowledges moral phenomena in their own reality instead of mistaking them for biological phenomena of social coordination, with which they cannot be equated. This is a philosophical mistake that cannot be balanced out through any scientific research.

However many trace elements of morality we might find among other creatures, it would be foolish to forget that the moral systems developed by human theorists (philosophers such as Plato, Aristotle or Kant in the past and Arendt, Nussbaum, Wolf and many other philosophers of the present day) are very different from the precursors of social cooperation among other living beings. No other living being writes books about ethics in which it justifies the idea of owing other beings moral respect because we can all put ourselves in another person's position. No other living being known so far is capable of scientifically coordinated systematic reflection which includes philosophical ethics. The emergence of philosophical ethics, for example, cannot be explained or described in evolutionary terms. The selection pressure to which the history of philosophy is subject is of a non-biological nature. Whether we ourselves consider morally justifiable what Plato or Aristotle, Hannah Arendt, Martha Nussbaum or Christoph Horn, and so on, considered morally justifiable is not determined by a genetic code but is, rather, a matter for philosophical research.

That the theory of evolution successfully explains how organic forms – and thus species – emerge and fade is not because it established itself via evolution but, rather, because it largely contains truths – that is, facts that exist independently of evolutionary theory. It is therefore unproductive to point out that Darwin's moral errors came simply from the prejudices of his time and that today, thanks to the advances in molecular biology in recent decades, we can use evolutionary theory to improve our moral reflections – like Richard Dawkins, who tries (along with many others) to describe moral phenomena in the language of molecular biology, especially genetics. For if we rely on our own philosophically and ethically untested moral convictions and then attempt to identify these in evolution, we are making the same mistake as Darwin and will rightly be accused of falling victim to the prejudices of our time.

This does not mean that biological facts have no bearing on our moral judgements; on the contrary.

One of the central theses of this book is that we must acknowledge non-moral facts if our moral reflection is to do justice to the complexity of our possible courses of action. The system of morally right judgements – that is, the ideal form of ethics – is thus never complete, since there will always be new discoveries and challenges.

Generally speaking, scientific-technological progress can encourage moral progress, but it need not do so. In the nineteenth and twentieth centuries, evolutionary biology contributed to the spread of biological racism. It provided the foundation for eugenics and its manifold violent excesses, including the sterilization of women based on a low IQ score, suggested by Darwin's cousin Sir Francis Galton, or Nazi eugenics, which led to the murder of people who were classified as 'unworthy of life'. Many have used (and still use) the insights of evolutionary theory to dehumanize people and seamlessly assign them to the animal kingdom.

Humans are animals; barely anyone has ever denied this, and it was known long before the theory of evolution. Classical ethics, such as the work of Plato and Aristotle, deals with the question of what kind of animals human are, not whether they are animals at all. Humans are not identical to any other animals, however, but are specifically the 'reluctant animals', as I have described it elsewhere.[50]

We have been transcending our animal survival conditions for millennia through intellectual and cultural achievements that have made us into historical beings.

Comparisons with other animals should not hide the fact that a human, as a spiritual and free being, goes far and fundamentally beyond any of the intellectual achievements of which all animals hitherto known to us are capable. No other animal practises science, writes novels and operas, argues about the desirability of digitalization or examines other animals using biological methods, to name only a few of the countless traits that distinguish humans.

There is not one *feature that sets humans apart from other animals; rather, there are many.*

Whenever people dehumanize other people or groups of people, sooner or later this affects moral and hence social conditions. If the moral understanding of rulers is defective, they can easily – like the British colonial masters in the USA, India and Africa or the German, Portuguese, Spanish or Dutch ones, whose morals were certainly no better – rely on dehumanizing interpretations of scientific facts to legitimize morally reprehensible systems with pseudo-arguments.

Human beings: who we are and who we want to be

The human being is the point of departure for ethics. The discipline of human self-examination is called **anthropology** (from ancient Greek *anthrōpos*, 'human'). Ethics is based on anthropology.

This does not mean that ethics is **anthropocentric** – that is, focused purely on humans. This would be a mistake, since we have moral obligations to other living beings as well as to the inanimate environment, even towards life that does not yet exist (such as future generations). Ethics, however, is **anthropogenic**: it comes from the self-examination of humans, and, as a rational, scientific subdiscipline of philosophy, it transcends the precursors of moral reflection that developed among other creatures as well as the primal hordes of early humanity, which had to care primarily for their offspring and close relatives. The latter still forms the core of ethics, but this intra-communal ethics has not corresponded to the state of ethical research for decades, for that research has long moved on to the risks of technology and science, to the environment, and thus to our obligations towards other animals. An intra-communal ethics of the primal horde does not even meet the requirement of addressing advanced religions, which have claimed for millennia that we have obligations towards a higher, divine order, meaning that the moral standard of humanity had been more advanced for millennia before the false reduction of morality to evolutionarily explicable altruism.

As far as we know, humans are the only living beings that occupy themselves systematically and rationally with the question of what or, rather, who we are and who we want to be. Of course, this does not apply to all members of the species *Homo sapiens*. For various reasons, some of our species are not capable of this, or are capable only to a limited extent, because not all people develop the ability to reflect on themselves.

The fact that humans are the point of departure for ethics does not entitle us to behave in a morally reprehensible fashion towards other species. On the contrary: because we can understand that it is morally wrong to be cruel to non-human animals and destroy their habitat, and that it is even necessary to do good to non-human animals, we are obliged to act morally towards other species. Our systematic, moral reflection – that is, ethics – extends beyond our species.

This does not mean (as claimed especially prominently by Peter Singer) that we are forced to subordinate the interests of our own species to those of other species for moral reasons. This would be a misguided, biologically rooted identity politics based on the schema of compensating for inflicting or having inflicted suffering on life forms by inflicting suffering on ourselves.

Singer's point of departure is a conception of humans, indeed an entire metaphysics, that is questionable in general or at least remains vague. For, like many others, he assumes that we essentially already know everything about the universe, humans, life and our planet, and that we have understood that humans are merely one form of cell cluster (albeit a complex one) among many others. From this perspective, there would no longer be any difference between newborn humans and a snake, and, if one had to choose between the two, one would – like Singer – even accept killing severely disabled human children whose short lives would consist only of suffering, for example, for the wellbeing of healthy snakes.[51] Singer is mistaken, for he misunderstands the non-moral facts about humans and commits the error of simply assigning us to the animal kingdom without considering that there is a reason why humans are capable of higher morality while other life forms are not. This is the source of the sanctity of human life – which Singer disputes – not the fact that we consider the mere biological survival of human animals sacred.

It is quite simply false, in any case, when the British evolutionary biologist Richard Dawkins claims that evolutionary biology has shown that the purpose of our individual lives consists exclusively in disseminating our genes through reproduction.[52] Like Darwin's statements, those made by Dawkins about genes, God and morality are based on misguided philosophical interpretations of biological knowledge, not on biological knowledge itself.

It is urgently necessary that we pool the powers and knowledge of the different disciplines in the natural sciences, technological science, the humanities and the social sciences and focus on the all-important question of who we are as humans and who we want to be.

In proposing a new enlightenment, then, I am certainly not demanding that we isolate philosophical ethics from other scientific knowledge or should entangle the former in a conflict of faculties. Rather, the new enlightenment calls for radical transdisciplinary cooperation with the aim of ascertaining what we know about humans today and what moral consequences follow from that.

No individual person or individual discipline can provide this; rather, it must emerge in forums of reflection that offer suitable research structures for this purpose. These could be universities, provided they focus on making sustainability and a successful, good life for humans and other beings their highest priority.

To achieve this, however, we must abandon the notion that universities exclusively pursue some research interests or other, without any societal aims, under the conditions of a socially isolated ivory tower. This contradicts both the everyday research in many disciplines and the original Enlightenment idea of the university, which is associated with the famous name of Wilhelm von Humboldt, who followed on from the German Idealists Fichte, Schelling and Hegel (all of whom were also vice-chancellors at universities and wrote about the purpose of universities).

Freedom of science does not mean that the sciences do not pursue any socially significant aims or show interest for what advances us as humans. A modern setting of objectives for universities would react to the great challenges of the twenty-first century, which we cannot meet unless we pool the knowledge of various disciplines. We cannot afford any more mistakes in this field of anthropological self-placement. If we continue to present one false, one-sided conception of humans after another (for example, the notion that the spirit is identical to neuronal processes; *Homo oeconomicus*; the denial of free will; the idea that society is legible in the language of evolutionary psychology, or that our thinking is a computation operation) and base our economy, politics and civil society on mistakes, we will slide into as yet unforeseeable disasters that will make the coronavirus seem like a common cold. Our time of crisis is thus also the hour of the university in an ambitious, philosophically substantial sense that we have forgotten since we began transforming higher education institutions into technical institutes, based on a neoliberal model that is especially common in England and the USA – a disastrous process that has led to moral regressions.

Errors about human nature have a massive impact on our powers of moral judgement. If we mistake human beings for a complex cluster of cells which can be fully explained, predicted and also controlled in the language of evolutionary theory, we automatically lose access to moral insight.

The principles on which the self-organization of living beings are based do not explain what we should or should not do on moral grounds. Certainly, it is true that the emergence of species on our planet, which we can explain via evolutionary biology today, has favoured the development of a capacity for moral judgement among humans and other beings. Darwin was right to suppose that our moral understanding depends substantially on the fact that we are social creatures who cooperate with one another for the continued survival of individuals and our species: we coordinate our actions for purposes that lie beyond our direct egocentric profit. This can also be found among many other living beings, as Darwin knew, for he closely observed the behaviour of all manner of creatures on his travels. In addition to humans, apes, dogs, birds, dolphins, bees and many others are organized in such ways that their cooperation follows proto-moral principles. For example, scientists have found a 'fairness detector' among many beings – behavioural reactions indicating that a just distribution of resources can be more important than egotistical advantage.

It would be a mistake, however, to conclude from this that our moral insights can be reconstructed as a simple continuation of social instincts on a linguistically and culturally coded level. Many of our moral insights go far beyond any clan- or tribe-based thinking. In particular, our higher moral understanding is not tied to so-called **instrumental reason** – that is, tactical and strategic considerations for improving our coordinated survival. Moral understanding is not some control mechanism for biologically explicable 'eating and fleeing machines', to use an ironic turn of phrase coined by my Bonn colleague Wolfram Hogrebe.[53]

To be sure, non-moral anthropological facts do not only include human-biological or otherwise physically measurable attributes of humans; as spiritual beings, humans have history. How we understand ourselves as human beings and as a part of reality is examined in the humanities. Art, religion, the diversity of our languages and lifeworlds – all this is differentiated in an unfathomably complex way. The reality of the spirit contributes at least as much to the self-determination of humans as does the scientific examination of our survival conditions and their technological optimization.

One especially important aspect of this is that, as spiritual beings, we do not seamlessly become part of nature in the sense of modern natural science. Against this background, I distinguish between the universe and nature. The **universe** is all that can be explored using the methods of modern natural science; it is limited to the measurable realm. Whatever cannot be proved by experimental measurement lies outside of the domain of modern natural science. This is not initially a weakness but, rather, a strength, for this methodological self-restriction enables the advancement of knowledge.

Nature goes beyond the universe. It is that which we attempt to know through measurement, but whose complexity always makes it more than we think we know at any time. It is fundamentally impossible to explore or control nature in its entirety by scientific means. We do not know how far it goes beyond what we know today, so I must agree once more with Hans Jonas, who recommended that we remain open to 'the thought that natural science may not tell the whole story about Nature.'[54] One can sense this thought behind one of the earliest pronouncements about nature, made by Heraclitus of Ephesus, one of the first philosophers of nature, who is presumed to have lived in the sixth and fifth centuries BCE on the territory of present-day Turkey. The saying reads, 'Nature loves to hide' (φύσις κρύπτεσθαι φιλεῖ).[55]

Whichever philosophy of nature is ultimately correct, humans, as spiritual beings, go beyond nature. This already follows from our moral demands, for these are not facts of nature: they cannot fundamentally elude our knowledge. In addition, the natural sciences are unsuitable for ascertaining moral facts using measuring procedures or mathematical theorizing. This in no way means that there are no moral facts, simply that there is a great deal that cannot be scientifically explored or technologically controlled.

Some will counter here that we are part of nature, and that there cannot be anything that lies outside the universe yet is effective within our universe. But this opinion, known in philosophy as the **assumption of causal closure**, is disputed by renowned physicists who instead insist that abstract, not physically measurable realities (such as mathematical structures, but also moral values) must be seriously taken into account if we are to describe and explain the measurable conditions of the universe correctly. One of the pioneers of quantum computers, the Oxford physicist David Deutsch, showed that our cognitive faculty goes far beyond the measurable and puts us in spiritual contact with the infinite, which by its nature is not experimentally measurable but can be grasped via the formation of abstract mathematical structures.[56] The South African cosmologist and mathematician George Francis Rayner Ellis, with whom I have been collaborating for a number of years, has shown with other, in part physical arguments that our spiritual life has a causal influence on the universe, which is precisely not some causally closed space in which elementary particles are simply pushed around according to laws of nature.[57]

This works because causality – the relationship between causes and effects – does not consist in material-energetic systems encountering other material-energetic systems. My desire to buy a cooling drink at the height of summer in order to quench my thirst is not only a neuronal impulse but is also connected to the fact that I know where there are drinks and form the intention to buy a drink, to my taste, to the existence of production chains for drinks, and so on. This constellation of factors contributes decisively to any successful explanation of one's actions: what people do cannot generally be explained in physical terms.[58]

It is indispensable to take into account the self-exploration of humans in the humanities, namely anthropology, if we want to find out who we are and who we want to be. As our historical situatedness determines non-moral facts that affect our courses of action, moral progress requires that we take these facts into consideration. For each morally significant concrete action situation consists of a complex allocation of non-moral facts and self-evident moral truths: if we determine the right relation between the non-moral and the moral in an actual given situation, we are capable of ascertaining what is morally right as precisely as possible.

Ethics for everyone

Philosophy means love of wisdom. **Wisdom** (*sophia*) is the fallible faculty to find the right balance. In the context of the moral philosophy of New Moral Realism outlined in this book, this means that wisdom consists in establishing the right relation between non-moral facts and the self-evident moral truths known so far. If this succeeds, we can discover hitherto partially concealed moral facts and thus achieve moral progress.

The ancient Greeks referred to relation and balance with the word *logos*, a term that also corresponds to what we call 'reason'. This is the source of **logic**, the foundational discipline of philosophy, whose task is to reflect on reflection in a rational, systematic and thus scientific fashion. The triad of philosophy, ethics and logic combines ways of thinking that are required in order to achieve moral progress. For, as we have seen, this progress consists in uncovering and recognizing moral facts that are concealed by the complexity of our action situation or deliberately through propaganda, manipulation or other forms of deception.

As the ancient Greeks already knew, ethics cannot exist without what they called physics. This refers to the systematic exploration of nature (*physis*) in relation to the position of humans in the cosmos; this later developed by a circuitous route into today's natural, technological and life sciences.

The love of wisdom (and thus wisdom itself) can, like logic and ethics, be practised as a disciplined, rational reflection on what we should or should not do – independently of our individual background. Ethics deals with **higher morality** – that is, with what we owe humans as such and what we should or should not do, given that we are all humans. It also takes other living beings into account, as well as the habitat we all share, Planet Earth. We have moral obligations towards other beings and our planet (the environment), whether we like it or not. If we violate these moral obligations, this has negative long-term consequences that will initially be palpable only for a few people and beings, but at some point for all.

This fact lies behind the mythically and religiously expressed idea of a **moral destiny**: we often have the impression of being punished for our morally reprehensible deeds not only by other people but by the universe or nature or God/the gods. This impression is not entirely false; while there is no hidden (divine or non-divine) mechanism that rewards us for good deeds and punishes us for bad ones according to a particular logic, it is in the nature of morally reprehensible actions to have a destructive effect.

This can be shown through a philosophical line of reasoning. An action changes the state of reality with reference to an aim that the actor has chosen more or less consciously and more or less intentionally. The action of buying rolls presupposes that someone has the intention of buying rolls and someone else has the intention of producing them. Further people cultivate the fields on which to grow the grain that is needed for the flour in the rolls. This means that there is a complex system of action without which we would be unable to buy rolls. This system of action encompasses many coordinated intentions and plans. Some of these coordinates have come about over millennia and are passed on from generation to generation.

If we do change the given reality in a morally reprehensible way through our actions, this means that we are causing harm to ourselves or others, for we are then intervening in the system of coordinates for human actions, which becomes unstable when we do not treat all of its elements as we should.

A concrete example is the sometimes atrocious pay for the staff involved in the production and sale of a cup of coffee with milk. Workers on coffee plantations are exploited, as are the underpaid dairy farmers (to say nothing of the cows kept under species-inappropriate conditions). The result is that the exploited and underpaid must come up with some explanation so as to live with the fact that they are being palpably wronged. This leads to ideologies, systems of delusion and self-delusion that allow those involved to maintain a moral imbalance that they often cannot resist without taking considerable risks. This makes the system of action unstable, which the Israeli philosopher Adi Ophir refers to as the 'order of evils' in his book of the same name.[59]

Of course, the sometimes insufficient payment given to staff in the food sector does not cause the system of action to break down on its own; it is a comparatively minor evil that is balanced out in the social market economy through such mechanisms as trade unions, solidarity, universal healthcare and other dimensions of the welfare state. In the chain of this system of action, however, we eventually encounter forms of exploitation that are not at all balanced out in this way, since not all of the chain is subject to the influence of the social market economy. The agricultural industry, for example, is tied to global production chains that are not fully covered either by the balancing mechanisms of the modern democratic law-based state or by the social market economy. For example, the agricultural equipment that is used to produce our daily bread comes from somewhere. In addition, the agricultural industry has long been affected by climate change. Even in Germany, there are now phases of drought (while I write these lines, in fact) that result from the actions of us all, one significant part of which is that the historical and current contribution of Germany to dangerous CO_2 emissions is gigantic. Even if this is chance thanks to the implementation of ecological insights, Germany is still among the top offenders when it comes to environmental destruction if one considers the global significance of our automobile industry. Even if the country's share in world pollution is currently around 2 per cent, and thus incomparable to those of China or the USA, German businesses manufacture products in China and the USA, which means that some of the percentage attributed to those countries can ultimately be attributed to Germany. Our energy balance is tied to those of other affluent and industrial nations, as the systems of action are interconnected, which makes it misleading to measure our emissions in terms of nation-state territories: if rainforests are cut down in Brazil for the sake of German meat consumption, we are also to blame. Through this interlocking, the global accumulation of sometimes smaller and sometimes greater morally reprehensible action causes the gradual self-extermination of humanity.

This is partly because, to this day, many of us fail to recognize that we, as actors, are part of nature, which is neither our friend nor our foe but, rather, the space on which we depend, in which we can realize our actions, and which we always also change through those actions. It is precisely because we are capable of higher morality that we can destroy the planet and our own survival conditions, something that Kant already pointed out with particular severity. In his *Critique of the Power of Judgement*, he observes:

> ... it is so far from being the case that nature has made the human being its special favourite and favoured him with beneficence above all other animals, that it has rather spared him just as little as any other animal from its destructive effects, whether of pestilence, hunger, danger of flood, cold, attacks by other animals great and small, etc.; even more, the conflict in the natural predispositions of the human being, reduces himself and others of his own species, by means of plagues that he invents for himself, such as the oppression of domination, the barbarism of war, etc., to such need, and he works so hard for the destruction of his own species ....[60]

Unless we see the moral and non-moral facts in the appropriate relation to one another, even moral achievements such as the modern democratic law-based state will not help us, since states must profit from morally reprehensible entanglements, especially in their relations with the rest of the world, in order to survive. Thus the overall moral balance is a negative one and continues its tendency towards self-extermination. All this can only be changed by a fundamental rethinking whose aim is to align the coordinates of our actions systematically with moral objectives, which need to be developed in global cooperation.

The so-called neoliberal world order, which, broadly speaking, refers to the global production chains for consumer goods, which are used especially by the affluent part of humanity, rests on the massively asymmetrical distribution of material and symbolic resources. These include citizenship: someone born a German citizen undoubtedly has better prospects of a life in prosperity than someone born with Ugandan or Libyan citizenship. Each of us bears a part of the responsibility for this asymmetry, and we must finally act on it. Just as we should protect lives in times of the coronavirus by interrupting infection chains through social distancing and strict hygiene (and doing this largely voluntarily), we should in future also interrupt the production chains that cause extreme poverty, for the protection of humans as well as the environment and other living beings.

This does not mean that we should cease to produce consumer and luxury goods and revert to a pre-modern lifestyle in order to do what is morally right. Rather, it means that the age of a new enlightenment requires each one of us to make all manner of efforts to set up sustainable production chains whose goals must always include dismantling unjust asymmetries.

We need a moral and systematically sustainable economic order whose creation of economic value is systematically tied to the ideal of moral progress for all people – a moral, humane market economy that is not geared towards infinite growth.

It cannot only be the task of NGOs and resistance fighters of all kinds to implement what is morally right through struggle. Rather, it is the task of every person, and of course also the responsibility of governments (as well as a constructive parliamentary opposition) to make sustainability and justice their highest priorities. As long as the misconception persists that wanting what is morally right is automatically connected to leftist or green politics, or is merely the domain of naïve do-gooders, we will keep walking towards the abyss of self-destruction. What is morally right by definition goes beyond party divisions; this does not rule out the possibility that various parties might pursue this goal particularly emphatically at various times.

That is why we need a cosmopolitics of the *radical centre*, as Gregor Dotzauer once put it in *Die Zeit* to describe the spirit of the New Realism.[61] We must acknowledge the idea that morally ambitious politics is possible and necessary as a non-partisan value basis. One important sign that this is gradually getting through is the large number of progressive projects being realized in Germany during the tenure of the grand coalition[62] (albeit not always in blissful harmony). This includes same-sex marriage, improvements in the pension system, the energy transition, the intake of refugees in 2015, and the solidarity measures during the first coronavirus wave in 2020.

I am adducing this not as a party-political statement, which is not my concern as a philosopher, but to show that the democratic law-based state is still a suitable forum in which to fulfil its aim of offering not only procedures and mechanisms of choice but also room for moral progress. The politics of the radical centre, however (which, as stated above, cannot be tied to a particular party or coalition, but must be universally valid), demands considerably more of us. In particular, we must consistently observe the **cosmopolitan imperative**, which calls upon all of us to see ourselves as inhabitants of the same planet and part of one gigantic, complex system consisting of countless connected subsystems. No one – no government, no research institution, no head of any church or religion – can grasp this interplay in its entirety. Thus cosmopolitans always live in a state of insecurity that can never be fully overcome, and that is precisely where they draw the motivation and power for change: because reality is ultimately irreducibly complex and we can never fully control it, there is always a possibility of further moral progress.

Philosophy, and thus ethics too, are global and hence cosmopolitan by nature. It is fundamentally impossible to have an ethics that deals exclusively what the inhabitants of a single nation state should or should not do.

Kant and that great philosopher of nature and master thinker of Romanticism Friedrich Wilhelm Joseph Schelling, who built on Kant's work, call an attack on the kingdom of ends '**radical evil**'. Radical evil destroys higher morality and therefore allows, whether directly or indirectly, the most morally reprehensible – evil – actions. Anyone who thinks one bears moral responsibility only for the fellow citizens cooped up in the same nation state is thus implicitly or explicitly declaring all other people (and beings) fair game. That is why nationalism is so reprehensible: it constitutes a gigantic error about the foundations of morality.

This somewhat abstract philosophical reflection has a very concrete application, for it can be used to demand the introduction of philosophy, especially ethics and logic for everyone, as a required subject in schools and for preparations at pre-school age.

The new enlightenment demands ethics for everyone, regardless of the specific school system and regardless of religion, background, wealth, gender or political opinion.

We should teach our children not only arithmetic, reading and writing but also thinking, which invites them to strive for wisdom, not just consumption and quantifiable success. Only in this way can one learn to be happy.

Philosophy, as the discipline that reflects on reflection, does not belong to the past but intervenes fundamentally in the structures of modernity and its development. Without the progress in philosophical logic in the nineteenth and twentieth centuries, for example, there would be no computer science or digitalization. That these, no longer restrained by ethical, philosophical reflection, have contributed massively to a dangerous crisis of democracy (Trump would most likely not have become president without Twitter and Facebook, and the world would probably also have been spared Bolsonaro without WhatsApp) shows how the society of knowledge can suddenly turn its own instruments on itself as weapons. Scepticism towards science and political abuse of scientific knowledge can best be debunked, criticized and overcome by philosophical methods – using epistemology, the philosophy of science, ethics, political philosophy, social philosophy, and so on.

Scepticism towards philosophy as a science is thus at least as disastrous as scepticism towards other disciplines of science. It is scandalous, then, that the German school system still promotes the idea that philosophy and ethics are some form of alternative to religion, and certainly optional. How on earth can one contrast philosophy and ethics with religion? Christianity, the most widespread religion in Germany, would not even exist in its present form without philosophy, and it would be terrible if Christianity were incompatible with ethics. Philosophy and religion are two different beasts; the relationship between them is determined in the philosophy of religion, a highly developed branch of philosophy. Philosophy is neither automatically critical of religion nor automatically well disposed towards it, and ethics is as religious as logic, mathematics, biology, physics or German lessons – that is, not at all. Offering it as an alternative to religion and a merely optional subject testifies to a systemically entrenched contempt for human reason in our school system.

We teach our children elementary arithmetic, reading and writing but not rational reflection on the foundations of our actions. In this way, we as a society accept producing moral illiterates. Children and young people gain access to *rational* moral understanding only by chance, since our educational system is fundamentally decent and sufficiently advanced to develop their rational faculties. Modern society is not collapsing, simply because there are self-evident moral truths. Much of what is good and evil is obvious to us, even if some of it may be concealed by systems of deception in dark times.

Many of the challenges of the twenty-first century – which include advanced digital technology (such as artificial intelligence), overpopulation, global production chains, cyberwars and (anti)social media – cannot be tackled without deeper transdisciplinary reflection. This presupposes learning the theoretical argumentation processes for philosophical ethics, which has matured over millennia and must continually prove itself in unpredictable action situations by dealing with new discoveries of non-moral facts.

This process of moral progress has no ultimate goal, nor does it automatically move in a single direction. The complexity of reality exceeds anything we might imagine, and the uncertainty that becomes especially obvious for everyone in crisis situations never disappears entirely. The different subsystems of society must therefore cooperate to create sustainable forms of coexistence. This cannot possibly work within the conceptual space of nation states and borders; rather, it demands a universal ethics that must also be worked out in transcultural conversations. One must – of course – listen to and read philosophers and other theorists from Africa, Latin America, Asia, and so forth, and take into account a variety of different traditions to reach an appropriate conception of humans that is not distorted by stereotypes. Here there are still countless deficits, even within the EU – for example, the fact that Italian or Spanish thinkers are barely acknowledged in Germany.

We must think globally and develop a global philosophy beyond well-rehearsed traditions and prejudices, for what matters in this century is to secure the survival of humanity and build a just global society. The problems hurtling towards us cannot be tackled effectively at a national level; this applies as much to present and future pandemics as it does to climate change and the upheavals resulting from digitalization.

In ethical matters, it is not enough for people to argue in the free-for-all of political opinion-forming about what we should do, for ethics as a discipline ultimately deals not with disputes but with finding the truth. The arena of political battles is not the best place to advance philosophical research. Virologists have learned in the coronavirus crisis what can happen when science becomes entangled in political battles: they have been played off against one another in the media and politics, even as they repeatedly insisted that their specialist knowledge should not be misused as a direct recommendation of political action.

It would be a scandal running through all the talk shows and statistics if the majority of people in Germany (which obviously includes not only German citizens) were unable to read, write or add up, simply because we were neglecting to teach our children how to read, write and add up. No one would defend it. It is equally intolerable and indefensible, however, that philosophy or ethics is not a universally required subject.

It is a scandal that the majority of people in Germany are ethically illiterate and have received no systematic training in logically disciplined philosophical reflection on moral issues.

We will refer to the assertion that democracy is merely an administrative act with a partially elected government apparatus as **bureaucratism**. It is wrong, for the democratic law-based state is not simply a system of legally coded procedures for the adjustment and coordination of institutional processes of resource distribution. Democracy is not identical to bureaucracy; rather, bureaucracy serves democracy by providing procedures for the separate execution of processes in order to ascertain and implement the so-called will of the people via surveys and public debates. This is the task and the expertise of elected politicians, who do not push through their private opinions; rather, they attempt, in complex negotiation processes, to do what they consider democratically legitimate with the instruments at their disposal. They apply their own moral understanding to this end, for politicians are not some distant, unworldly elite, simply citizens who take on a particular task that is very demanding and carries considerable responsibility. They have to make far-reaching decisions under conditions of uncertainty and time pressure and in the arena of geopolitical and national-political conflict. Alongside public opinion-forming and debating culture, politicians must be informed about philosophical and ethical research (among other things); this is possible if we offer ethics for everyone, so that each individual can form a rational idea of the state of research.

As scientific disciplines, philosophy and ethics are tied to fallible knowledge claims and truth claims; philosophers cannot unilaterally issue prophetic declarations (on solitary walks in the woods, like Nietzsche) that are erratically acknowledged by society. We would never accept such a thing in STEM subjects (science, technology, engineering and mathematics) because we want to incorporate scientific-technological progress systematically into the fabric of our overall social action coordination (and loudmouths are the last thing we need for that).

The modern democratic law-based state came about as the result of the Enlightenment, and thus, among other things, of the French Revolution and its complex historical consequences. Countless people have sacrificed their lives for resistance and freedom struggles in order to enable a form of organization that now makes the principle of human dignity its priority. Our political order rests on moral progress, which it implements in the bureaucratic forms of the democratic law-based state. Where these do not correspond to moral facts, or no longer do so, we are entitled, as citizens of democratic law-based states, to demand a change of course – which fortunately succeeds on occasion.

Naturally one can have heated debates about abortion or assisted dying to establish the exact arguments for and against certain measures as well as their legal formulation. Decisions to introduce new laws and duties in a democratic law-based state are fallible but based on specific reasons.

The goal of a democratic debate is to find the truth by listening to reasons.

This is something that the democracy theorists Julian Nida-Rümeln and Rainer Forst have repeatedly emphasized in Germany. In each case we must establish which reasons are capable of truth and which complex considerations lead to which results. Specifically, such things as abortion, same-sex marriage and assisted dying are allowed under certain circumstances, because the reasons in favour of them outweigh those against them.

Admittedly, this is partly because the democratic law-based state must use ideologically neutral arguments (and, above all, must not base its decisions on any of the many religions represented in our countries). I am arguing in favour neither of atheism nor of the abolition of religious education, but we must understand that we need to make major changes to the school system.

Religion and ethics cannot be in conflict; having to choose between them is a disastrous decision, and a choice between philosophy and ethics is even worse. The school subject must be called 'philosophy', and it is concerned with learning how to address the fundamental questions of human life rationally. This includes ethics, but also logic, argumentation and epistemology.

By introducing ethics for everyone across the board, we could advance the democratic body politic not only as an administrative system but above all as a value system. The aim of this cooperation should be to develop a sustainable form of economic management and coexistence that allows humanity to live together peacefully in wellbeing and prosperity for many generations.

Epilogue

In this book I have tried to show with various examples how philosophical-ethical reasoning relates to our concrete everyday concerns and ways of thinking and how we can critically examine and overcome prejudices. My concern was not to offer an exhaustive study and develop a system of ethics for the twenty-first century – this is a Herculean task to which I will continue making contributions, especially in working out an ethics for socially disruptive information technologies (such as social media and artificial intelligence in general).

I will have reached my goal for now if you have understood that moral progress in dark times is possible, and that there are objectively existing moral facts that address us as humans and neither have nor need any justification through evolution, God or universal human reason. Ethics requires no substantiation outside of itself; its claims collapse if one does not acknowledge that rational, systematic, open-ended and fallible reflection is the best way to find out what we should or should not do for ethical reasons. This practice of reflection rests on a millennia-old history that began on the European continent with the ancient Greeks, but which is found in many cultures and also developed in the interwoven histories of other parts of humanity.

The aim and meaning of human life is a good life. A **good life** is one in which we make ourselves responsible actors in the kingdom of ends and understand ourselves as living beings that are capable of higher, universal morality. Such a conception of humans is the foundation of all enlightenment, which has occurred in various phases in all parts of the world at different times. Today, faced with the dark times we are experiencing, enlightenment is more essential than it has been for a long time; because of our morally reprehensible actions in the last two centuries of modernity, which have helped to erect disastrous systems of unjust resource distribution, we face the threat of self-extermination. If we wish to prevent this, it is crucial that we begin a new chapter of a *global enlightenment beyond nationalist distortions* (including Eurocentrisms).

I will therefore end by appealing to us all to participate in the project of a new enlightenment. After the coronavirus, our society cannot be the same as before; it is now even clearer that humanity is a global community of fate.

Spirit and higher morality are real, and they are interwoven with the factual structure of the material-energetic universe, with nature as a whole, in a never wholly explicable fashion. Reality is much too complex for that, which is why there is no 'end of history' either. Reality, as the place that cannot possibly be escaped from because there is no elsewhere, is not a utopia. It is the reality of the 'we', that which necessarily unites individuals into a 'we'.

What matters most is for us to realize this and to articulate that realization. I am optimistic about this, for it is still in our hands to do the right thing. Will we hear the wake-up call? Or will we soon be turning on one another again like greedy predators? It is up to us. Humans are free.

Glossary

The key terms listed here form the framework of the book's argument. Definitions of each term may be found on the pages indicated.

Notes

Preface to the English Edition

1 Francis Fukuyama, *The End of History and the Last Man* (London: Penguin, 1992).

2 Francis Fukuyama, *Liberalism and its Discontents* (London: Profile Books, 2022).

3 G. W. F. Hegel, *Lectures on the Philosophy of World History*, vol. I, ed. and trans. Robert F. Brown and Peter C. Hodgson (Oxford: Oxford University Press, 2011), p. 88.

4 On this concept, see Adi Ophir: *The Order of Evils: Toward an Ontology of Morals*, trans. Rela Mazali and Havi Karel (New York: Zone Books, 2005).

Introduction

1 See the famous thesis of the end of history in Francis Fukuyama, *The End of History and the Last Man* (London: Penguin, 1992). Contrast this with the more recent work by Ivan Krastev and Stephen Holmes, *The Light That Failed: A Reckoning* (London: Penguin, 2019).

2 See the calculations in Maja Göpel, *Unsere Welt neu denken: Eine Einladung* (Berlin: Ullstein, 2020), p. 50; naturally it was too early to take the coronavirus crisis into consideration.

3 The American philosopher Robert B. Brandom recently took a new interpretation of Hegel's philosophy as a point of departure for a sophisticated philosophy of trust whose socio-ontological deep structure might become part of the blueprint for a successful global socialization. See Robert Boyce Brandom, *A Spirit of Trust: A Reading of Hegel's Phenomenology* (Cambridge, MA: Harvard University Press, 2019).

4 See Thomas M. Scanlon's ground-breaking book *What We Owe to Each Other* (Cambridge, MA: Harvard University Press, 1998). For a defence of a moral realism similar to the position I develop in the present book, see, by the same author, *Being Realistic about Reasons* (Oxford: Oxford University Press, 2013). In his most recent book, Scanlon shows why, from an ethical perspective, socioeconomic inequality leads to moral imbalances. See *Why Does Inequality Matter?* (Oxford: Oxford University Press, 2018).

5 This goes hand in hand with a far-reaching revolution in ethics that was first brought to light in all its clarity by Hans Jonas. It implies that we need a new form of bio- and techno-ethics that goes far beyond what was conceivable in classical and modern philosophy, when human actions mostly affected only small groups. The effects of modern advanced technology apply to everyone, however, which makes it a more urgent task than ever to develop universal values for the twenty-first century. I would recommend Hans Jonas's central work to all my readers: *The Imperative of Responsibility: In Search of an Ethics for the Technological Age*, trans. Hans Jonas and David Herr (Chicago: University of Chicago Press, 1984).

6 See the at times remarkably irrational and fairly unsubstantiated overview of fictitious scenarios of a coming superintelligence in Nick Bostrom, *Superintelligence: Paths, Dangers, Strategies* (Oxford: Oxford University Press, 2014). Contrast with Markus Gabriel, *Der Sinn des Denkens* (Berlin: Ullstein, 2019). For an introduction to the novel thematic complex of the ethics of artificial intelligence, see Mark Coeckelbergh, *AI Ethics* (Cambridge, MA: MIT Press, 2020).

7 See the highly topical book by the Harvard economist Shoshana Zuboff, *The Age of Surveillance Capitalism: The Fight for a Human Future at the New Frontier of Power* (London: Profile Books, 2019).

8 In English in the original text (trans.).

9 Regarding the digital 'structural transformation of the public sphere' with reference to the famous book of that name by the social philosopher Jürgen Habermas, see Markus Gabriel, *Fiktionen* (Berlin: Suhrkamp, 2020), §§16f., as well as Armin Nassehi, *Muster: Theorie der digitalen Gesellschaft* (Munich: C. H. Beck, 2019).

10 See Bruno Latour, 'On the partial existence of existing and non-existing objects', in Lorraine Daston (ed.), *Biographies of Scientific Objects* (Chicago: University of Chicago Press, 2000), pp. 247–69. The American philosopher has gone to the trouble of thoroughly refuting Latour's fallacies, contradictions and false assumptions. See Paul A. Boghossian, *Fear of Knowledge: Against Relativism and Constructivism* (Oxford: Clarendon Press, 2007).

11 Bruno Latour, *Politics of Nature: How to Bring the Sciences into Democracy*, trans. Catherine Porter (Cambridge, MA: Harvard University Press, 2004).

12 I have already laid out the New Realism in (hopefully) easily understandable terms in my trilogy *Why the World Does Not Exist*, *I Am Not a Brain* and *The Meaning of Thought*, published [in the original German] from 2013 onwards. For an overview, see also Markus Gabriel (ed.), *Der neue Realismus* (Berlin: Suhrkamp, 2014), as well as Markus Gabriel and Matthias Eckoldt, *Die ewige*

Wahrheit und der Neue Realismus: Gespräche über (fast) alles, was der Fall ist (Heidelberg: Carl-Auer, 2019).

13 'AfD' is the abbreviation for Alternative für Deutschland [Alternative for Germany], the largest far-right party in Germany (trans.).

14 The politician Walter Lübcke, a member of the conservative CDU party, was murdered by a far-right terrorist in June 2019 on account of his efforts to help refugees (trans.).

15 In February 2020, a far-right assassin murdered nine young people with migrant backgrounds at two hookah lounges in Hanau (near Frankfurt). He subsequently killed himself (trans.).

16 See, for two examples among many, Michael Hampe, *Die Dritte Aufklärung* (Berlin: Nicolai, 2018), and Steven Pinker, *Enlightenment Now: The Case for Reason, Science, Humanism, and Progress* (New York: Penguin, 2018). I disagree with both on significant details and cite these books here only to point out that there is a palpable, factually based need for a new enlightenment.

17 Stanley Cavell, *The Claim of Reason: Wittgenstein, Skepticism, Morality, and Tragedy* (Oxford: Oxford University Press, 1999), p. 109.

Chapter 1 *What Values Are, and Why They Are Universal*

1 Terms that appear in bold type in the main text are listed in the glossary, which can also be used after reading the book in order to retrace the development of the argumentation via its basic concepts.

2 In the context of the New Realism – i.e., the philosophical position that forms the background of this book, there is also a fourth core thesis (**core thesis 4**): moral facts are *sui generis*; they cannot be attributed to any occurrence in the universe. They form their own field of meaning in the realm of the human spirit. The combination of these core theses and their integration into a more comprehensive philosophical panorama makes the overall position an innovation in the research landscape of moral realism. These are secondary aspects for an understanding of the reflections in the main text and will be developed more comprehensively elsewhere in relation to other current strains of moral realism.

3 By contrast, the *morally absolutely necessary, absolute good*, is something that one should do in **any** given situation.

4 This can be distinguished from the *morally absolutely forbidden, radical evil*, which is something that must not be done in any given situation.

5 Martha C. Nussbaum, *The Cosmopolitan Tradition: A Noble but Flawed Ideal* (Cambridge, MA: Harvard University Press, 2019).

6 Bertolt Brecht, *The Threepenny Opera*, trans. Ralph Manheim and John Willett (London: Bloomsbury, 2015), p. 55.

7 Jean-Paul Sartre, *Existentialism Is a Humanism*, trans. Carol Macomber (New Haven, CT: Yale University Press, 2007), p. 29.

8 However, not every form of state regulation necessarily prevents institutions from viewing us as people who are capable of moral understanding. The respective understanding that individuals implement in their way of life is not in opposition to the state, for, in a representative democracy, the state consists of a series of individual decisions made by individuals who are themselves, ideally, acting on moral understanding. When institutions such as the constitutional court or the federal government decide on steps for the implementation of moral understanding, they are not automatically dehumanizing the citizens.

9 John Leslie Mackie, *Ethics: Inventing Right and Wrong* (London: Penguin, 1990).

10 On the history of value nihilism, see Winfried Schröder, *Moralischer Nihilismus: Radikale Moralkritik von den Sophisten bis Nietzsche* (Stuttgart: Reclam, 2005).

11 In 2016, Böhmermann read out a satirical poem on television in which he accused Erdoğan of, among other things, beating girls, having sex with goats and watching child pornography (trans.).

12 www.morgenpost.de/berlin/article228228491/Diese-16-Sprueche-muss-sich-Kuenast-weiterhin-gefallen-lassen.html.

13 The *Reichsbürger* [Citizens of the Reich/Empire] movement is a loosely organized far-right tendency in Germany that denies the legitimacy of the modern German state and its democratic principles, regarding it as a betrayer of national values (trans.).

14 That is why Kant, in *The Metaphysics of Morals*, where he develops his philosophy of ethics and right, defines 'right' as the 'sum of conditions under which the choice of one can be united with the choice of another in accordance with a universal law of freedom' (Immanuel Kant, *The Metaphysics of Morals*, trans. Mary Gregor [Cambridge: Cambridge University Press, 2017], p. 27).

15 Samuel P. Huntington, *The Clash of Civilizations and the Remaking of World Order* (New York: Simon & Schuster, 2011) and *Who Are We? The Challenges to America's National Identity* (New York: Simon & Schuster, 2005).

16 See Amartya Sen, *Identity and Violence: The Illusion of Destiny* (New York: W. W. Norton, 2006).

17 In classical democracy, the Sophists were consciously used to shape opinion; they were a sort of cross between cunning lawyers and spin doctors, comparable to American figures such as Roger Stone or Rudolph Giuliani. Another example of an extreme sophist is the Canadian psychologist Jordan Peterson, who is on a crusade against political correctness; he poses as a white male victim of neo-Marxist colleagues and has generated millions of fans with this show.

18 Plato, *Republic*, trans. Robin Waterfield (Oxford: Oxford University Press, 1998), p. 16.

19 Ibid., p. 18.

20 Ibid., p. 19.

21 See, for example, the famous statements in Karl Marx and Friedrich Engels, *The German Ideology* (New York: International, 1970), p. 47: 'Morality, religion, metaphysics, and all the rest of ideology and their corresponding forms of consciousness, thus no longer retain the semblance of independence. They have no history, no development; but men, developing their material production and their material intercourse, alter, along with this their real existence, their thinking and the products of their thinking. Life is not determined by consciousness, but consciousness by life.' Ibid., p. 247: 'communists do not preach *morality* at all. They do not put to people the moral demand: love one another, do not be egoists ....' Rather, the discoveries of the authors of *The German Ideology* 'shattered the basis for all morality' (ibid., p. 115). For a discussion of Marx's critique of morality, which at times itself seems moralistic, see Denis Mäder, *Fortschritt bei Marx* (Berlin: Akademie, 2010), pp. 255ff.

22 Paul A. Boghossian, *Fear of Knowledge: Against Relativism and Constructivism* (Oxford: Clarendon Press, 2007), and 'Der Relativismus des Normativen', in Markus Gabriel (ed.), *Der neue Realismus* (Berlin: Suhrkamp, 2014).

23 Boghossian, 'Der Relativismus des Normativen', pp. 366f.

24 'Valuing Diversity – Fostering Cohesion'. Speech by Federal President Christian Wulff on the twentieth anniversary of German reunification on 3 October 2010 in Bremen, www.bundespraesident.de/SharedDocs/Reden/EN/ChristianWulff/Reden/2010/101003-Deutsche-Einheit-englisch.html.

25 For incisive comments on the USA, see Brian Leiter, *Why Tolerate Religion?* (Princeton, NJ: Princeton University Press, 2014).

26 *The Baghavad Gita*, trans. Bibek Debrory (New Delhi: Penguin Books India, 2005).

27 This epithet refers to Armin Meiwes, who in 2001 killed and partly ate a man (who participated voluntarily) (trans.).

28 John Rawls, *A Theory of Justice* (Cambridge, MA: Harvard University Press, 1971).

29 See, for example, the study by Edmond Awad, Sohan Dsouza, Azim Shariff, Iyad Rahwan and Jean-François Bonnefon, 'Universals and variations in moral decisions made in 42 countries by 70,000 participants', in *Proceedings of the National Academy of Sciences* 117/5 (2020), pp. 2332–7.

30 See the seminal investigation by Victor Farías, *Heidegger and Nazism* (Philadephia: Temple University Press, 1989), and Emmanuel Faye, *Heidegger:*

The Introduction of Nazism into Philosophy, trans. Michael B. Smith (New Haven, CT: Yale University Press, 2009). For an overview of the more recent debate, see *Heidegger's Black Notebooks: Responses to Anti-Semitism*, ed. Andrew J. Mitchell and Peter Trawny (New York: Columbia University Press, 2017).

31 Carl Schmitt, *The Tyranny of Values*, ed. and trans. Simona Draghici (Washington, DC: Plutarch Press, 1996).

32 For those who are unfamiliar with my own critique of metaphysics: because the world does not exist, metaphysics fails as a theory of absolutely everything, of reality as a whole. That is what *Why the World Does Not Exist* and *Meaning and Existence* deal with. In the same books, however, I also argue that there are non-physical objects which are genuinely and even measurably effective – this is the subject matter of *I Am Not a Brain*, *The Meaning of Thought*, *Neo-Existentialism* and *Fiktionen*. On the various understandings of metaphysics and their connection to the ontology of conceptual fields, see Markus Gabriel, 'Metaphysik oder Ontologie?', in *Perspektiven der Philosophie: Neues Jahrbuch* 42 (2016), pp. 73–93. My reading of the Schmitt quotation rests on the assumption that Schmitt here understands 'the metaphysical' as something that is not physically measurable, which is connected to the contrast between positivism and metaphysics.

33 For an introduction, see Kant's classic, *Groundwork of the Metaphysics of Morals*. Kant's concept of metaphysics as a whole is difficult to pin down, for he argues that there are also 'metaphysical foundations of natural science', and he worked on a scientific metaphysics throughout his life. It is surely one of Kant's basic operations, however, to locate the *ought* outside of what can be known and explained through natural science, while reconciling this with the fact that we, as organisms, are part of what can be known and explained through natural science.

34 See Christoph Möllers, *The Possibility of Norms*, trans. Alex Holznienkemper (Oxford: Oxford University Press, 2020). For an engagement with this approach, see Markus Gabriel, *Fiktionen* (Berlin: Suhrkamp, 2020), §14.

35 Martin Heidegger, *Anmerkungen I–IV (Schwarze Hefte 1942–1948)* (Frankfurt: Klostermann, 2015), p. 20.

36 One of the most prominent and extreme figures in the AfD (trans.).

37 Höcke used this phrase in his verbal attack on the Holocaust memorial in Berlin (trans.).

38 Co-leader of the AfD (with Jörg Meuthen) from 2017 to 2019 and co-leader of the AfD's parliamentary group (with Alice Weidel) from 2017 to 2021 (trans.).

39 Friedrich Nietzsche, *On the Genealogy of Morals*, trans. Douglas Smith (Oxford: Oxford University Press, 1996), p. 5.

40 Johann Wolfgang von Goethe, *Faust: Part One*, trans. David Luke (Oxford: Oxford University Press, 1998), p. 42.

41 Nietzsche, *On the Genealogy of Morals*, p. 8.

42 See, for example, Jason Stanley's theory of propaganda in *How Propaganda Works* (Princeton, NJ: Princeton University Press, 2015), as well as his book *How Fascism Works: The Politics of Us and Them* (New York: Random House, 2018).

Chapter 2 Why There Are Moral Facts but Not Ethical Dilemmas

1 Donald Davidson, 'On the very idea of a conceptual scheme', in *Proceedings and Addresses of the American Philosophical Association, 1973–4*. Julian Nida-Rümelin, in *Demokratie und Wahrheit* (Munich: C. H. Beck, 2006), develops a definition of the relationship between democracy and truth on a similar basis.

2 On the discovery of the universal before and outside of the European cultural sphere, see Jan Assmann, *Achsenzeit: Eine Archäologie der Moderne* (Munich: C. H. Beck, 2018). For an overview of the African discussion, see Kwasi Wiredu, *Cultural Universals and Particulars: An African Perspective* (Bloomington: Indiana University Press, 1996), as well as the essays in Franziska Dübgen and Stefan Skupien (eds), *Afrikanische politische Philosophie* (Berlin: Suhrkamp, 2015). For the Chinese context, see Zhao Tingyang, *All Under Heaven: The Tianxia System for a Possible World Order*, trans. Joseph E. Harroff (Oakland: University of California Press, 2021).

3 See Michael Zeuske, *Sklaverei: Eine Menschheitsgeschichte von der Steinzeit bis heute* (Stuttgart: Reclam, 2018).

4 Regarding torture from a philosophical perspective, see Jay Bernstein, *Torture and Dignity: An Essay on Moral Injury* (Chicago: University of Chicago Press, 2015).

5 Anyone interested in the theoretical details of the social ontology underlying this book should consult the third part of Markus Gabriel, *Fiktionen* (Berlin: Suhrkamp, 2020).

6 One can argue about this principle in certain exceptional cases, but it applies fully in the vast majority of cases. I am thinking of the following: in philosophy, there is a central discussion on whether we can be mistaken about whether we are conscious, which takes us deep into the theory of self-consciousness and has an impact on the theory of action. Anyone interested in this should investigate the philosophical conception articulated by the philosopher Sebastian Rödl, who teaches in Leipzig; he seeks to show that we are far less mistaken about ourselves than one might think, for there is a core area of error-proof self-knowledge. See Sebastian Rödl, *Self-Consciousness and Objectivity: An*

Introduction to Absolute Idealism (Cambridge, MA: Harvard University Press, 2018).

7 Anne Will is a well-known German political talk-show host and former newsreader (trans.).

8 Aristotle, *Metaphysics*, trans. Hugh Lawson-Tancred (London: Penguin, 1998), p. 107 (1011b).

9 For an introduction to the field of epistemology, which deals with the scope and structure of human truth claims, see Markus Gabriel, *Die Erkenntnis der Welt: Eine Einführung in die Erkenntnistheorie* (Freiburg: Alber, 2012).

10 Thomas Nagel, *The View from Nowhere* (Oxford: Oxford University Press, 1986).

11 For more details, see Gabriel, *Die Erkenntnis der Welt*, chapter II.1.

12 See Markus Gabriel, *Why the World Does Not Exist* (Cambridge: Polity, 2015), chapter V.

13 Peter Singer, *Practical Ethics* (Cambridge: Cambridge University Press, 2011), pp. 4f.

14 G. W. Leibniz, *New Essays on Human Understanding*, ed. and trans. Peter Remnant and Jonathan Bennett (Cambridge: Cambridge University Press, 1996), p. 7: 'Nothing takes place suddenly, and it is one of my great and best confirmed maxims that nature never makes leaps.' For a recent treatment of the evolutionary prehistory of morality, see Patricia S. Churchland, *Conscience: The Origins of Moral Intuition* (New York: W. W. Norton, 2019).

15 Sharon Hewitt Rawlette, *The Feeling of Value: Moral Realism Grounded in Phenomenal Consciousness* (CreateSpace Independent Publishing Platform, 2016).

16 On 19 February 2020, a far-right extremist went on a killing spree at two hookah lounges in the German town of Hanau, killing nine people with migrant backgrounds and wounding five others before killing his mother and himself (trans.).

17 Johann Wolfgang von Goethe, *Werke: Hamburger Ausgabe*, vol. 2 (Munich: C. H. Beck, 1998), p. 330.

18 SED stands for *Sozialistische Einheitspartei Deutschlands* (Socialist Unity Party of Germany), the founding and ruling party of the GDR (trans.).

19 Renate Künast is a Green Party MP and former minister of food and agriculture (2002–5). In 2019 she unsuccessfully sued Facebook over abusive, frequently sexist comments made by various users (trans.).

20 Immanuel Kant, *Groundwork of the Metaphysics of Morals*, ed. and trans. Mary Gregor (Cambridge: Cambridge University Press, 1997), p. 31 (translation modified).

21 Ibid., p. 38.

22 Markus Gabriel, *Der Sinn des Denkens* (Berlin: Ullstein, 2019), pp. 178–87.

23 Immanuel Kant, *Grounding for the Metaphysics of Morals: with On a Supposed Right to Lie because of Philanthropic Concerns*, trans. James W. Ellington (Indianapolis: Hackett, 1993), pp. 63–8.

24 Robert Habeck is co-leader of the German Green Party. Following the 2021 general election he was appointed minister of economic affairs and climate action as well as vice-chancellor (trans.).

25 Slavoj Žižek, 'My dream of Wuhan', *Die Welt*, 5 February 2020, www.welt.de/kultur/article205630967/Slavoj-Zizek-My-Dream-of-Wuhan.html.

26 Thaddeus Metz, 'Auf dem Weg zu einer Afrikanischen Moraltheorie', in Franziska Dübgen and Stefan Skupien (eds), *Afrikanische politische Philosophie: Postkoloniale Positionen* (Berlin: Suhrkamp, 2015), pp. 300–3. Metz lists further moral demands, though they express local social normativity rather than universal principles, as he himself concedes. The overall weakness of this approach is that it adduces local 'African' moral judgements instead of arguing that these judgements and ways of thinking found in Africa are well founded and thus morally universal. In ethics, it is a matter not of playing Africa off against Europe, or vice versa, but of ascertaining what is universally right. To be sure, one can often find some moral insights outside of Europe and the so-called West that are superior to some of our moral ills, which applies especially to principles I) and J) in Metz's catalogue, but also to the environmental ethics of many peoples who have been living in the Amazon region for millennia. Modern scientific-technological progress leads equally to moral regressions and in no way guarantees that inhabitants of affluent territories are automatically morally superior. Obviously we Europeans can learn a great deal from Africans, Latin Americans and Asians. What matters in the twenty-first century is to develop the foundations of a morally tenable cosmopolitics. Nationalist presumption and the notion that any continent enjoys moral superiority are clearly moral ills and thus make no positive contribution to the ethical grounding of moral judgements.

27 Gertrude Elisabeth Anscombe, *Intention* (Cambridge, MA: Harvard University Press, 2000).

28 See Andreas Rödder, *Konservativ 21.0: Eine Agenda für Deutschland* (Munich: C. H. Beck, 2019), and Thomas Bauer, *Die Vereindeutigung der Welt: Über den Verlust an Mehrdeutigkeit und Vielfalt* (Stuttgart: Reclam, 2018). Unfortunately, Bauer's argumentation rests on a whole array of postmodern errors about truth that he makes on pp. 26–30. The following result of his anti-truth reflections is also unacceptable: 'Democratic decisions cannot stake any claims to truth, purity or timeless validity' (p. 84). This view is irreconcilable with the

foundations of the democratic law-based state, especially the recognition of clear universal human rights. The internal contradiction of Bauer's approach has consequences here, for he is very unambiguously against disambiguation [*Vereindeutigung*] and even makes rather strident truth claims, such as when he claims (without any supporting sources): 'In over a thousand years before the late twentieth century, there was [in legal systems based on Islamic law] almost no stoning of adulterers, let alone any executions because of consensual homosexual acts' (p. 37). There is reason to doubt this, and I would be very surprised if there were reliable statistics for such executions and corporal punishments documenting this practice over the last thousand years.

29 All anonymous references to the (federal) chancellor in this book refer to Angela Merkel, who held the position until December 2021 (trans.).

30 Immanuel Kant, *Critique of Pure Reason*, ed. and trans. Paul Guyer and Allen W. Wood (Cambridge: Cambridge University Press, 1998), p. 542.

31 Crispin Wright, *Truth and Objectivity* (Cambridge, MA: Harvard University Press, 2009), pp. 1f.

32 For an overview, see the introduction by Mark Coeckelbergh, *AI Ethics* (Cambridge, MA: MIT Press, 2020).

33 Kant, *Groundwork of the Metaphysics of Morals*, p. 41.

34 Ronald Dworkin, 'Objectivity and truth: you'd better believe it', *Philosophy & Public Affairs* 25/2 (1996), pp. 104f.

35 Ernst Tugendhat, *Vorlesungen über Ethik* (Frankfurt: Suhrkamp, 1994).

36 Ibid., p. 87.

37 See www.ekd.de/Zehn-Gebote-10802.htm. This order and division of commandments follows Lutheran and Catholic traditions, while other Christian and Jewish denominations insert 'You shall not make a graven image' as the second commandment and combine the last two into one (trans.).

38 See https://en.wikipedia.org/wiki/Fundamental_Law_of_Vatican_City_State.

39 Regarding this position, which denies the existence of a higher morality – that is, one that goes beyond our clan-based notions – see Richard Dawkins, *The Selfish Gene* (Oxford: Oxford University Press, 1976).

40 On this concept of spirit, see Markus Gabriel, *I Am Not a Brain* (Cambridge: Polity, 2017) and *Neo-Existentialism* (Cambridge: Polity, 2018), as well as the second part of *Fiktionen*.

41 Concerning the more technical philosophical point arising especially from Robert Brandom's philosophy, see Markus Gabriel, *An den Grenzen der Erkenntnistheorie: Die notwendige Endlichkeit des objektiven Wissens als Lektion des Skeptizismus* (Freiburg: Alber, 2014), and, by way of introduction, Gabriel, *Die Erkenntnis der Welt*.

Chapter 3 Social Identity

1 For an impression of recent argumentation, see Kwame Anthony Appiah, *The Lies That Bind: Rethinking Identity* (London: Profile Books, 2018). Regarding the emergence of the understanding that the concept of race is sociologically untenable, see Jürgen Kaube, *Max Weber: Ein Leben zwischen den Epochen* (Reinbek: Rowohlt, 2014), pp. 190–224.

2 See the famous analysis of the contingency of our everyday world in Peter L. Berger and Thomas Luckmann, *The Social Construction of Reality: A Treatise in the Sociology of Knowledge* (London: Penguin, 1991). Both Husserl and Berger and Luckmann overplay their hand, because they do not take into account that our everyday lifeworld follows on from our biological life form and is thus by no means entirely socially constructed. But that is a different issue; for a more detailed discussion, see Markus Gabriel, *Fiktionen* (Berlin: Suhrkamp, 2020).

3 A provincial Bavarian town with particular importance for the cultivation of Bavarian traditions (trans.).

4 The word *Kartoffel* [potato] is used as a slang term for (white) ethnic Germans, as opposed to people from migrant backgrounds (trans.).

5 Though rather obscure in its derivation (*kanaka*, Hawaiian for 'human'), the word *Kanake* is a well-established ethnic slur for people from Middle Eastern and Southern European backgrounds, especially from Turkey. It was introduced following the influx of migrant workers from Greece, Turkey and Italy in the 1950s and 1960s and has also been reclaimed as a self-identifying term (trans.).

6 *Weissbier* is a typically Bavarian wheat beer and *Weisswurst* is a typically Bavarian soft, white sausage usually eaten with sweet mustard (trans.).

7 Walter Lippmann, *Public Opinion* (New York: Simon & Schuster, 1997), p. 69.

8 Ibid., p. 59.

9 Ibid., p. 97.

10 Markus Gabriel, 'Der Hygienismus kann in eine Gesundheitsdiktatur umschlagen', *Die Welt*, 21 April 2020.

11 The ontology of non-existent objects is rather complex in its details; those interested in them should see Gabriel, *Fiktionen*, §§1–5.

12 For a more extensive discussion, see Gabriel, *Der Sinn des Denkens* (Berlin: Ullstein, 2019), pp. 223–41.

13 Unfortunately, one does find racist mentalities in the work of Fichte, Schelling and Hegel (to name the most famous thinkers active in Jena), but they also argued against the racism of their time, such as the theory of phrenology, which was popular at the time and attempted to attribute human character traits and races to the shape of the skull.

14 Martin S. Fischer, Uwe Hossfeld, Johannes Krause and Stefan Richter, 'Jenaer Erklärung – Das Konzept der Rasse ist das Ergebnis von Rassismus und nicht dessen Voraussetzung', *Biologie in unserer Zeit* 49/6 (2019), pp. 399–402.

15 Ibid., pp. 400f.

16 In the original German, the author uses the English word 'race' here and notes the difference between the biologically understood German word *Rasse* (which is also used for animals) and its more socially defined use in English (trans.).

17 A famous German television and film actor (trans.).

18 A German Green Party MP of Turkish parentage. Following the 2021 general election he was appointed minister of food and agriculture (trans.).

19 An Eritrean-born German radio and television presenter (trans.).

20 Nina Power, *One Dimensional Woman* (Winchester: O Books, 2009).

21 See especially Richard Rorty, *Philosophy and the Mirror of Nature* (Princeton, NJ: Princeton University Press, 2009) and *Contingency, Irony and Solidarity* (Cambridge: Cambridge University Press, 1989).

22 Immanuel Kant, 'An answer to the question: what is enlightenment?', in *Political Writings*, ed. H. S. Reiss, trans. H. B. Nisbet (Cambridge: Cambridge University Press, 1991), p. 54.

23 Ludwig Wittgenstein, *Philosophical Investigations*, ed. P. M. S. Hacker and Joachim Schulte, trans. G. E. M. Anscombe, P. M. S. Hacker and Joachim Schulte (Oxford: Blackwell, 2009), p. 110e.

24 See his masterpiece *A Spirit of Trust* (Cambridge, MA: Harvard University Press, 2019), though it is not recommended for laypersons. For an introduction, see Robert B. Brandom, *Articulating Reasons: An Introduction to Inferentialism* (Cambridge, MA: Harvard University Press, 2000).

25 Wittgenstein, *Philosophical Investigations*, p. 49e.

26 Thomas Sturm, '"Rituale sind wichtig": Hans-Georg Gadamer über Chancen und Grenzen der Philosophie', *Der Spiegel* 8/2000.

27 Max Weber, *Economy and Society*, ed. Guenther Roth and Claus Wittich (Berkeley: University of California Press, 1978).

28 Ibid., p. 395.

29 Ibid., p. 389.

30 Ibid., p. 387.

31 Ibid., p. 389.

32 Ibid.

33 Ibid. (translation modified).

34 Concerning the social *person* as opposed to the non-social *individual*, see Gabriel, *Der Sinn des Denkens*, pp. 183–7. On society as an imaginary space, see Cornelius Castoriadis, *The Imaginary Institution of Society*, trans. Kathleen

Blamey (Cambridge, MA: MIT Press, 1997), as well as Gabriel, *Fiktionen*, §§12–17.

35 The expression *das Volk der Dichter und Denker* is a traditional German self-description promoted by cultural patriots (trans.).

36 Anyone wishing to understand the scale of Hegel's philosophizing under the present conditions of philosophical theory should plough through the brilliant masterpiece by the American philosopher Robert B. Brandom. In his 2019 book, he succeeded in analytically deciphering Hegel's *Phenomenology of Spirit* and reconstructing it at the theoretical level of the present day. See Brandom, *A Spirit of Trust*.

37 Thilo Sarrazin, the former SPD finance senator in the Berlin Senate and holder of various positions in the financial world, was in fact expelled from the party on 31 July 2020. This was the culmination of a prolonged conflict over the anti-immigrant and anti-Muslim rhetoric with which he became associated from roughly 2010 onwards, displayed in several books. Boris Palmer is the mayor of Tübingen and has likewise been criticized heavily by his party comrades for insensitive or offensive remarks. Proceedings to expel him from the Green Party were initiated in November 2021 (trans.).

38 For an overview and introduction, see Manuel Anselmi, *Populism: An Introduction* (Abingdon: Routledge, 2018).

39 Gabriel, *Fiktionen*, §13.

40 See Gabriel, *I Am Not a Brain* (Cambridge: Polity, 2017), *Fiktionen* and *Neo-Existentialism* (Cambridge: Polity, 2018). It is possible that we share spirit with other living beings, but that is a different issue; for we certainly do not share all specifics with all living beings, which means that the presence of spirit is common in the animal kingdom and maybe beyond that, depending on whether God and an immortal soul exist. If that is the case, spirit is not even tied to embodiment. This does not have to be decided here, however, since we are dealing with the terrestrial conditions of our moral responsibility and embeddedness. I would at least point out, however, that the fact that we are animals of a particular kind does not mean that we are *only* animals. There are no findings in natural science which prove that neither God nor an immortal soul exist. The possible character of the scientifically observable universe has no bearing on the metaphysical question of whether there are dimensions of reality that go beyond what can be scientifically observed. Furthermore, the answer to this question is still yes, since mathematical, aesthetic and indeed moral facts, for example, are not scientifically observable. There are certainly connections between scientifically observable processes and other conceptual fields of reality, but these connections are not the same as identity; numbers, for example, are

not identical to groups of material objects. The number 4 is not the amount of all groups of material objects of which there are four, but rather an abstract structure. The mathematician and philosopher Gottlob Frege proved this for mathematics in his brilliant treatise *The Foundations of Arithmetic*. For moral facts, it should really be enough to refer to Plato, who showed convincingly in many of his dialogues, such as the *Republic*, the *Euthyphron*, the *Phaedo* and the *Apology*, that there are moral facts which, independently of our respective opinions, pass judgement on the moral value of our actions. Like it or not, there is justice beyond court cases.

41 This is not intended to justify immoral behaviour towards other animals. Rather, animal ethics is based on the fact that we, as humans, have a special capacity for moral understanding. A principle formulated by Hans Jonas applies here: *we have moral responsibility for all those over whom we have power.* As science and technology give us power over other living beings, we are also responsible for them.

42 Bernard Williams, *Morality: An Introduction to Ethics* (Cambridge: Cambridge University Press, 1972), p. 53.

43 See Gabriel, *Why the World Does Not Exist* (Cambridge: Polity, 2015) and *Fiktionen.*

44 Identity politics must first be undone through difference politics. This is a first step towards progress and was in fact one of the aims of the difference philosophies of the previous century, associated especially with names such as Emmanuel Levinas, Jacques Derrida and Luce Irigaray. Paradoxically, the identity politics of our time is a regressive reaction to the advances made by these theorists of difference, who – especially Derrida – were committed to a form of what I call indifference politics. Derrida, incidentally, along with Saint Augustine, Albert Camus and Alain Badiou – probably the most influential French philosopher today – is one of the most important North African philosophers engaged with in Europe and the USA. Especially in his late work *The Politics of Friendship*, Derrida developed a universalist ethics on the basis of a theory of hospitality, an ethics whose full potential has not yet been uncovered. See the important study by Philip Freytag, *Die Rahmung des Hintergrunds: Eine Untersuchung über die Voraussetzungen von Sprachtheorien am Leitfaden der Debatten Derrida–Searle und Derrida–Habermas* (Frankfurt: Klostermann, 2018).

Chapter 4 Moral Progress in the Twenty-First Century

1 For more detail, see Gabriel, *I Am Not a Brain* (Cambridge: Polity, 2017), *Der Sinn des Denkens* (Berlin: Ullstein, 2019) and *Fiktionen* (Berlin: Suhrkamp, 2020).

2 For an introduction to this wide-ranging subject, see Jan Rehmann, *Einführung in die Ideologietheorie* (Hamburg: Argument, 2008). On contemporary theorizing, see Gabriel, *Fiktionen*, §§12–17.

3 See Shoshana Zuboff, *The Age of Surveillance Capitalism: The Fight for a Human Future at the New Frontier of Power* (New York: Public Affairs, 2019); Yvonne Hofstetter, *Der unsichtbare Krieg: Wie die Digitalisierung Sicherheit und Stabilität in der Welt bedroht* (Munich: Droemer, 2019), *Das Ende der Demokratie: Wie die künstliche Intelligenz die Politik übernimmt und uns entmündigt* (Munich: C. Bertelsmann, 2016) and *Sie wissen alles: Wie intelligente Maschinen in unser Leben eindringen und warum wir für unsere Freiheit kämpfen müssen* (Munich: C. Bertelsmann, 2014).

4 This is not to say that art, culture and religion automatically have an emancipatory effect. There is good and bad art, good and bad religion; art, culture and religion are only morally valuable if they are based on good. To the extent that they are tied to human practices, they always express how humans see themselves at a particular time. For more detail, see Gabriel, *Why the World Does Not Exist* (Cambridge: Polity, 2015), chapters V–VII.

5 Hans Jonas, *The Imperative of Responsibility* (Chicago: University of Chicago Press, 1984), pp. 2f. (translation modified).

6 For an in-depth treatment, see Michael Zeuske, *Sklaverei* (Stuttgart: Reclam, 2018).

7 Stephen Cave, 'Intelligence: a history', *Aeon* (2017), https://aeon.co/essays/on-the-dark-history-of-intelligence-as-domination.

8 Thilo Sarrazin, *Feindliche Übernahme: Wie der Islam den Fortschritt behindert und die Gesellschaft bedroht* (Munich: FinanzBuch, 2018), p. 277.

9 Ibid., p. 143.

10 Andreas Urs Sommer, *Werte: Warum man sie braucht, obwohl es sie nicht gibt* (Stuttgart: J. B. Metzler, 2016).

11 Ibid.

12 Ibid.

13 The details of the historical situation are more complicated, however, as the concept of slavery gathers together different forms of asymmetrical dependency. There are various forms of slavery that change over history and are manifested differently in different contexts; this does not make slavery any better, but it needs to be taken into account for a comprehensive study and reconstruction of the moral weaknesses of such dependencies. This has been a research topic since 2019 at the Bonn Excellence Initiative 'Beyond Freedom and Slavery: Asymmetrische Abhängigkeiten in vormodernen Gesellschaften'. From this research context, see the excellent book by Zeuske, *Sklaverei*.

14 Which Aristotle seems to mean, as the following famous passage from the *Politics* suggests: 'For he who can be, and therefore is, another's, and he who participates in reason enough to apprehend, but not to have, is a slave by nature' (Aristotle, *The Politics and The Constitution of Athens*, ed. Stephen Everson [Cambridge: Cambridge University Press, 1996], p. 17).

15 Zeuske, *Sklaverei*, p. 7.

16 Ibid., p. 25.

17 Aristotle, *The Politics*, p. 15.

18 The concept of capitalism admittedly has many meanings, and it is not always clear what its defenders and critics are actually arguing about. For a philosophical clarification at the level of contemporary social philosophy, see Nancy Fraser and Rahel Jaeggi, *Capitalism: A Conversation in Critical Theory* (Cambridge: Polity, 2018).

19 On the morally reprehensible market logic of the health system, see Giovanni Maio, *Geschäftsmodell Gesundheit: Wie der Markt die Heilkunst abschafft* (Berlin: Suhrkamp, 2015).

20 Markus Gabriel, 'Die meisten liberalen Demokratien haben eine Ausgangssperre verhängt – doch ist sie, ethisch betrachtet, wirklich gerechtfertigt?', *Neue Zürcher Zeitung*, 26 March 2020, and 'Der Hygienismus kann in eine Gesundheitsdiktatur umschlagen', *Die Welt*, 21 April 2020.

21 David Runciman, 'Coronavirus has not suspended politics – it has revealed the nature of power', *The Guardian*, 27 March 2020, www.theguardian.com/commentisfree/2020/mar/27/coronavirus-politics-lockdown-hobbes.

22 See the precise reconstruction of the legal-philosophical and state-philosophical situation for theory in this field in Christoph Menke, *Kritik der Rechte* (Berlin: Suhrkamp, 2015).

23 For an introduction to the neoliberal school of thought, see Matthew Eagleton-Pierce, *Neoliberalism: The Key Concepts* (Abingdon: Routledge, 2016).

24 I refer the reader once again to the calculations in Maja Göpel, *Unsere Welt neu denken* (Berlin: Ullstein, 2020).

25 Ibid., p. 152.

26 Scholarship on Smith has shown that Smith himself did not pave the way in any relevant sense for *Homo oeconomicus*, as his conception of humans is, rather, based on the premise that society comes from morality, which latter consists in the fact that we always assess ourselves in the light of others and depend on mutual assistance. Smith does not hold the mistaken view that humans are primarily selfish by nature. For a more detailed account, see Reiner Manstetten, *Das Menschenbild der Ökonomie – Der homo oeconomicus und die Anthropologie von Adam Smith* (Freiburg: Alber, 2002).

27 For one prominent voice among many, see Amartya Sen, *The Idea of Justice* (London: Penguin, 2010).

28 See the introductory description in Göpel, *Unsere Welt neu denken*, pp. 55–73.

29 See www.margaretthatcher.org/document/106689.

30 John Blundell, *Margaret Thatcher: A Portrait of the Iron Lady* (New York: Algora, 2008), p. 193.

31 Luciano Floridi, *The Fourth Revolution: How the Infosphere is Reshaping Human Reality* (Oxford: Oxford University Press, 2014).

32 See the world bestseller by the Nobel laureate Daniel Kahnemann, *Thinking, Fast and Slow* (New York: Farrar, Straus & Giroux, 2011).

33 Adam Smith not only presented an economic theory based on egotism, which one can find in his work *The Wealth of Nations* (New York: Bantam Books, 2003); as a moral philosopher, he crucially also wrote a central work of ethics, *The Theory of Moral Sentiments* (New York: Cosimo, 2007), in which he examines our ability to put ourselves in the position of others and develop empathy with them. The relationship between the two works is a matter of dispute among Smith scholars. For an introduction to these issues, see Craig Smith, *Adam Smith* (Cambridge: Polity, 2020).

34 Gilbert Ryle, *The Concept of Mind*, 60th anniversary edn (Abingdon: Routledge, 2009).

35 The relationship between sociology, social intelligence and everyday ethics is spelt out by the cultural sociologist Clemens Albrecht using familiar everyday examples in *Sozioprudenz: Sozial klug handeln* (Frankfurt: Campus, 2020).

36 One especially prominent and welcome exception to this is Thomas Piketty, *Capital and Ideology* (Cambridge, MA: Harvard University Press, 2020), in which the author seeks to show that excessive social inequality is economically harmful and morally reprehensible.

37 One should note that Adam Smith, who introduced the phrase 'invisible hand' into national economy, by no means meant that market mechanisms driven by egotism automatically benefit the general public. In his theory, the invisible hand is shaped by the interplay of morality, economy and politics.

38 For a philosophical overview of the field of happiness studies in the social sciences (including economics), which has long since become established as a discipline at leading anglophone universities, see the book by the Cambridge philosopher of science Anna Alexandrova, *A Philosophy for the Science of Well-Being* (Oxford: Oxford University Press, 2017). See also the conception in Julian Nida-Rümelin, *Die Optimierungsfalle: Philosophie einer humanen Ökonomie* (Munich: Irisiana, 2011).

39 Jonas, *The Imperative of Responsibility*, p. 27.

40 See 'There is such a thing as society, says Boris Johnson from bunker', *The Guardian*, 29 March 2020, www.theguardian.com/politics/2020/mar/29/20000-nhs-staff-return-to-service-johnson-says-from-coronavirus-isolation.

41 Paul J. Crutzen and Eugene Stoermer, 'The "Anthropocene"', *IGBP Global Change Newsletter* 41 (2000), pp. 17f.

42 Peter Sloterdijk, *You Must Change Your Life*, trans. Wieland Hoban (Cambridge: Polity, 2013), p. 452.

43 Christoph Horn, *Einführung in die Moralphilosophie* (Freiburg: Alber, 2018), p. 24.

44 Ibid., pp. 24f.

45 Ibid., p. 18.

46 Other life forms, as well as inanimate nature, must also often be taken into account in our reflections, albeit for different reasons. These reasons are explained in animal and environmental ethics. I do not share the opinion, espoused prominently by Peter Singer, that we adopt moral attitudes towards other life forms for the same reasons as towards people. Showing moral preference for humans is not a morally reprehensible 'speciesism', as he calls it, which is supposedly even on a par with racism, for a fundamental difference is that races do not exist, but species do. The abstruse implications of Singer's radical position have been criticized from a range of perspectives, especially because he approves of euthanasia for severely disabled newborns and infants and assigns a lower moral status to severely disabled persons in general than to healthy animals of other kinds, such as chimpanzees. This only follows, however, if one accepts his mistaken equation of racism and speciesism; because he is wrong, we are justified in rejecting the conclusions he draws from it. This in no way means that we have no moral obligations towards other life forms.

47 Susan Wolf, 'Moral saints', *Journal of Philosophy* 79/8 (1982), pp. 419–39.

48 Charles Darwin, *The Descent of Man: Selection in Relation to Sex* (London: Penguin, 2004), p. 135.

49 See, for example, ibid., p. 142:

> Most savages are utterly indifferent to the sufferings of strangers, or even delight in witnessing them. It is well known that the women and children of the North American Indians aided in torturing their enemies. Some savages take a horrid pleasure in cruelty to animals, and humanity is an unknown virtue. Nevertheless, beside the family affections, kindness is common, especially during sickness, between the members of the same tribe, and is sometimes extended beyond these limits. Mungo Park's touching account of the kindness of the negro women of the interior to him is well known. Many instances could be given of the noble fidelity of savages

towards each other, but not to strangers; common experience justifies the maxim of the Spaniard, 'Never, never trust an Indian.'

50 Gabriel, *Der Sinn des Denkens*, p. 17.

51 Peter Singer, *Practical Ethics* (Cambridge: Cambridge University Press, 2011), pp. 151–4. Singer states that 'our present absolute protection of the lives of infants' is 'a distinctively Christian attitude rather than a universal ethical value' (p. 153), though he does not adduce any source or supporting evidence for this abstruse claim.

52 Richard Dawkins, *The Selfish Gene* (Oxford: Oxford University Press, 1976).

53 Conversational remark.

54 Jonas, *The Imperative of Responsibility*, p. 8.

55 Heraclitus, Fragment 123, at http://heraclitusfragments.com/.

56 David Deutsch, *The Beginning of Infinity: Explanations That Transform the World* (London: Penguin, 2012), as well as Gabriel, *Der Sinn des Denkens*, pp. 46–50.

57 George Ellis, *How Can Physics Underlie the Mind? Top-Down Causation in the Human Context* (Berlin: Springer, 2016). See also the similar argumentation by the philosopher of science Jennan T. Ismael, *How Physics Makes Us Free* (Oxford: Oxford University Press, 2016).

58 See the theory of free will in Gabriel, *I Am Not a Brain*, pp. 178–219. More recently, Christian List has presented similar arguments in *My Free Will Is Real* (Cambridge, MA: Harvard University Press, 2019).

59 Adi Ophir, *The Order of Evils: Toward an Ontology of Morals*, trans. Rela Mazali and Havi Carel (New York: Zone Books, 2005).

60 Immanuel Kant, *Critique of the Power of Judgement*, trans. Paul Guyer and Eric Matthews (Cambridge: Cambridge University Press, 2000), p. 298.

61 Gregor Dotzauer, 'Radikale Mitte: Der Philosoph Markus Gabriel erklärt, warum es die Welt nicht gibt', *Die Zeit*, 14 August 2013.

62 From 2013 to 2021, Germany was governed by a coalition of SPD and CDU (trans.).

Index

moral progress (*cont.*)
  recognition of non-moral facts, 205
  science and, 208, 227
  self-knowledge and, 189
  sociocritical analyses and, 187
  threats to, x, 189–91
moral progress in dark times, 67, 184, 245
moral psychology, 112
moral questions, 4–5, 102–4, 107, 109
moral realism, 18, 29, 70–1, 78–9, 107, 122
moral reflection, 222, 224, 226
moral regression, 201, 203, 205, 208, 231, 257n26
moral tension, 75–7
moral universalism, 68, 224
moral values
  definition, 26
  vs. economic values, 5, 26–7, 61, 213
  God and, 121–2
  Nietzschean approach to, 59–61
  non-negotiable nature of, 61
  religion and, 124–5
  universality of, 26, 101
morality
  altruism and, 223–4, 229
  atheism and, 126
  communist view of, 253n21
  definition of, 223
  development of, 87
  economy and, 27–8
  vs. ethics, 24
  vs. law, 25
  majority and, 34–5
  norms and, 25
  relation to good, evil and neutral, 25–6
  universality of, 67
morally necessary action, 26
morally permissible action, 26
morally reprehensible action, 26, 32

morally unambiguous situations, 107–8
Moro, Sergio, 176
multiculturalism, 98–9
Musk, Elon, 7
Muslims *see* Islam

Nagel, Thomas, 81
nation state, 138, 139
national identities, 146
National Socialism, 52–3, 70–1
National Socialist German Workers' Party (NSDAP), 50
nationalism, 164, 168
naturalistic fallacy, 54
nature
  development of biological forms in, 88
  humans and, 233, 237
  systematic exploration of, 234
  vs. universe, 232–3
Nazi machine, 50
Nazism, 50, 56, 98, 199
negative discrimination, 139–40
neo-Kantianism, 53–4, 55, 56
neoliberalism, 176, 206, 209, 210, 217, 237–8
neutral, 4, 25–6
new enlightenment *see* New Moral Realism (NMR)
New Moral Realism (NMR)
  conception of, xi, 13, 220
  core theses of, 18, 251n2
  definition of, 94
  idea of, 6
  interim goal of, 33
  project of, 230, 246
Nietzsche, Friedrich, 171, 172, 197
  equivocation of, 58–60
  idea of nihilism, 56, 57–8
  influence of, 195
  on moral values, 58, 59–61
  On the Genealogy of Morals, 58
nihilism, 56, 57–8